PRAISE FOR *SUSTAI*
HUMAN RESOURCE
MANAGEMENT

CU00922103

'One of the most comprehensive and up-to-date textbooks on sustainable HRM. Students will understand what sustainable HRM means, how it is measured and reported on, why it is strategically relevant for organizations, what happens if it is ignored and how it unfolds in diverse cultural contexts. Teachers will receive a text that they can ask students to prepare before class – ideal for inverted-classroom and problem-based learning type of courses.'
Ina Aust-Gronarz, Professor of Human Resources, University of Louvain, Belgium

'An outstanding book about sustainable HRM that not only explains the theoretical and practical aspects of the discipline but also engages students with its discussion of the complexities and developments in a range of geographical regions. The examples, discussion questions and ideas for workshops bring the various aspects of sustainable HRM alive and enable students to understand its complexities and its scope. A welcome addition to the literature on sustainable HRM.'
Robin Kramar, Adjunct Professor, University of Notre Dame, France

'The United Nations invites us to consider sustainability in development efforts across micro-individual, meso-organizational and macro-national levels. Rafal Sitko's book responds to the urgent need to consider stakeholder-based sustainability in framing human resource management policies and practices. An unmissable read.'
Mustafa F Özbilgin, Professor of Organizational Behaviour, Brunel Business School, UK

Sustainable Human Resource Management

Using HRM to achieve long-term social, environmental and business goals

Rafal Sitko

KoganPage

Publisher's note

Every possible effort has been made to ensure that the information contained in this book is accurate at the time of going to press, and the publishers and author cannot accept responsibility for any errors or omissions, however caused. No responsibility for loss or damage occasioned to any person acting, or refraining from action, as a result of the material in this publication can be accepted by the editor, the publisher or the author.

First published in Great Britain and the United States in 2023 by Kogan Page Limited

Apart from any fair dealing for the purposes of research or private study, or criticism or review, as permitted under the Copyright, Designs and Patents Act 1988, this publication may only be reproduced, stored or transmitted, in any form or by any means, with the prior permission in writing of the publishers, or in the case of reprographic reproduction in accordance with the terms and licences issued by the CLA. Enquiries concerning reproduction outside these terms should be sent to the publishers at the undermentioned addresses:

2nd Floor, 45 Gee Street	8 W 38th Street, Suite 902	4737/23 Ansari Road
London	New York, NY 10018	Daryaganj
EC1V 3RS	USA	New Delhi 110002
United Kingdom		India

www.koganpage.com

Kogan Page books are printed on paper from sustainable forests.

© Rafal Sitko, 2023

The right of Rafal Sitko to be identified as the author of this work has been asserted by him in accordance with the Copyright, Designs and Patents Act 1988.

ISBNs

Hardback   978 1 3986 0671 5
Paperback   978 1 3986 0649 4
Ebook   978 1 3986 0670 8

British Library Cataloguing-in-Publication Data
A CIP record for this book is available from the British Library.

Library of Congress Cataloging-in-Publication Data
Names: Sitko, Rafal, author.
Title: Sustainable human resource management : using HRM to achieve
  long-term social, environmental and business goals / Rafal Sitko.
Description: 1 Edition. | New York, NY : Kogan Page Inc, 2023. | Includes
  bibliographical references and index.
Identifiers: LCCN 2022049914 (print) | LCCN 2022049915 (ebook) | ISBN
  9781398606494 (paperback) | ISBN 9781398606715 (hardback) | ISBN
  9781398606708 (ebook)
Subjects: LCSH: Personnel management. | Organizational change. | Social
  responsibility of business.
Classification: LCC HF5549 .S658 2023 (print) | LCC HF5549 (ebook) | DDC
  658.3/01–dc23/eng/20221014
LC record available at https://lccn.loc.gov/2022049914
LC ebook record available at https://lccn.loc.gov/2022049915

Typeset by Integra Software Services, Pondicherry
Print production managed by Jellyfish
Printed and bound by CPI Group (UK) Ltd, Croydon, CR0 4YY

CONTENTS

LIST OF FIGURES AND TABLES

Figures

Tables

Introducing Sustainable HRM

1

> **LEARNING OBJECTIVES**
>
> After completing this chapter, you should be able to:
> - Start recognizing limitations of the traditional model of managing people.
> - Provide a definition of sustainable HRM.
> - Explain what sustainability and HRM are.
> - Evaluate the importance of sustainable HRM as a management topic.
> - Describe key challenges to the field of sustainable HRM.
> - Describe key opportunities for developing sustainable HRM practices.
> - Critically discuss whether sustainable HRM represents a new step in the evolution of people management.

Introduction

People make organizations, and organizations are only as good as the people who work in them. Without their members, organizations would be empty spaces with stacks of furniture, or possibly less than that. The basic premise of human resource management (HRM) is that people are key to organizational success. However, in practice, employees and their well-being are often of secondary consideration for their employers.

In 2021, Microsoft published results from their global Work Trend Index survey which collected data from over 31,000 full-time or self-employed workers. The study found that 54 per cent of respondents felt overworked and 39 per cent felt outright exhausted (Microsoft, 2021). In the UK (CIPD, 2022) one in four employees reported that work has a negative impact on their physical health and 27 per cent of survey respondents said work has a negative impact on their mental health. Seventy-one per cent of women and 62 per cent of men said that in the last year they have experienced some form of non-physical work-related health condition, such as anxiety, depression or panic attacks. This data highlights the importance of exploring HR practices that will help achieve an organization's business goals, but not at the expense of their employees.

The negative impact of work also 'spills over' on employees' family members. Behaviours such as work-related stress and anxiety are transferred to the family domain (Lawson et al, 2013). In a large study, conducted by Mental Health America (2017) in the United States, 81 per cent of respondents reported that stress from their job affects relationships with their friends or family, and 63 per cent of the respondents said that frustration or stress from their job causes them to cry regularly or engage in unhealthy behaviours such as habitual drinking.

Overworking staff not only puts a burden on employees, their families and wider communities, but also on the employers themselves. The same study conducted by Mental Health America (2017) found that workplace mental health problems cost US employers an estimated $500 billion annually in lost productivity. This financial expense is manifested, for example, in the form of staff absenteeism. A third of the surveyed US employees admitted that they missed work two or more days a month because their work environments are so stressful. Among those who reported that they stayed away from work because of a stressful environment, 35 per cent said they missed three to five days a month, and 38 per cent said they missed six working days or more.

Every generation laments the daunting difficulties in the world of management. Have a look at books and articles from a few decades ago. Many covered dangerous geopolitical situations, new technology disrupting markets, threats and opportunities created by globalization – all these concerns are also common themes in the current business world. At the organizational level, trying to solve ethical and social problems while at the same time achieving ambitious business goals, comes to the fore. This book recognizes that managing people is one of the major challenges for organizations today and hopes to provide another perspective on it.

Issues of employee health problems, stress at work or difficulties in achieving work–life balance lead us to once again rethink HRM and search for more sustainable and socially responsible approaches. At the same time, with the growing concerns about the natural habitat, it is also crucial to explore in more depth how we can use people management to help organizations achieve their environmental goals. The need for HRM practices to consider the interests of a wider range of stakeholders brings us to the subject of sustainable human resource management.

What is sustainable HRM?

Stankevičiūtė and Savanevičienė (2018) explained that sustainable HRM is 'an umbrella term that covers multiple dimensions, diverse contexts, and multiple levels of analysis and can be understood in terms of a number of complimentary frameworks.' Ehnert et al (2016) defined it as:

> the adoption of HRM strategies and practices that enable the achievement of financial, social and ecological goals, with an impact inside and outside of the organization and over a long-term time horizon while controlling for unintended side effects and negative feedback.

There is a range of perspectives and definitions describing sustainable HRM (see e.g. Mariappanadar, 2003; Ehnert, 2009; Kramar, 2014). For the purposes of this book a broader definition is applied. Here, *sustainable human resource management* is concerned with the use of HRM to achieve long-term social, environmental and business goals. It is perceived as a specific approach to managing employees and all people who provide work to the organization. (For a list of key definitions and terms marked with a *bold italic font*, see also the Glossary at the back of the book.)

In order to fully unpack the scope of the term 'sustainable HRM' we first need to explain its key components, i.e. 'sustainability' and 'HRM', and then we will link them together.

Historical snapshot of sustainability

The general concept behind sustainability is very old. We know that in approximately 400 BC, Aristotle was already popularizing the idea of living in a manner that was self-sustaining. The ancient Greek philosopher did not use the term 'sustainability' but he encouraged a responsible use of resources and strongly condemned excessive consumption. For centuries since, literature dedicated to fishery and forestry has explored ideas related to finding a balanced way to use ecosystems. Good practices were promoted related to careful utilization of wood and fish, with a pace and amount that would allow the resources to be regenerated (Ehnert, 2009).

In modern history, in 1987 the Brundtland Commission (The United Nation's World Commission on Environment and Development) raised awareness of how economic, social and environmental systems are inter-linked. The Commission and its report also became known for defining sustainable development as a 'strategy of social development that meets the needs of the present without compromising the ability of future generations to meet their own needs' (Brundtland, 1987).

While the Brundtland Commission identified three pillars of sustainable development as *economic*, *social* and *environmental*, in the following decades the ecological challenges received primary attention. With its roots in the environmental movement, the word 'sustainability' for many academics and practitioners still means protection of natural habitats.

Nevertheless, there is a body of literature taking a broader perspective on the subject. For example, Crane et al (2019) defined **sustainability** as 'the long-term maintenance of systems according to environmental, economic and social considerations'. This definition highlights that sustainability is more than a term for environmental management. The above conceptualization is also closely connected with ideas of 'corporate social responsibility' and 'triple bottom line', which we will explore in more detail in Chapter 2. For now, let's explore why organizations are concerned with sustainability.

General rationale for sustainable organizations

There are two main lines of argument supporting sustainability initiatives in organizations. The first is related to the 'business case'. This includes all points explaining how sustainability policies and practices can have a positive impact on achieving business goals. From this perspective sustainability is desirable because it can help to:

- **Increase productivity and morale.** Studies suggest that an adoption of environmental and social sustainability initiatives increases employees' productivity (Delmas and Pekovic, 2018). According to Delmas and Pekovic, investment in even one of the following practices – teamwork, interorganizational relations or training – combined with environmental practices is correlated with higher labour productivity. Meanwhile, Burchett et al (2010) found that greening the workspace with even one plant has a significant positive impact on employees' morale.

- **Improve brand image and avoid loss of social legitimacy.** Unsustainable practices can damage an organization's reputation. This could create financial burden in the form of lost revenue or increased costs of managing public relations. Investment in sustainability protects organizations from damaging incidents and allows them to better meet customers' demands. Capgemini (2020) conducted a survey in nine countries (US, UK, Sweden, France, Germany, Netherlands, Italy, Spain and India) and found that 79 per cent of customers are changing their purchase preferences based on sustainability. Sustainable operations can also improve relations with the local community and the government. In an attempt to create desired change in society, some governments offer tax incentives and subsidies to sustainable organizations.

- **Reduce costs.** Sustainability highlights reduction of waste. More sustainable operations can lead to higher efficiency, streamlined efforts and conservation of resources. Reduced consumption of resources and energy-saving strategies can require initial investment, to provide more substantial savings long term. However, in some cases, sustainable cost reduction practices can be inexpensive and require primarily a change in employees' habits: for example, training staff to switch off devices that are not currently being used.

- **Create value.** By developing sustainable products and services organizations can add value to their offerings and charge higher prices. Meeting the market's demands for sustainable organizations and products, companies create opportunities for increased profit.

The second main line of argument is related to the 'ethical case' (also called the 'moral case' or 'social case'). From this perspective sustainability is perceived as a correction for organizational actions which cause, or could cause, harm to individuals, communities and the environment. The ethical case refers to the role that organizations play in society and the accountability for the impact they make. Thus, 'sustainable' is often used synonymously with the term 'socially responsible'. With limited human and natural resources, it becomes an organization's ethical and social duty to adopt more future-oriented practices.

It is questionable to what extent a solely business or solely ethical rationale is sufficient. On the one hand, the narrow focus on the business case is what caused the need to develop a sustainable agenda in the first place. If economic goals are the only reason for introducing sustainability practices it may not be possible to achieve meaningful social and environmental changes.

Furthermore, using sustainability only for the purpose of economic gains could erode the public's trust in such initiatives. On the other hand, exclusive focus on the social case can meet with resistance from organizational actors who do not share the same ethical values. This approach can also conflict with businesses' logic to operate according to the economic rationale. The business and social perspectives for sustainability should not be seen as mutually exclusive but rather interconnected and complementary. Both sides of the argument are important to consider in sustainable management.

So far, we have introduced the concept of sustainability and located it in the organizational context. Let's now turn to HRM.

Skill check

Understanding the rationale for sustainable organizations. This is a key skill to develop because sustainability practices help to achieve organizational objectives and can be embedded in many strategies and policies.

Defining human resource management

There is a vast array of different conceptualizations of HRM. Numerous books and articles have been written about HRM, each of them presenting its own explanation of the subject. Notable examples include:

Storey (1995) for whom human resource management is 'a distinctive approach to employment management which seeks to achieve competitive advantage through the strategic deployment of a highly committed and capable workforce, using an array of cultural, structural and personnel techniques.'

Dessler (2016) who wrote 'Human resource management is the process of acquiring, training, appraising, and compensating employees, and of attending to their labor relations, health and safety, and fairness concerns.'

Armstrong and Taylor (2020) who said HRM is 'concerned with all aspects of how people are employed and managed in organizations'.

Torrington et al (2020) provided a more detailed explanation of the concept of HRM by referring to its six groups of objectives and how they are carried out by HR professionals. The areas of HRM responsibility can be summarized as:

- **Staffing objectives.** The HR team ensures that the organization is appropriately staffed. This involves recruiting, selecting and developing people with the right skills to provide the services needed. This area of responsibility is also related to developing employment and reward packages that will attract, retain and motivate staff.

- **Performance objectives.** According to Torrington et al (2020), the second main area of HRM objectives is related to maximizing employees' performance. This can be done through ensuring motivation and commitment of staff, as well as providing the necessary training and development opportunities. The HR staff also need to assist the organization in disciplinary matters, where employees' conduct or performance are not satisfactory.

- **Change management objectives.** This is related to effectively managing change, such as structural reorganization of activities for staff, or introduction of people to their new roles. In other instances, HRM may be responsible for introducing cultural changes in the organization, altering employees' attitudes, norms or habits.

- **Administration objectives.** This involves a range of administrative tasks necessary for the smooth operation of any organization, for example: maintaining accurate and comprehensive data on employees; complying with legal requirements; administering pay; allowing staff to take leave; and implementing accurate taxation. HRM is also involved in ensuring that the organization meets the necessary health and safety standards (e.g. complying with working time regulations).

- **Reputation objectives.** This is still a relatively new area of responsibilities for HRM, which is required to support the organization in its efforts to create a brand and develop a desirable reputation. For example, the HR function should play a role in building its organization's reputation of being ethical and socially responsible.

- **Well-being objectives.** These objectives involve improving working lives and providing more diligent care for employees' mental health.

McKenna and Beech (2014) highlighted that while there is no single definition of the term, HRM can be seen as a form of management that considers people as the key 'resource'. The word 'resource' is captured here in quotation marks to highlight that this terminology is problematic. Many academics have criticized the practice of referring to employees as resources. For example, Osterby and Coster (1992) argued that:

> The term 'human resources' reduces people to the same category of value as materials, money and technology – all resources, and resources are only valuable to the extent they can be exploited or leveraged into economic value.

When people are called a *resource*, even if qualified as 'the most important' resource, they may become subject to the same strict managerial rationale that minimizes costs of inventory. This language can help business owners and managers to conveniently forget that employees, unlike equipment, have mental well-being which needs to be considered. Treating people only as a means to an end, and as factors of production, inevitably lends itself to harming staff.

In line with the criticism of the name 'HRM', Boxall and Purcell (2016) proposed that:

> People are not human resources. On the contrary, people are independent agents who possess human resources, which are the talents they can deploy and develop at work and which they take with them when they leave the organization.

According to this perspective, **human resources** are all the assets and characteristics that people possess and contribute to an organization, for example knowledge, passion, motivation, technical abilities, soft skills, social networks or experience (note, however, that the acronym 'HR' is commonly used to refer to the part of the organization responsible for recruiting, selecting and training employees). The semantic discussion is important because the language we use shapes how we think and behave.

Even when its rhetoric is empowering, the HRM practice can be exploitative. Legge (1995) has extensively examined the gap between the positive language of HRM, which is people centred, and common HRM practices, which often focus on excessive cost reduction. The HRM rhetoric is based around the idea of developing your employees and investing in them because their talents provide the competitive advantage. However, according to Legge, the HRM policies that are meant to provide 'empowerment' in reality often lead to work intensification. For instance, 'ownership for career development' is a diplomatic phrase used by HR teams and managers to shift responsibility for career development from the employer to the employee and 'flexible work arrangements' can mean decreased pay and employment security (e.g. contracts with no guaranteed pay).

Similar arguments were presented by Bolton and Houlihan (2007) in their book *Searching for the Human in Human Resource Management*. When we define the employment relationship only in terms of economic principles, the humanity is 'squeezed out' of work. This potentially exploitative nature of many HRM practices is closely connected to the short-term orientation of organizations and limited assumptions of what role HRM should play in organizations. When HRM was developed, its task was to prove that it is, above anything else, an 'excellent business discipline' (Logan, 2008). The focus on economic imperative, and perceiving people as mere means to achieve organizational objectives, has led to development of irresponsible practices in people management (Ehnert, 2009; Richards and Sang, 2021). At the same time, many organizations today attempt to maintain their reputation as good employers. This tension between the economic rationale and maintaining a positive image can lead to policies showing only superficial care for employees' well-being. For example, offering free online Zumba classes to employees who, due to persistent work stress, are facing professional burnout.

Linking sustainability with HRM

The term sustainable HRM has been used for two decades but the literature on this subject is still in its early stages of development. While the discussion on sustainability in management is well established in the broader literature of business ethics, a comprehensive link with HRM has between created only recently. Nonetheless, sustainable HRM is increasingly gaining popularity. In response to the external pressures from customers, investors, business partners, policymakers and society as a whole, organizations need to rethink their responsibility towards key stakeholders. Sustainability in the field of HRM is no longer a 'nice-to-do' but rather a 'need-to-do'. This message is supported, for example, by a series of reports on 'employment and environmental sustainability' published by the International Labour Organization (ILO, 2021). Similarly, according to the CIPD's (2020) research, 'sustainability, purpose and responsible business' is one of the key future trends influencing the HR profession. CIPD (2020) said:

> People professionals should be at the forefront of driving responsible business that creates value for all stakeholders, including employees.

CIPD (2020) highlighted the role that HRM should play in supporting organizational efforts to achieve social but also environmental goals. This is where so-called '**Green HRM**' (GHRM) comes in. It focuses on enhancing positive environmental outcomes in the organization through responsible people management, and it should be a key component of sustainability initiatives in HRM.

Sustainable HRM does not challenge the premise that the primary purpose of HRM is helping organizations to survive and develop. Sustainable HRM explores and promotes social and environmental solutions that are balanced with economic outcomes. Desirable social and environmental outcomes introduced for their own sake can, and should, be encouraged. However, sustainable HRM recognizes the inescapable reality that resources in organizations are finite, and therefore they require financial and strategic deliberation.

Unlike traditional approaches to HRM, sustainable HRM puts more emphasis on the interconnectedness of different aspects within the organization and the external environment. The contribution to an organization's survival and development is achieved by preserving and nurturing a quality human resource base. This includes the emphasis on soft issues such as treating the well-being of the employees and the community as one of the values of organizational culture and then enacting those values in practice. As Ehnert explained (2009), sustainability in HRM is about 'the balance of "consuming" (or deploying) and "reproducing" human resources'.

Earlier in the chapter we looked at popular, broad rationales for sustainable organizations. In the next section we will collect and summarize key arguments explaining why organizations should care specifically about sustainable HRM.

Why is sustainable HRM important?

There are many reasons why sustainable HRM is an important topic. For managers and policy makers, sustainable HRM can provide an array of ideas for new policies and practices. For students and academics this could be a crucial field to discuss and evaluate organizational wastefulness, consequences of irresponsible management and solutions for it, as well as tensions between short-term and long-term business orientations.

Here is a list that summarizes 10 key arguments for organizations to engage with sustainable HRM. Note that many of the points are closely connected with each other:

1 **People and their 'human resources' are essential for organizational success.** People management is at the heart of any successful organization. This raises the stakes for a consideration of how to sustainably manage people who provide labour for your organization.

2 **HRM malpractice can inflict significant harm on people who provide work for the organization, the wider community and the natural environment as well as organizations themselves.** Irresponsible people management can cause enormous damage to a range of stakeholders, including employees. In many contemporary organizations, work intensification and overworking are the norm, leading to significant health harm (Mariappanadar, 2016). According to a joint research project conducted by the World Health Organization (WHO) and the ILO (International Labour Organization), every year approximately three-quarters of a million people die due to coronary heart disease and stroke caused by working long hours (Pega et al, 2021). This is summed up by the BBC article, 'How overwork is literally killing us' (BBC, 2021). The harm and negative effects of work practices cross over to employees' family members and healthcare costs (Mariappanadar, 2014).

3 **Organizations are facing changing demographics.** Population ageing is a phenomenon observed worldwide. While demographic trends differ between countries, according to the United Nations (2020), 'All regions will see an increase in the size of the older population between 2020 and 2050'. By 2050 it is estimated that the global population of persons aged 65 years or over will double its current value and reach 1.5 billion. This is coupled with falling fertility in many countries such as the UK (Vollset et al, 2020). Due to the decreasing supply of young employees and the growing number of the elderly, organizations will have to plan how to make work more attractive for their staff long term. Managers may have to learn how to transition from short-term high-intensity HRM practices to people management that allows employees to 'regenerate' and 'sustain' their energy and well-being.

4 Tight labour markets increase competition for talent. Due to the changing demographics and high demand for qualified and experienced employees, many industries experience a 'tight' labour market (Oxford Analytica, 2021). A *'tight' labour market* is one where demand for employees is relatively high and the supply is relatively low. In other words, it is a labour market where there is a lot of competition between organizations to hire employees. This is opposite to a *'loose' labour market* where the demand for labour is relatively low but the supply of labour is high. In a loose labour market there is a surplus of people looking for employment. Organizations operating in a tight labour market face fierce competition for finding, hiring and retaining employees (Taylor, 2021). Sustainable HRM can help employers compete for talent and this is especially important for organizations operating in challenging labour markets.

5 Sustainable HRM helps organizations build a positive reputation. More critical practice of HRM can improve treatment of employees, allowing managers to create a positive, lasting brand of a good employer. *Un*sustainable HRM creates a poor reputation, making it harder to recruit and retain staff. As Taylor (2021) highlighted, no amount of image building will be effective in attracting employees if the terms and conditions of work are not improved. Furthermore, research suggests that job seekers prefer organizations with socially valued characteristics. According to Lis (2012), 'If organizations are willing to provide sustainable HRM practices they can become an employer-of-choice'.

6 Recognition of long-term perspective helps to meet complex demands of stakeholders. For many stakeholders, achieving economic success is no longer enough for claiming organizational viability. Investors, customers, business partners and wider community members increasingly demand that organizations engage in socially responsible practices. Managing complex relationships with stakeholders and balancing their demands is one of the challenges for today's businesses. This requires people management that 'reflects a commitment to going beyond the regular practice' (Richards, 2022) and beyond the minimum compliance with employment law. Sustainable HRM is 'extending the notion of strategic success in HRM' (Ehnert, 2009). A sustainable approach to management and HRM reflects a societal vision of what is 'desirable'.

7   **Sustainable HRM practices have a positive impact on customer satisfaction and innovation.** A study conducted on Swedish hotels found that allocating resources into sustainable HRM is key for achieving both customer satisfaction and innovation (Wikhamn, 2019). Managers working in hotels may perceive investing money in employees as a financial dilemma, because of the traditionally high staff turnover. However, as Wikhamn argued, responsible HRM practices are crucial for shaping positive employee and customer interactions, which in turn are fundamental for organizational success in the hospitality industry. The research also found that investment in human resources has direct impact on innovation. In hotels, innovation can take the form of improving services, processes or marketing. As explained by Wikhamn (2019), 'firms striving after innovation need to invest in people'.

8   **Sustainable HRM helps to keep up with the competition and set trends for others to follow.** Market leaders like DHL highlight the importance of financial, environmental and social sustainability, setting the example for other organizations. Cisco uses myriad ways to instil value in their employees – through training, meaningful and creative interaction with peers and finding flexible arrangements that benefit both employees and employers.

9   **Sustainable HRM helps to comply with changing institutional and legislative context.** Organizations and their people management are subject to a range of local and international regulations. Moreover, large institutions such as the United Nations call organizations to action with programmes such as Sustainable Development Goals (SDGs, also known as 'Global Goals') (UN, 2015). Sustainable HRM allows employers to operate within the law and to be proactive in meeting demands imposed by legislative and regulatory institutions.

10   **Sustainable HRM is the 'right thing' to do.** Maintaining employees' physical and mental well-being, as well as protecting the natural environment, are employers' ethical duties. Most basic employee rights include fair remuneration, due process, participation and association, freedom from discrimination, privacy, and a healthy and safe work environment (Crane et al, 2019). Respecting these rights represents not only good business practice but also the moral obligations employers have towards their employees. Sustainable HRM is deeply concerned with ethics and sets guidelines explaining how to treat employees with

dignity. It also plays a central role in creating the awareness and organizational change necessary for environmental management. Ignoring the role that HRM can play in combatting environmental pollution and ongoing climate change could be seen as a form of ethical neglect.

The last point on the list raises an important question: how is *sustainable HRM* similar to or different from *ethical HRM*?

Sustainable HRM and ethical HRM

Crane et al (2019) argued that ethics is the study of morality where 'morality is concerned with the norms, values and beliefs embedded in social processes which define right and wrong for an individual or community'. Fundamentally, ethics stems from an individual's or organization's moral conviction.

Sustainable HRM has evolved out of discussions about ethical practices and, consequently, it overlaps with ethical HRM. For example, both sustainability and ethics are concerned with issues such as how to treat employees fairly. Like the sustainable approach, the ethical dimension of HRM highlights the limitations of irresponsible people management.

However, ethics focuses on what is *morally right* and the economic rationale is either an afterthought or nonexistent. Conversely, traditional HRM overemphasizes business needs, often with little consideration of employee, community and environmental welfare. Sustainable HRM presents practices and policies that consider both ethical standards and practical organizational objectives. In this book, sustainable HRM is conceptualized as an approach to HRM that is broader than ethical HRM.

Challenges and opportunities for sustainable HRM

Showing willingness to engage in sustainable practices and expanding the efforts to maintain social legitimacy and positive image are not enough. To meaningfully practise sustainable HRM, organizations need to demonstrate their ability to maintain and regenerate resources. However, balancing social, environmental and economic dimensions can add complexity to people management practices. Chapter 7, which is dedicated to the implementation of sustainable HRM, addresses this in more detail.

Furthermore, regional disparities need to be considered when planning and applying sustainable HRM. Dominant management styles upheld in different parts of the world should be taken into account. Legal and economic conditions can also present challenges for organizations as they seek to adopt a new approach to HRM. We discuss this in Chapter 9, which is dedicated to external forces shaping sustainable HRM in different national contexts.

On the other side of this discussion, there are signs of opportunity for the development and introduction of sustainable HRM. Firstly, CEOs are increasingly acknowledging that sustainability is crucial for their organizations. A study conducted by Accenture and the UN Global Compact (2019) examined how CEOs perceive sustainability. The project surveyed more than 1,000 top executives from across 21 industries and 99 countries and found that:

> 99 per cent of CEOs from companies with more than $1 billion in annual revenues believe sustainability will be important to the future success of their business (Accenture and UNGC, 2019).

In a similar vein, the EY 2022 survey of MENA (Middle East and North Africa) CEOs found that 97 per cent of executives see sustainability as 'extremely or more important' for driving value over the coming years (EY, 2022). Accenture (2019) conducted more than 100 in-depth interviews with CEOs, chairpersons and presidents of UN Global Compact companies. The results showed that CEOs are concerned about the role that their companies play in society. Sustainability is now firmly established on organizational agendas. The denial of organizations' responsibility to achieve balance between financial, social and environmental goals has significantly shrunk. According to the report, 94 per cent of surveyed CEOs now feel personal responsibility for ensuring their company has a core purpose and a role in society.

Organizations recognizing the wider meaning of sustainability coincides with calls to action made by academics. For example, Pfeffer (2010) urged companies to broaden the focus of their sustainability policies and concentrate not only on issues such as polar bears and melting icebergs but also on people.

Sustainability is also high on the agenda of national and pan-national governments. According to the official website of the European Union (European Commission, 2021a),

> Sustainable development is a core principle of the Treaty on European Union and a priority objective for the Union's internal and external policies. The United Nations 2030 Agenda includes 17 Sustainable Development Goals (SDGs) intended to apply universally to all countries. It is a commitment to eradicate poverty and achieve a sustainable world by 2030 and beyond, with human well-being and a healthy planet at its core.

This is achieved, for example, through tying research and innovation to SDGs. The EU's key research funding programme, Horizon Europe, has a budget of €95.5 billion and it helps to achieve the UN's SDGs (European Commission, 2021b). In its 2018 budget, the Government of Canada committed new funding over 13 years for establishing an SDGs Unit within the government ($49.4 million) and for delivering SDGs ($59.8 million) (Government of Canada, 2021). In 2021 Canada released 'Moving Forward Together', a National Strategy for achieving SDGs. This is a follow-up and reiteration of already existing efforts to support the UN's sustainability agenda.

Further investigations are required to examine the scope to which the above government actions and policies create real change for sustainable people management in organizations. Nevertheless, the examples illustrate that many governments recognize the importance of sustainability.

More of the same or the next step in the evolution of people management?

A particular challenge that sustainable HRM is facing is a perception that this approach is just 'old wine in a new bottle'. Is sustainable HRM just a new name for practices that have been long established in HRM? In order to answer this question, we need to take a step back and briefly acknowledge the rich history of people management.

The discussion of modern people management often begins with a recognition of Robert Owen (1771–1858), a famous industrialist. As a manager of New Lanark mill in Scotland, he introduced a series of progressive practices such as the 10-hour day. This was a considerable improvement, as in large factories at the time employees would work up to 16 hours a day. By 1817, he formulated a new goal of eight hours of work and coined the slogan 'Eight hours labour, eight hours recreation, eight hours full rest'. Owen, together with James Montgomery and Lord Shaftsbury, represented social reformers concerned with people's working conditions. They promoted ideas of achieving organizational goals and efficiency through management of workers' welfare. In 1896, the English confectionery firm Rowntree's appointed the first industrial welfare worker, Mary Wood. Her job was to care for the well-being of women and children in the factory. Soon other employers started to follow this example and also chose to appoint welfare workers (sometimes called 'welfare officers' or 'welfare secretaries'). In 1913, at a conference for employers, the 'Welfare Workers' Association' was formed. This was a forerunner of what we know today as the CIPD (Chartered Institute of Personnel and Development), a British professional body for human resource management professionals. In the early stages of managerial practice development, the rhetoric of *industrial betterment* was often linked to religious values such as the Protestant notion of duty (Barley and Kunda, 1992). Investment in welfare was also seen as a means to avoid adversarial industrial relations. However, what is key to recognize is that the roots of HRM come from acknowledging businesses' limitations and attempts to improve people's quality of work.

In the first half of the 20th century, welfare management began to transform into *personnel management* (PM). With the growth of organizations, employers needed better administration of staff. There was a need for a more structured and formal approach to timekeeping, employee discipline, payment systems, maintaining personnel records and retaining staff. Personnel managers were also tasked with consulting and mediating between employees and employers. In cases where a dispute would arise, the personnel officer's job would be to react to it and solve the immediate problem. The welfare work and employment management were combined into the broad role of personnel management.

PM played mostly an operational, rather than strategic, role. In other words, even though personnel managers had specialized knowledge and understanding of staff, they were not in a position to influence changes in the organization. According to Evans and Cowling (1985), British personnel managers were not usually given the opportunity to use initiative or advise on changes. With time the PM role gradually evolved. In the 1960s and 1970s, personnel managers developed practices focusing on staff training, motivation and retention. Some PMs started to specialize in reward management or resourcing. This period also saw the development of systematic *workforce planning*, which is a process of analysing the current staff, determining future personnel needs and identifying gaps between the labour demand and supply.

The 1980s saw a gradual increase in the popularity of 'Human Resource Management'. HRM was presented as a more strategic, proactive, business-oriented version of PM. Although HRM was introduced as a replacement for PM, they had much in common. In fact, many practitioners and scholars have debated the extent to which these two approaches to people management are different or only represented a change of name. Guest (1987) and Storey (1995) argued that HRM shows a distinct form of people management, based on unitarism (an assumption that employees share the same interests as employers) individualism, high commitment, and integration of HR and business strategy. The advocates of the new trend argued that the HRM conceptual framework was enriched with a number of new theories from the studies of strategic management, organizational behaviour and human capital. Moreover, Armstrong (1987) pointed out that

> HRM is regarded by some personnel managers as just a set of initials or old wine in new bottles. It could indeed be no more and no less than another name for personnel management, but as usually perceived, at least it has the virtue of emphasizing the virtue of treating people as a key resource, the management of which is the direct concern of top management as part of the strategic planning processes of the enterprise. Although there is nothing new in the idea, insufficient attention has been paid to it in many organizations.

The development of HRM continued. Storey (1989) argued that we can differentiate between the 'soft' and 'hard' HRM. The hard approach focused on tight control and quantitative performance management. This view represented employers who are not concerned with employees' needs and see them merely as a resource and cost to the organization. Characteristic of this approach are minimum pay and little empowerment of employees (Geary, 1992). On the other hand, the soft HRM approach puts emphasis on gaining competitive advantage through investing in people. According to this approach, employers should motivate and develop their staff. The main features of soft HRM include employee involvement and personal commitment to organizational goals and missions. Here close managerial control is replaced with an organizational culture of self-responsibility, granting autonomy, promoting positive workplace conditions and enhanced employee engagement. However, Truss et al (1997) argue that in practice all organizations have a mixture of both hard and soft approaches. While the precise balance between those two approaches can be unique to each organization, according to Truss et al (1997), hard and soft HRM complement each other and can be seen in any company. They summarize:

> One conclusion of our study, therefore, is that even if the rhetoric of HRM is 'soft', the reality is almost always 'hard', with the interests of the organization prevailing over those of the individual.

Sustainable HRM is inspired by a long tradition of re-humanizing work. It is built on the efforts and ideas of employee welfare approaches as well as the 'soft' HRM models. Sustainable HRM is a new perspective on old trends in management (Aust et al, 2020). In addition to the arguments presented by welfare management and soft HRM, sustainable HRM highlights the importance of a broader group of stakeholders. Sustainable HRM adds a consideration of societal and ecological challenges. Unlike welfare management or soft HRM, sustainable HRM also draws on the specialized fields of diversity management, talent management, green HRM and corporate social responsibility. Similar to welfare management or soft HRM, sustainable HRM is a product of its times. However, the new approach reflects society's current concerns about long-term sustainable development. For example, in the UK there has been a rise of in-work poverty over the last two decades. According to the Joseph Rowntree Foundation report (Innes, 2020), in 1996 approximately 11.2 per cent of working-age adults in a working family lived in poverty. In 2018 this figure had risen to 14.7 per cent.

It is true that the concept of sustainability has become a 'buzzword' in political, management and academic circles. It appears frequently in publications and events, providing an angle that resonates with audiences' interest. Sustainability sounds familiar and is catchy. These are important qualities for ideas in management and academic literature to spread and be widely discussed. The new approach draws on the logic and terminology which now has been well accepted by many organizations. The open-ended nature of sustainable HRM, and the fact that it can be applied to all aspects of the HRM function, shows potential for innovative thinking and space for further detailed developments. All in all, it can be concluded that while sustainable HRM is built on decades of attempts to re-humanize work, it is a new step in the evolution of responsible people management.

While sustainable HRM gains popularity it still requires more systematic adaptation into the educational curriculum. According to Jepsen and Grob, (2015),

> There has been little integration of sustainability practices into mainstream HR education, at both undergraduate and practitioner levels. Only when set into a syllabus, and promulgated through relevant professional development will these practices become normative.

This book attempts to address this issue and make a contribution to the HRM education syllabus.

Summary

This chapter introduced sustainable HRM and placed it within the contemporary debate about people management. First, we recognized how the current practice of people management can have a negative impact on employees, organizations and society as a whole. As part of this discussion, we defined a new approach to managing employees and all people who provide work. From there we took a step back and provided a brief historical overview of sustainability and the rationale for considering it in organizations. We also introduced the concept of HRM and linked it with the theme of sustainability.

The second main section of the chapter was dedicated to further discussion on why the topic of sustainable HRM is necessary. The chapter outlined 10 main reasons for organizations to engage with sustainable HRM. We also clarified the difference between ethical and sustainable HRM. We summarized some of the main challenges and opportunities for the field of sustainable HRM. One of the challenges was unpacked in more depth in this chapter, i.e. the perception that the new approach to people management is just 'old wine in a new bottle'. In order to address this issue, the discussion had to revert to basics. We briefly reviewed how modern people management developed with a particular recognition of the rich history of re-humanizing work. The chapter ended with the conclusion that while sustainable HRM relies on past progress, it represents a new contemporary perspective on how to make people management more responsible.

In Chapter 2, we shall move on to examine specific key concepts, theories and approaches to sustainable HRM. This will include the framework of corporate social responsibility.

Study questions

1 Define HRM and explain limitations related to the traditional way of managing people.

2 Provide a brief historical outline of sustainability and discuss the 'business case' and 'ethical case' for sustainable organizations.

3 What is sustainable HRM and why should organizations care about it?

4 Is ethical HRM the same as sustainable HRM? Is sustainable HRM just a new name for old practices? Discuss.

5 Explore contemporary challenges and opportunities for the field of sustainable HRM.

6 Present a brief historical overview of people management practices that have provided foundations for the contemporary practice of sustainable HRM.

Key reading

Accenture and UNGC (2019) The decade to deliver a call to business action, the United Nations Global Compact — Accenture strategy CEO study on sustainability 2019, https://www.accenture.com/_acnmedia/PDF-109/Accenture-UNGC-CEO-Study.pdf (archived at https://perma.cc/79LM-SRC7)

Ehnert, I (2009) *Sustainable Human Resource Management: A conceptual and exploratory analysis from a paradox perspective*, Physica-Verlag, Berlin/Heidelberg, Germany

References

Accenture and UNGC (2019) The decade to deliver a call to business action, the United Nations Global Compact – Accenture strategy CEO study on sustainability 2019, https://www.accenture.com/_acnmedia/PDF-109/Accenture-UNGC-CEO-Study.pdf (archived at https://perma.cc/SR46-NAAZ)

Armstrong, M (1987) Human resource management: a case of the emperor's new clothes, *Personnel Management*, August, pp 30–35

Armstrong, M and Taylor, S (2020) *Armstrong's Handbook of Human Resource Management Practice*, 15th edn, Kogan Page, London

Aust, I, Matthews, B and Muller-Camen, M (2020) Common good HRM: a paradigm shift in sustainable HRM? *Human Resource Management Review*, 30 (3), p 100705

Barley, S R and Kunda, G (1992) Design and devotion: surges of rational and normative ideologies of control in managerial discourse, *Administrative Science Quarterly*, 37 (3), pp 363–99

BBC (2021) How overwork is literally killing us, https://www.bbc.com/worklife/article/20210518-how-overwork-is-literally-killing-us (archived at https://perma.cc/QSL6-RX93)

Bolton, S C and Houlihan, M (eds.) (2007) *Searching for the human in Human Resource Management: Theory, Practice and Workplace Contexts*, Macmillan International Higher Education, New York

Boxall, P and Purcell, J (2016) *Strategy and Human Resource Management*, 4th edn, Palgrave, London and New York

Brundtland, G (ed.) (1987) *Report of the World Commission on Environment and Development: Our common future*, Oxford University Press, Oxford

Burchett, M, Torpy, F, Brennan, J and Craig, A (2010) *Greening the Great Indoors for Human Health and Wellbeing*, University of Technology Sydney, Sydney, Australia

Capgemini (2020) Consumer products and retail – how sustainability is fundamentally changing consumer preferences, https://www.capgemini.com/wp-content/uploads/2020/07/20-06_9880_Sustainability-in-CPR_Final_Web-1.pdf (archived at https://perma.cc/ME55-YFGF)

CIPD (2020) People Profession 2030: A collective view of future trends, https://www.cipd.co.uk/Images/people-profession-2030-report-compressed_tcm18-86095.pdf (archived at https://perma.cc/RE24-HJB3)

CIPD (2022) CIPD Good Work Index 2022, UK working lives survey, executive report June 2022, https://www.cipd.co.uk/Images/good-work-iIndex-executive-report-2022_tcm18-109897.pdf (archived at https://perma.cc/8WYA-VZDD)

Crane, A, Matten, D, Glozer, S and Spence, L (2019) *Business Ethics: Managing corporate citizenship and sustainability in the age of globalization*, 5th edn, Oxford University Press, Oxford

Delmas, M A and Pekovic, S (2018) Organizational configurations for sustainability and employee productivity: a qualitative comparative analysis approach, *Business and Society*, 57 (1), pp 216–51

Dessler, G (2016) *Human Resource Management*, 13th edn, Pearson, Harlow, Essex

Ehnert, I (2009) *Sustainable Human Resource Management: A conceptual and exploratory analysis from a paradox perspective*, Physica-Verlag, Berlin/Heidelberg, Germany

Ehnert, I, Parsa, S, Roper, I, Wagner, M and Muller-Camen, M (2016) Reporting on sustainability and HRM: a comparative study of sustainability reporting practices by the world's largest companies, *The International Journal of Human Resource Management*, 27 (1), pp 88–108

European Commission (2021a) Sustainable Development Goals, https://ec.europa.eu/info/strategy/international-strategies/sustainable-development-goals_en (archived at https://perma.cc/LD9K-QHZQ)

European Commission (2021b) Horizon Europe, https://ec.europa.eu/info/research-and-innovation/funding/funding-opportunities/funding-programmes-and-open-calls/horizon-europe_en (archived at https://perma.cc/8NC4-NBNS)

Evans, A and Cowling, A (1985) Personnel's part in organization restructuring, *Personnel Management*, January, pp 14–17

EY (2022) 97% of MENA CEOs say sustainability is important as a driver of value, www.ey.com/en_lb/news/2022/03/ey-97-of-mena-ceos-say-sustainability-is-important-as-a-driver-of-value (archived at https://perma.cc/G9DJ-UQYC)

Geary, J F (1992) Employment flexibility and human resource management: the case of three American electronics plants, *Work, Employment and Society*, 6 (2), pp 251–70

Government of Canada (2021) Moving forward together: Canada's 2030 Agenda National Strategy, https://www.canada.ca/en/employment-social-development/programs/agenda-2030/moving-forward.html (archived at https://perma.cc/7XAS-554H)

Guest, D E (1987) Human resource management and industrial relations, *Journal of Management Studies*, 24 (5), pp 503–21

ILO (2021) Issue briefs, https://www.ilo.org/asia/publications/issue-briefs/lang--en/index.htm (archived at https://perma.cc/YJL2-4UXJ)

Innes (2020) What has driven the rise of in-work poverty? Joseph Rowntree Foundation, https://www.jrf.org.uk/file/54061/download?token=7Onk5EZF&filetype=full-report (archived at https://perma.cc/F5WL-CQV2)

Jepsen, D M and Grob, S (2015) Sustainability in recruitment and selection: building a framework of practices, *Journal of Education for Sustainable Development*, 9 (2), pp 160–78

Kramar, R (2014) Beyond strategic human resource management: is sustainable human resource management the next approach? *The International Journal of Human Resource Management*, 25 (8), pp 1069–89

Lawson, K M, Davis, K D, Crouter, A C and O'Neill, J W (2013) Understanding work–family spillover in hotel managers, *International Journal of Hospitality Management*, 33, pp 273–81

Legge, K (1995) *Human Resource Management: Rhetoric and realities*, Macmillan, London

Lis, B (2012) The relevance of corporate social responsibility for a sustainable human resource management: an analysis of organizational attractiveness as a determinant in employees' selection of a (potential) employer, *Management Revue*, 23 (3), pp 279–95

Logan, G (2008) CIPD vows to raise HR profile with Government, *Personnel Today*, 7 October, 4

Mariappanadar, S (2003) Sustainable human resource strategy: the sustainable and unsustainable dilemmas of retrenchment, *International Journal of Social Economics*, 30 (8), pp 906–23

Mariappanadar, S (2014) Stakeholder harm index: a framework to review work intensification from the critical HRM perspective, *Human Resource Management Review*, 24 (4), pp 313–29

Mariappanadar, S (2016) Health harm of work from the sustainable HRM perspective: scale development and validation, *International Journal of Manpower*, **37** (6), pp 924–44

McKenna, E F and Beech, N (2014) *Human Resource Management: A concise analysis*, 3rd edn, Pearson, Harlow, Essex

Mental Health America (2017) Mind the workplace – MHA workplace health survey 2017, https://www.mhanational.org/sites/default/files/Mind%20the%20 Workplace%20-%20MHA%20Workplace%20Health%20Survey%20 2017%20FINAL.PDF (archived at https://perma.cc/CMQ2-PAWN)

Microsoft (2021) The Work Trend Index, the next great disruption is hybrid work—are we ready? https://www.microsoft.com/en-us/worklab/work-trend-index/hybrid-work (archived at https://perma.cc/V8MF-6522)

Osterby, B, and Coster, C (1992) Human resource development – a sticky label, *Training and Development*, April, pp 31–32

Oxford Analytica (2021) Tight US job market may persist due to demographics, *Expert Briefings*, https://dailybrief.oxan.com/Analysis/ES262915/Tight-US-job-market-may-persist-due-to-demographics (archived at https://perma.cc/QW64-TGVG)

Pega, F, Náfrádi, B, Momen, N C, Ujita, Y, Streicher, K N, Prüss-Üstün, A M and Woodruff, T J (2021) Global, regional, and national burdens of ischemic heart disease and stroke attributable to exposure to long working hours for 194 countries, 2000–2016: a systematic analysis from the WHO/ILO joint estimates of the work-related burden of disease and injury, *Environment International*, **154**, p 106595

Pfeffer, J (2010) Building sustainable organizations: the human factor, *Academy of Management Perspectives*, **24** (1), pp 34–45

Richards, J (2022) Putting employees at the centre of sustainable HRM: a review, map and research agenda, *Employee Relations*, **44** (3), pp 533–54

Richards, J and Sang, K (2021) Socially *irresponsible* human resource management? Conceptualising HRM practice and philosophy in relation to in-work poverty in the UK, *The International Journal of Human Resource Management*, **32** (10), pp 2185–212

Stankevičiūtė, Ž and Savanevičienė, A (2018) Raising the curtain in people management by exploring how sustainable HRM translates to practice: the case of Lithuanian organizations, *Sustainability*, **10** (12), p 4356

Storey, J (1989) Human resource management in the public sector, *Public Money and Management*, **9** (3), pp 19–24

Storey, J (1995) Human resource management: still marching on, or marching out? In J Storey (ed.) *Human Resource Management* (pp 3–32), Routledge, London

Taylor, S (2021) *Resourcing and Talent Management*, 8th edn, Kogan Page, London

Torrington, D, Hall, L, Taylor, S and Atkinson, C (2020) *Human Resource Management*, 11th edn, Pearson, Harlow, Essex

Truss, C, Gratton, L, Hope-Hailey, V, McGovern, P and Stiles, P (1997) Soft and hard models of human resource management: a reappraisal, *Journal of Management Studies*, **34** (1), pp 53–73

UN (2015) Resolution adopted by the General Assembly on 25 September 2015, transforming our world: the 2030 agenda for sustainable development, https://sdgs.un.org/2030agenda (archived at https://perma.cc/XQF6-JB7A)

UN (2020) World population ageing 2020 highlights, https://www.un.org/development/desa/pd/sites/www.un.org.development.desa.pd/files/undesa_pd-2020_world_population_ageing_highlights.pdf (archived at https://perma.cc/75AS-8F7L)

Vollset, S E, Goren, E, Yuan, C W, Cao, J, Smith, A E, Hsiao, T and Murray, C J (2020) Fertility, mortality, migration, and population scenarios for 195 countries and territories from 2017 to 2100: a forecasting analysis for the global burden of disease study, *The Lancet*, **396** (10258), pp 1285–306

Wikhamn, W (2019) Innovation, sustainable HRM and customer satisfaction, *International Journal of Hospitality Management*, **76**, pp 102–10

Sustainable HRM: key concepts, theories and models

2

LEARNING OBJECTIVES

After completing this chapter, you should be able to:

- Explain the meaning of corporate social responsibility (CSR).

- Discuss if corporations should have social responsibility.

- Explain what the triple bottom line framework is and how it can be translated into the respect, openness, continuity (ROC) model.

- Understand stakeholder theory and its significance for the sustainable HRM approach.

- Understand institutional theory and its significance for the sustainable HRM approach.

- Critically evaluate organizational paradoxes that influence the practice of sustainable HRM.

Introduction

As discussed in Chapter 1 the tradition of sustainability has long historical roots and has been practised for centuries, for example in fishery and forestry. Over the years, the subject has been expanded beyond the focus on the natural environment. Today, many CEOs recognize the importance of holistic sustainable development. Professional bodies and academics call for organizations to adopt a more sustainable approach to people management, which would balance long-term social, environmental and business goals.

Sustainable HRM has evolved out of a discussion of ethical practices and is closely related to the idea of corporate social responsibility (CSR). This prompts us to ask: what is CSR and what role does sustainable HRM play in furthering it? Do organizations have obligations only to their owners, or do they also need to consider internal and external groups of stakeholders? What implications does this have for the practice of human resource management? What paradoxical tensions can we observe in organizations when an attempt is made to implement sustainable HRM?

In this chapter we will answer these questions and by doing so we will explore the theoretical underpinnings of sustainable HRM, such as CSR, triple bottom line, the ROC (respect, openness and continuity) model, stakeholder theory, institutional theory and paradox theory.

What is corporate social responsibility?

Firstly, let's consider what a corporation is. A corporation is a specific type of business organization, registered with relevant authorities. From a legal perspective, a corporation is regarded as a separate entity, an 'artificial person' or a 'legal person'. For example, a corporation, as a legal entity, may need to pay taxes, can sue and be sued, can hold property in its own name, etc. At the same time the law recognizes that corporations are not 'real people', meaning there are limitations to corporations' rights and responsibilities. For instance, corporations cannot vote in elections.

Another feature of a corporation is that it is owned by shareholders. Some corporations are private, and these business entities are in the hands of a single or a small group of shareholders. However, most people are familiar with public corporations, where shares are publicly traded. In these cases, there are thousands of shareholders holding a small portion of the ownership of the corporation.

When a business is 'incorporated' it receives a special status of a corporation which legally separates the business and its owners. In the eyes of the law, shareholders have limited liability for the actions and finances of their business. For example, a shareholder in a corporation is not liable with their own assets for the debts of the company. Shareholders are also not involved in running the organization (unless they hold other roles). They appoint a board of directors, which represents their interest. Then, the board of directors appoints management of the corporation that runs day-to-day operations. Managers and directors are expected to protect the investment of the shareholders and the company as a whole. This framework, and owners' limited liability, can lead to corporations taking on excessive risk and causing harm to third parties (e.g. employees, local communities, the environment) to maximize financial gains. Hence, an idea was born that businesses should also act in a socially responsible manner and follow the rules of *corporate social responsibility*.

There is no universally accepted definition of CSR. However, it is commonly used as an umbrella term describing theories and practices that emphasize that corporations have not only financial but also social, environmental and ethical responsibilities. According to the European Commission (2021), CSR is 'the responsibility of enterprises for their impact on society'. CSR can be seen as general conviction, a set of practices and polices forming self-regulation for organizations, or a specific theoretical framework. As a conviction, CSR is not a new concept. Keynes wrote in 1923 that 'The business man is only tolerable so long as his gains can be held to bear some relation to what, roughly and in some sense, his activities have contributed to society.' Fans of history can find examples of CSR ideas even in ancient history. In approximately 1700 BC, Hammurabi, the king of Ancient Mesopotamia, introduced a code that provided standards for social and professional responsibilities of constructors, doctors, innkeepers or farmers.

The key idea behind CSR is that businesses are interwoven with society. As a result, the society has expectations for businesses to conduct their operations in a socially responsible manner, rather than merely meeting the minimum legal requirements. According to CSR, organizations should pursue actions that align with societal objectives. Even though CSR has traditionally focused on private sector businesses, its key principles can be used for setting management standards for different types of organizations, including public bodies (Hawrysz, 2013). The meaning of CSR can also vary by region and culture (Matten and Moon, 2008). Depending on the context in which CSR is used there can be differences related to: What is the purpose of an organization? To whom is the organization responsible? What role(s) does it play in the society? Reflecting on numerous definitions and interpretations, Godfrey et al (2010) called CSR an empirically and theoretically 'tortured concept', but the authors also acknowledged CSR's increasing importance in managerial practice.

CSR and sustainable HRM

Organizations engage in sustainable practices to further their CSR, and vice versa. According to CIPD (2021), 'These two factors are intrinsically linked because a business that damages the systems on which it depends will ultimately be unsustainable.' By supporting CSR, HRM can assist organizational efforts to operate in a sustainable way.

HRM plays a crucial role in advancing CSR and putting it into action. For CSR to be effective it needs to be embedded in the organization's culture. One of the functions of HRM is to communicate policies, and cultural and behavioural changes. As a link between top, middle and line managers, HR professionals are ideally positioned to influence attitudes towards CSR and sustainability. Furthermore, 'the way a company treats its employees will contribute directly to the picture of a company that is willing to accept its wider responsibilities' (CIPD, 2003). Hence, one of the first steps in achieving CSR can be to ensure that an organization manages its employees in a sustainable fashion.

In practice, how CSR and sustainable HRM are linked will depend on the internal resources, as well as the nature and strategy of the organization. Figure 2.1 illustrates four types of basic relationships between CSR and sustainable HRM. Firstly, sustainable HRM can shape the agenda of CSR practices: (1). This could happen in organizations where there is no clear owner

Figure 2.1 Basic relationships between CSR and sustainable HRM

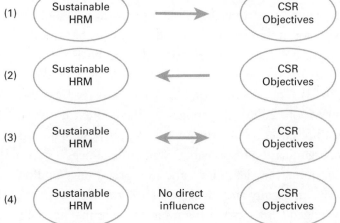

of CSR and the HR team steps up to the challenge and leads the CSR planning, implementation and reporting. This type of relationship can also occur in organizations where highly skilled employees are key to organizational success and CSR practices focus primarily on the social dimension. In the second type of relationship, CSR is the dominant force and it shapes sustainable HRM practices: (2). We can observe this in organizations with a firmly established CSR unit or strategy, which influences the HR function and how line managers supervise their employees. Thirdly, CSR and sustainable HRM initiatives influence each other and develop in parallel: (3). Finally, HRM is practised in a sustainable manner but there is no connection between it and the CSR efforts. This last form of relationship can exist, for example, in organizations where HRM focuses only on the social dimension of sustainability and CSR efforts are only concentrated on environmental or charitable actions: (4).

CSR pyramid

To better understand how sustainable HRM can support CSR objectives we need to explore in more detail what social responsibilities corporations have. The most popular and established model that explains this was introduced by Archie Carroll (1991, 2016). According to Carroll, CSR can be seen as a four-level pyramid. Each tier creates different obligations and opportunities for corporations. To achieve full social responsibility, corporations would need to satisfy obligations related to all four levels. These are: economic, legal, ethical and philanthropic responsibilities:

- **Economic responsibility.** This is the foundation of Carroll's CSR pyramid. In order to fulfil other obligations businesses need to survive and meet their economic responsibilities towards owners and other key stakeholders. Businesses that do not meet their basic financial responsibilities perish.

- **Legal responsibility.** According to Carroll, this level represents regulations that companies must comply with in order to operate. Businesses are required to respect their legal obligations, for example, related to employment laws or health and safety regulations. Carroll stresses that in a free-market economy the first two layers of responsibilities (economic and legal) are closely connected with each other. Failure to meet legal obligations could have a negative impact on corporations' first set of obligations covered by the model. The society *requires* all corporations to meet their economic and legal duties.

- **Ethical responsibility.** This is related to engaging in what is right even when the law and regulations do not require such actions. Companies are *expected* by the society to follow ethical norms when they are pursuing their business goals. Even though the model depicts ethical responsibilities as a separate third layer, these obligations are meant to be seen as cutting through the whole pyramid. For example, corporations that only meet the minimum legal requirements may still be perceived as socially irresponsible if their actions are perceived by the public as morally dubious. One of the ethical responsibilities of businesses would be to not exploit legislative loopholes and differences in international legal standards. A key element of ethical responsibility is to 'be responsive to the "spirit" of the law, not just the letter of the law' (Carroll, 2016).

- **Philanthropic responsibility.** At the top of the CSR pyramid, Carroll places philanthropy. This form of responsibility captures the idea that companies, just like everyone else, have obligations to support communities that they are a part of. The frequency and size of these generous actions will vary since they are voluntary. In practice, when businesses engage in this form of CSR they often use it as an opportunity to enhance their reputation and public image. According to Carroll's model, 'giving back' is not necessarily required but it is increasingly *desired* by the society. It is preferred for a business to engage in philanthropic activities, but the public would not label it 'unethical' if the company did not fulfil this obligation.

While Carroll's framework focuses on corporations, we can see how the obligations described in the model may also be applicable to other types of organizations. Non-profit organizations need to meet economic obligations to reinvest money back into their social causes. They need to provide goods and services that will attract donations, customers or financial grants. Public organizations can survive without turning a profit. However, they still need to follow economic responsibilities dictated by the budget that is provided for them. Moreover, all the above types of organizations have economic responsibilities towards their employees and business partners. Similarly, legal, ethical and philanthropic responsibilities are not exclusive to corporations.

One of the strengths of Carroll's model is its recognition that, among different responsibilities, organizations still need to meet their economic obligations. This makes the framework fairly pragmatic (Crane et al, 2019). In terms of limitations, Carroll (2016) admitted that the model was developed primarily 'with American-type capitalistic societies in mind'. For other national and cultural contexts, the order of pyramid levels may have to be reconsidered. For example, Visser (2006) argued that in some African countries philanthropic responsibilities of businesses are given higher priority than legal or ethical obligations.

CSR pyramid and sustainable HRM

Like any theoretical framework Carroll's model has its strengths and limitations. Nevertheless, it can be a useful starting point for linking sustainable HRM with CSR.

- HRM can assist organizations in achieving their *economic responsibilities* in a sustainable way. However, to do this the HR team needs to be ready to question 'business as usual'. HR professionals should understand the economic model of their organization and help search for a strategy that considers the social and environmental impact. This involves producing, communicating and delivering plans for achieving economic responsibilities for a wider range of stakeholders. For example, managers actively practising stress management and improving employee well-being can reduce work absences and staff turnover, thus contributing to economic goals.

- HRM plays a key role in helping organizations meet their *legal responsibilities*. In addition to basic employment law, compliance HR can prepare and analyse different scenarios for going beyond the minimum requirements. The HR team can conduct an internal audit of existing compliance levels and explore best practices related to employment law. Exercising sustainable HR best practices can save organizations from litigation.

- All elements of properly carried out sustainable HRM contribute towards fulfilment of an organization's *ethical responsibilities*. For example, taking on a sustainable approach an organization can integrate environmental objectives into all aspects of HRM, such as recruitment, selection, induction, training, rewarding employees and managing employees' performance. Using sustainable HRM to make the organization environmentally conscious can be seen as ethically desirable.

- Sustainable HRM can also aid with *philanthropic responsibilities*. The HR team can lead or facilitate projects that provide training, mentoring and development for demographic groups who are underrepresented in a given profession or industry. Alternatively, organizations can contribute their employees' time to help local communities and support charitable work. For example, in 2021/2022, British transport company HS1 dedicated over 700 hours to staff volunteering (HS1, 2022).

When the social responsibility of the organization is framed in relation to economic, social and environmental objectives, this is often referred to as triple bottom line (TBL).

Skill check

Linking CSR and sustainable HRM. People management can play a key role in helping achieve CSR objectives. HR teams and line managers need to consider how this can be accomplished in their organization.

Triple bottom line

The *triple bottom line* (TBL) is a term that was coined in 1994 by John Elkington, a British author and one of the leading experts on corporate responsibility and sustainable development. In finance, the term 'bottom line' is often used in reference to a company's earnings. Improving the bottom line would mean to increase business profits. In the spirit of sustainable development, Elkington advanced an idea that instead of concentrating only on the financial goals, businesses should watch over three bottom lines: financial (profit), social (people) and environmental (planet). Hence, TBL is also sometimes referred to as '3Ps' (Elkington, 1997):

- **Profit.** In a narrow sense this economic bottom line focuses on measuring a business's financial profit. However, from a broader perspective it refers to the positive and negative impact of the organization on the local and international economy.

- **People.** The people bottom line refers to measuring the impact that the organization has on its employees, community, customers and other stakeholders.

- **Planet.** The planet bottom line refers to measuring the positive and negative impacts the organization has on the natural environment.

The TBL, or 3Ps, reflect the pillars of sustainability highlighted by the Brundtland Commission (1987), as outlined in Chapter 1. In practice, the TBL is often used as an accounting framework evaluating either 'profit' or 'loss' in each of the three Ps. While quantifying progress in the social and environmental categories can be challenging, many organizations use the TBL as a tool for reporting their sustainability policies and practices. However, with the mark of the 25th anniversary of the term TBL, the author John Elkington (2018) argued that we need to 'recall' the model, because he did not intend it to be used *just* as an accounting framework. According to Elkington, '[TBL] was supposed to provoke deeper thinking about capitalism and its future, but many early adopters understood the concept as a balancing act, adopting a trade-off mentality.' Elkington argues that the TBL needs some 'finetuning' although he does not clarify what exact changes need to be introduced to the model. His essay points out that the TBL or similar frameworks are not enough if they 'lack the suitable pace and scale'.

ROC model

In the field of sustainable HRM the TBL can be translated into a model formed by De Lange and Koppens (2007). They argue that the things that separate traditional HRM from sustainable HRM are:

- **Respect.** A renewed emphasis on respect for internal stakeholders, specifically the employees. This involves but is not limited to appreciation of and engagement with employees.

- **Openness.** An outside-in perspective on HRM with environmental awareness.

- **Continuity.** A long-term approach, in terms of both economic and societal sustainability, concentrating on individual employability.

According to De Prins et al (2014), the ROC model will aid promotion and implementation of sustainable HRM, similar to how the TBL/3Ps vocabulary has gained popularity among scholars and managers. The ROC model can be used as a bridge between the CSR tradition and the principles of 'next-generation HRM' (De Prins et al, 2014).

De Prins (2019) identifies the following three main assumptions of the ROC model.

1 According to the ROC model, sustainable HRM represents the next stage in the evolution of HRM. The model revises the mainstream principles of strategic HRM: 1) the link between HRM and financial performance; 2) the fit between HRM and strategy; and 3) HRM and the sustainable competitive advantage (De Prins, 2019). The narrative of traditional strategic HRM is dominated by the employers' perspective and needs. However, more recent discussions of people management are concerned with sustainable HRM which provides a balanced view that the employer, employees and society/external stakeholders need.

2 Sustainable HRM and the ROC model help organizations find balance between two extremes of a paradox of maximizing profits through strategic HRM and reducing harm of people management practices (Mariappanadar, 2014). The ROC model proposes that these two elements are not mutually exclusive but reinforcing.

3 According to De Prins (2019), sustainable HRM is a social-constructivist concept. From this perspective knowledge is constructed through interaction with others, rather than discovered. Knowledge is actively developed by adding new information and expanding our understanding. De Prins (2019) highlights this assumption to clarify that they intend to stimulate a discussion on sustainable HRM rather than present a normative or descriptive solution to the subject.

The first key element of the ROC model is *respect*, which urges organizations to adopt a smarter and more responsible approach towards management of human resources. As mentioned in Chapter 1, authors such as Legge (1995) and Bolton and Houlihan (2007) argued that there is a disjunction between HRM theory and practice, with humanity being 'squeezed out' from work. ROC, and especially the first pillar (R), derives from a tradition of critical analysis of HRM and a recognition of the role that ethics plays in people management.

While HRM was developing as a professional practice, research and managerial experience were demonstrating that HRM can provide value for organizations and help achieve financial outcomes. However, as HRM was

competing with other organizational functions for the spotlight and resources, gradually the emphasis on employees was being neglected. The ROC
model proposes to revisit and reinvigorate the resourced-based view, positioning employees and their resources 'as a critically important asset to the
organization' (Cleveland et al, 2015). According to Stankevičiūtė and
Savanevičienė (2018), 'Bringing the H back to HRM requires a different approach to HRM or even a paradigm change.'

Examples of HRM practices related to 'respect' include talent development, employee engagement and empowerment, proactive health and well-
being management, work–life balance, mutually beneficial flexibility,
constructive stress management and a culture of cooperation.

The second key element of the ROC model is *openness*. It underscores organizations' role in society and recognizes the need to consider a wider range
of stakeholders, beyond just the owners of the business. Openness implies a
consideration of social issues and communities' concerns such as the protection of the natural environment or equality, diversity and inclusion. 'O' is also
dedicated to the institutional pressures that are exerted on organizations to
incorporate sustainability into HRM. In order to be perceived as legitimate,
organizations need to conform to internal and external environment demands. As the concepts of sustainability and CSR become relevant in society,
this puts pressure on organizations to accept ideas of sustainability. With this
in mind, the key question for the second block of the model is: 'How can we
connect our HRM policy (even more) with our other stakeholders and the
underlying values, standards and developments in society?' (De Prins, 2019).

Examples of HRM practices related to 'openness' include diversity management, accommodating an ageing workforce, implementing environmentally
friendly solutions, transparency of labour relations, unity of business, society
and education, as well as responsible interaction with local communities.

Continuity, which is the third pillar of the model, discusses how sustainable
HRM aids organizations' long-term survival and development. De Prins
(2019) argues that sustainable HRM requires a balanced approach between
economic and institutional perspectives. Rather than concentrate exclusively
on short-term financial performance, organizations can subscribe to a long-
term perspective which considers the needs of different groups of stakeholders, including one of the major internal groups, i.e. employees.

The framework recognizes that practices of lifetime employment are a
thing of the past. Nevertheless, in the process of mutual value creation, organizations can cultivate individuals' employability and work ability (De

Prins, 2019). *Employability* represents attributes that would allow a person to gain and maintain employment. On the other hand, ***work ability*** refers to a combination of good health and occupational competencies that allows an individual to perform work tasks. Management of employees' work ability requires a holistic, proactive approach including training as well as care for the quality of their working lives and work conditions.

Examples of HRM practices related to 'continuity' include developing employability, transfer of experience, long-lasting employment relations, being an attractive employer and compliance beyond labour regulations.

The ROC model's theoretical roots are deeply embedded in stakeholder theory and institutional theory. Each of these deserves a separate discussion, as they are a part of the theoretical foundation that forms sustainable HRM.

WORKSHOP DISCUSSION 1

Plante Moran

Plante Moran is a large American public accounting and business advisory firm. It employs more than 3,300 people, has 20 offices in the US and four international offices in Mexico, India, Japan and China. Plante Moran is well known for its sustainable HRM practices. It has received numerous local and national awards for best employer. Perhaps the most impressive achievement is featuring for 24 consecutive years on the *Fortune* magazine list of '100 Best Companies to Work For' in the US.

In 2021, 93 per cent of surveyed employees said that Plante Moran is a great place to work. This compares against the average 57 per cent of employees who feel the same about a typical US-based company. Moreover, 98 per cent of employees say that the management at Plante Moran is honest and ethical in its business practices.

These achievements are the result of Plante Moran leaders' continued commitment to create a great workplace. In 2017, Jim Proppe succeeded Gordon Krater and became the new managing partner of Plante Moran. Under Proppe's leadership the company significantly grew in size (increasing the number of employees by approximately 30 per cent) while maintaining culture and workplace excellence. Proppe explained:

> We continue to see the benefits of investing in programmes and policies that can be tailored to each staff member and give people the ability to grow personally and professionally, (...) We want to maintain and enhance our 'whole person comes to

work' culture, especially during challenging times, to attract and retain best-in-class professionals who provide excellent service to our clients.

Work–life balance

Scott Behson, a management professor at Fairleigh Dickinson University, is one of the authors promoting the whole-person workplace idea. According to this concept, organizations have the responsibility to honour employees as full people. We all juggle different roles and identities in our professional and private lives, and employers should use different practices and policies to create a welcoming and inclusive workplace for all staff.

At Plante Moran the idea of recognizing employees as full people was firmly set by the company's founders and remains relevant today. For decades the company has had workplace flexibility programmes that allow staff to balance work and family responsibilities. During the Covid-19 pandemic, the company also added a new 'flexible time off' policy.

Key work–life balance policies at Plante Moran include:

Flexible time off – staff can take time off when they need it most and do not need to bank time or worry about paid time off availability. Staff need to remain committed to the provided work objectives, but these can be achieved with the simultaneous focus on employees' well-being.

Alternative work arrangements – an option to tailor the work schedule around private responsibilities. This can include telecommuting, compressed workweeks, part-time schedules and putting in extra hours during tax season with reduced summer schedules.

Enhanced parental leave – six weeks' paid parental leave for all new parents, including adoptive parents. This is in addition to the six to eight weeks of short-term disability benefits the firm provides to birth mothers.

Tax-season day care – on tax-season Saturdays, at some of the offices, the company offers free on-site childcare.

Dress for your day – based on their own schedule (e.g. no meetings with clients), employees can follow a more relaxed dress code and wear denim at the office.

Athletic reimbursement – the company reimburses 50 per cent of athletic expenses up to a maximum of $80 per month.

The company also has a WorkFlex Committee which gathers ideas related to improving work–life balance, brings suggestions to the management team and champions practices that support employees.

Plante Moran work–life balance policies do not exist just on paper. Employees are aware of them and use them. According to one of the staff members,

The firm has been very supportive of me throughout the years. I recently decided to switch service groups, and my new group welcomed me with open arms. The firm was willing to listen to what I wanted, and it was a good fit for both me and my new service group. I've been fortunate to have flexibility to be able to be present in my children's lives and have been offered a generous flexible time off benefit.

On top of large strategic policies, the company is also looking for more symbolic ways through which it can show appreciation to its staff. Sometimes it is picking up the tab on food service delivery fees. At other times it is shipping ice cream to staff members across the globe to say 'thank you' for their extraordinary efforts during the pandemic.

The company uses its workplace culture as a top tool for recruitment and retention. 'In this job market, we know giving our team flexibility, independence, and recognition for all the great work they do maximizes career satisfaction,' Proppe said.

Diversity, equity and inclusion

Plante Moran is strongly committed to diversity, equity and inclusion. The company has a DEI Council which releases a report every year summarizing the company's DEI achievements.

Plante Moran is partnering with the Exceptional Academy (EA) – a local, one-year programme that offers Cisco certification and cybersecurity and network training for adults with autism and other neurodiverse attributes. Plante Moran promotes the benefits of hiring individuals with disabilities and directly offers internships and employment opportunities to EA graduates. For example, after John Ferella completed the EA programme, due to his skills and accomplishments, he was able take his career to the next level. He left behind working in the fast-food industry and received a full-time cybersecurity position with Plante Moran.

Plante Moran also supports local nonprofit organizations and by doing so provides its own employees with the opportunity to make a difference in the communities where they live and work. In 2022 some of the organizations that Plante Moran supported included OneGoal, Youth Opportunities Unlimited, Equality Toledo and Leader Dogs for the Blind.

Employees at Plante Moran can join groups ('Staff Resource Groups', abbreviated as SRGs) which celebrate diversity. So far, four groups have formed: Pride, African American, Veterans and Satellite. The last one is dedicated to employees who always work remotely. SRGs help staff members feel a deeper sense of community and promote their visibility at the company.

Questions

1 Use the ROC model discussed in this chapter to analyse the case of Plante Moran. What examples of Respect, Openness and Community can you identify in Plante Moran HRM practices?

2 What do you think prompted Plante Moran to shape their HRM practices in a sustainable manner discussed in the case study?

3 At Plante Moran the 'WorkFlex Committee' is a part of the DEI Council. How do you think work–life balance policies can help the employer to support their DEI objectives?

Sources

www.greatplacetowork.com/certified-company/1000203

https://go.plantemoran.com/rs/946-CTY-601/images/PM_DEI_Annual_Report_2022.pdf

www.plantemoran.com/explore-our-thinking/areas-of-focus/the-power-of-diversity-equity-and-inclusion

www.plantemoran.com/explore-our-thinking/insight/about-us/awards

www.plantemoran.com/get-to-know/news/2017/07/jim-proppe-assumes-role-as-plante-moran-managing-partner

www.plantemoran.com/explore-our-thinking/insight/careers/work–life-balance

www.plantemoran.com/get-to-know/news/2022/04/plante-moran-named-to-fortunes-100-best-companies-to-work-for-list

www.plantemoran.com/explore-our-thinking/insight/2021/05/beyond-fast-food-students-with-autism-find-careers

Behson, S (2021) *The Whole-Person Workplace: Building better workplaces through work–life, wellness, and employee support*, Authors' Place Press, Wilmington, NC

Stakeholder theory

Another key theoretical framework for the field of sustainable HRM is stakeholder theory. First, we need to recognize that stakeholder theory has many similarities to CSR. For CSR the starting point is the evaluation of corporations' responsibilities. Likewise, the stakeholder approach aims at recognizing different groups towards which organizations have responsibility. According to stakeholder theory, rather than focusing exclusively on the demands of owners, organizations should respond to the expectations of all stakeholders. Thus, in a similar way to CSR, stakeholder theory questions the assumption that organizations should only be concerned with pursuing profit. Moreover, much the same as CSR, stakeholder theory forces us to consider how organizations affect society. The main difference is that stakeholder theory emphasizes building and maintaining relationships with stakeholders.

Stakeholder theory was developed and popularized by Edward Freeman (1984). He argued that the management theories that were available in the 1980s were not suitable to address 'the quantity and kinds of change which are occurring in the business environment' (Freeman, 1984). One of the key insights of the theory is that capitalist organizations operate due to the inter-dependent interests of investors, employees, customers, suppliers, communities and governmental bodies. From this perspective the role of the manager is to recognize the nature of the joint interest and create value for all stakeholders (Laplume et al, 2008). The theory concentrates on examining cooperation and co-creation. According to Freeman (1984), while it is possible for organizations to operate in the short term by paying attention only to the interests of owners, in the long run such organizations (especially corporations) lose their social legitimacy. The consequences for organizations neglecting the stakeholder approach can be considerable, for example, due to potential litigation and loss of customers to competitors who are able to better satisfy the needs of different interest groups.

There are multiple explanations of who is a stakeholder (see e.g. Laplume et al, 2008). However, Freeman (1984) defined a *stakeholder* as 'any individual or group who can affect or is affected by actions, decisions, policies, practices or goals of an organization'. The range and nature of stakeholders can vary between organizations, different parts of the organization or even between projects. In practice, with finite resources and a range of constituencies that can be affected by an organization's actions, distinguishing which stakeholders are relevant may be necessary. One of the popular methods for identifying key stakeholders was presented by Mitchell et al (1997). According to the authors, the degree to which managers pay attention to a stakeholder (salience) is dependent on that stakeholder's attributes of power, legitimacy and urgency. These three qualities can be used to identify which stakeholders need to be prioritized:

- **Power.** This the extent to which a stakeholder can influence organizational behaviour and decision making.

- **Legitimacy.** This represents the extent to which the relationship with the stakeholder is perceived as desirable or appropriate.

- **Urgency.** This is the extent to which stakeholder claims or actions require immediate attention.

Stakeholder theory and sustainable HRM

Järlström et al (2018) applied the stakeholder salience framework in the field of sustainable HRM. They found that power and legitimacy are attributes that may be more critical for identification of key stakeholders, rather than urgency (situation based). They found that top management identifies sustainable HRM key stakeholders as employees, legislators, customers, trade unions and employee representatives, as well as organizational leaders and managers. The findings suggest that while managers show intent to promote ethical and sustainable practices, many of them still do not make a connection between HRM and a wider community or natural environment.

Stakeholder theory is consistent with the focus on sustainability. If an organization is concerned with sustainable development, it needs to recognize its wider environment with the interest of different internal and external stakeholders.

While sustainability and the stakeholder approach are closely connected they have different purposes. According to Guerci et al (2014), 'sustainability refers to principles and requirements that an organization must satisfy for being considered sustainable, whereas stakeholder theory is based on interactive and negotiation processes that result in an integration of the stakeholders' claims with the corporate interest.'

Guerci et al (2014) also explained the four main reasons why HRM should adopt a stakeholder perspective. Consider the following.

- First, successful HRM cannot concentrate on the interest of only employees but rather helps to meet the needs of all key stakeholders. When an organization recognizes the context in which it operates and responsibly manages its relationships with a range of stakeholders, the HRM function must follow the same approach.

- Second, by embracing the stakeholder approach, the HRM function gains another vital aspect through which it can create value in the organization. With organizations recognizing the role of stakeholder management, it is no longer enough for HRM to monitor performance and contribute to the financial bottom line. HRM needs to oversee and report the intended and unintended impacts on stakeholders.

- Third, incorporating the stakeholder perspective into HRM broadens our understanding of the relationship between the employer and employee, highlighting the importance of other stakeholders such as political actors, employee families, and local communities (Ferrary, 2009).

- According to Guerci et al (2014), the fourth reason for making the connection between stakeholder theory and sustainable HRM is to further ethical practices and social justice.

We can expand this list and identify one more key reason. Namely, Mariappanadar (2014) argued that the stakeholder perspective in HRM is necessary to fully recognize harm and the associated social costs of unsustainable people management practices, such as work intensification. We explore this idea in more depth in Chapter 3, in the discussion of negative externalities.

Institutional theory

Institutional theory explains how organizations navigate norms and rules of the social system in order to gain legitimacy and acceptance. Similar to the previously discussed theoretical frameworks, institutional theory casts light on why employers may choose to engage in sustainable HRM.

Institutional theory was introduced by John Meyer and Brian Rowan (1977). They suggested that formal structures can have symbolic properties. For example, organizations can have formal structures of recruitment, training and reward management infused with cultural meaning, signalling the importance of diversity and inclusion or sustainability. Organizations can plan to adopt specific structures and practices to signal commitment to associated values. As more organizations adopt a particular structural element (or practice), it gains social acceptance and becomes 'institutionalized'. This then exerts pressure on entities that have not yet introduced the given solution (Tolbert and Zucker, 1983). The key idea behind institutionalism is that many organizational actions represent a trend that evolves and with time becomes established as a convention or norm in an organization and its environment. Institutional theory provides a framework for understanding existing pressures to adopt a more sustainable approach to people management, but it can also be used to explain norms and forces that maintain *un*sustainable management practices (see, for example, Kobayashi and Eweje, 2021).

Before we move on with our discussion, we should quickly clarify what is meant by an 'institution' in this theoretical perspective. Scott (1995) explained that 'institutions are social structures that have attained a high degree of resilience'. Institutions offer legitimate scripts for actions. These can be seen as formal or informal rules and norms of specific systems in a given environment. Institutions define, for organizations and their members, what behaviour is appropriate or unacceptable (DiMaggio and Powell, 1991). Those organizations that can conform to institutional pressures are seen as legitimate and can receive support from other actors in the environment (e.g. government, shareholders, customers, community, etc.). According to institutional theory, for organizations to survive they need to achieve social legitimacy, which in turn requires them to conform to the expectations of their institutional environment. For example, as CSR becomes a relevant issue in a society, organizations respond to those environmental pressures and attempt to incorporate CSR policies and practices. This leads to institutional *isomorphism*, a phenomenon where organizations in a given environment resemble one another because they conform to similar pressures. According to DiMaggio and Powell (1983), we can identify three main types of institutional mechanisms that lead to isomorphism: coercive, normative and mimetic forces. These pressures can be imposed by different stakeholders, e.g. government and non-government organizations, suppliers, shareholders or customers:

- **Coercive forces.** This is when an organization is required by another organization to adopt a particular structure. Coercive force can be imposed, e.g. by trade unions or the government. For instance, in the UK under the Health and Safety at Work etc. Act (1974) employers have a duty to provide systems of work that are, so far as is reasonably practicable, safe and without risks to health.

- **Normative forces.** These are pressures brought about by organizational training and socialization. These are also forces that originate from the exchange of knowledge and practices through professional networks and through flow of workers between organizations. For example, managers in the banking industry following the practice of demanding first-year employees to work excessively long hours (*Financial Times*, 2021).

- **Mimetic forces.** This occurs when organizations, due to uncertainty, copy others. Imitating behaviours can happen because of the belief that others' actions are rational and successful or because of fear of appearing deviant or backward. In HRM this includes copying competitors' HRM strategies and practices in order to follow trends in the field.

Institutional theory suggests that organizations' social, environmental and economic performance is affected by the context in which they operate. The framework can be used to explain the system of norms, rules and beliefs that affect organizations and their management practices and policies. Mariappanadar (2019) identified the web of institutional contexts to which organizations respond to decide if they should develop sustainable HRM (see Figure 2.2).

Skill check

Analysing institutional mechanisms. This is an important skill because it helps to explain how formal structures and standard organizational practices are developed and popularized. Understanding institutionalization helps to recognize trends that lead to sustainable HRM or maintain unsustainable practices.

Figure 2.2   An institutional context framework for sustainable HRM

Institutional forces for sustainable HRM		
Organizational and industry context	*National context*	*International context*
• Role of organizational image • Investment incentives • Diversity of employees • Labour market conditions, e.g. high competition for talent • Business competition • Capital intensity • Industry growth • Reliance on external stakeholders, e.g. local community • Crisis response	• Laws and regulations • Necessity of compliance • Employment relations, e.g. trade union membership • Stakeholder activism • Market demand for ESG (environment, social and governance) businesses • National culture and its values of sustainability • Legitimacy of HRM practices	• Trust in sustainability standards and frameworks • Sustainability reporting standards, e.g. Global Reporting Initiative (GRI) • Sustainability frameworks, e.g. UN Global Compact, SDGs • Sustainability rankers and raters, e.g. World Benchmarking Alliance, Environmental Performance Index • Civil society organizations • Pressures from foreign subsidiaries of the organization

SOURCE Adapted and expanded from Mariappanadar (2019)

Paradox theory

When managers integrate sustainability practices with HRM they often encounter organizational tensions. These tensions can be paradoxical, i.e. involving dualities that are contradictory. One example is the need to cut costs in the short term and the need to invest for the future. When these elements are considered in isolation, each of them seems logical. However, when juxtaposed they can seem irrational, inconsistent and even absurd (Smith and Lewis, 2011). According to the paradox framework, managers too often persist on 'either/or' choice when encountering tensions. Instead, embracing a more complex 'both/and' mentality can be more fruitful. Insisting on taking a one-sided resolution to the paradoxical tension can resolve it only temporarily, because the tension will subsequently recur (Poon and Law, 2020). The theory allows managers to identify paradoxical tensions in the field of HRM and also to develop coping strategies promoting a more sustainable approach to people management.

The idea of organizational paradoxes has been differently conceptualized in academic literature. For example, Ehnert (2009) talks about the paradox *theory*, Hughes (2019) focuses on the paradox *perspective*, and Lewis (2000) proposes a three-part paradox *framework*. Lewis's framework represents a foundation for a discussion of contradictory and complex relationships in organizations. It describes: a) the nature of paradoxical tensions, b) the reinforcing cycles (the negative dynamics of a paradox) and c) the management of paradoxical tensions:

The nature of paradoxical tensions
According to Lewis, paradoxical tensions in organizations are perceptual. They are socially constructed polarities 'that obscure the interrelatedness of the contradictions' (Lewis, 2000). Contradictions are highlighted through simple binary logic, not capable of comprehending the intricacies of paradox. The 'either/or' thinking fails to recognize the 'wholeness composed of contradictions'. To illustrate the nature of paradoxical tensions in organizations Lewis refers to the Taoist symbol of Yin and Yang. Lewis emphasizes the *interaction* between interdependent contradictions in organizational paradoxes.

The reinforcing cycles: the negative dynamics of a paradox
According to Lewis (2000), 'the dynamics of paradox are often vicious'. As actors attempt to 'resolve' a paradoxical tension, this can further perpetuate

and exacerbate the tension. The challenge for employees and managers is how to cope with paradoxical tensions in a way that would turn negative reinforcing cycles into organizational opportunity.

Management: tapping the positive potential of paradox

Lewis (2000) argues that 'managers need to recognize, become comfortable with, and even profit from tensions and the anxieties [paradoxes] provoke'. The paradox framework suggests a shift in narrative and practice from 'resolving' to 'coping' with tensions. Instead of linear problem solving, the suggestion is to stay with the paradox, examine in more detail polarized perceptions, find a link between opposing forces and create a framework that gives meaning to the interconnected contradictions (Vince and Broussine, 1996).

Paradoxical tensions in sustainable HRM

In management and organizational literature, paradox theory has been used to examine issues such as change, competition or success. Ehnert (2009, 2014) proposes to apply paradox theory to improve our understanding of complex interrelationships in HRM and to achieve sustainable people management. Ehnert (2009, 2014) draws on Lewis's work and identifies three main paradoxes of sustainable HRM.

Efficiency versus substance paradox

This paradox illustrates a classic tension in HRM between deploying human resources efficiently, according to economic rationale, while at the same time sustaining the human resource base. This paradox includes a potential dilemma between financial pressures and attention to development of employees' competencies. The paradox also describes tensions between employees dedicating efforts to work processes or investing time into regeneration which will allow them to maintain mental and physical well-being. A one-sided resolution of this paradox would be to focus on financial objectives but neglect actions necessary to ensure availability of resources in the future.

Efficiency versus responsibility paradox

This paradox refers to tensions between satisfying economic rationale, while also maintaining social legitimacy. Ehnert (2014) points out here that behaving in a way that allows maintenance of social legitimacy does not always overlap with resource regeneration. For example, organizations can ask employees to engage in CSR activities after work hours in addition to regular duties (Poon and Law, 2020).

Present versus future paradox

The last paradox is concerned with tensions between short-term profit making and long-term organizational viability. An example of one-sided resolution of this paradox would be to prioritize lowering labour costs at the expense of poor investment in developing human resources (Ehnert, 2009, 2014).

Ehnert highlights how interconnected the three paradoxes of sustainable HRM are. In fact, we could argue that the shared base of these paradoxes is the short-term economic rationale that creates tensions with the regeneration of the HR base, maintenance of social legitimacy and recognition of the long-term economic rationale (see Figure 2.3). From the perspective of sustainable development, resolving these paradoxical tensions by paying attention to only one side could be detrimental to organizations. Thus, let's consider alternative coping strategies.

Figure 2.3   Paradoxical tensions of sustainable HRM

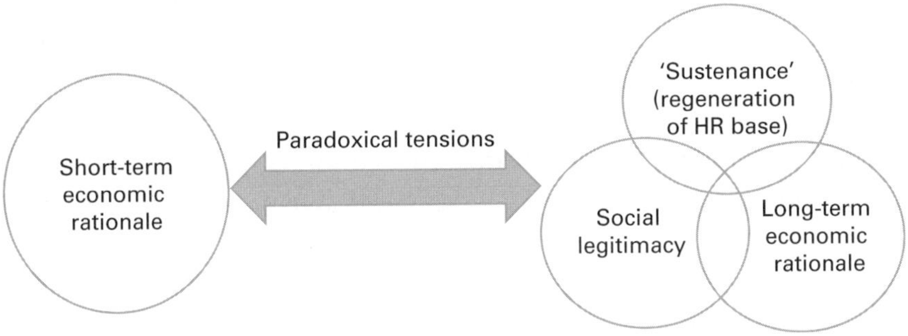

SOURCE Based on Ehnert (2009)

Strategies to cope with paradoxical tensions

According to Ehnert (2014), accepting the co-existence of opposite values is the first step in active management of tensions in sustainable HRM. Then, organizations need to plan how they wish to approach the identified tensions. Drawing on the work of Poole and Van de Ven (1989), Ehnert (2009) explained four main strategies that can be applied to the identified paradoxes of sustainable HRM: balancing, layering, sequencing and integrating.

Balancing

This is 'a coping strategy which opposes the poles of a paradox and emphasizes their co-existence' (Ehnert, 2009). This approach relies on accepting the tensions and searching for balancing tactics. The tension does not disperse but rather is accounted for and managed. For example, in a tension between a short economic rationale and resource sustenance, this approach would focus on a balance between high staff performance and improving employees' work–life balance. The strategy would also suggest a more levelled approach to the pursuit of economic objectives and social legitimacy, as well as balancing short- and long-term economic rationales.

Layering

This is a form of coping strategy that involves spatial separation of contradictions. This could help to reduce tensions between contradictory elements, while at the same time maintain some attention to both sides of the equation. However, the strategy only partly avoids the interrelated nature of the paradox. An example of layering in practice would be having separate units responsible for human resource deployment and 'reproduction'. For example, line managers would control how employees' performance is utilized and the HR department and/or external partners would be responsible for resource regeneration. The tension between short-term economic rationale and social legitimacy would be managed by having separate departments for HR and CSR. Whereas the tension between short- and long-term economic rationale would be managed by 'building the future into the present in different locations' (Ehnert, 2009).

Sequencing

Similar to layering, this is a coping strategy that uses separation of contradictions, although in this case the separation is temporal rather than spatial.

The poles of a paradox are considered one after the other. In this approach, the organizational pendulum swings from one to the other opposing quality, over time creating a process that can be represented by a wave or cycle. An example of this strategy would involve maximizing performance and profits in peak seasons while developing employee skills and providing more resource regeneration at off-peak times. Organizations adopting this strategy would prioritize economic rationality in busy periods and social responsibility when there is a need to build or protect the organization's legitimacy.

Integrating

This involves the introduction of new terms for reconciling the paradoxical tension. Unlike *balancing*, which accepts the paradox and attempts to use pole opposite positions simultaneously, *integrating* focuses on eliminating the opposition (at least temporarily) between the poles by introducing a new perspective (Ehnert, 2009). Real paradoxes cannot be permanently resolved. Hence, it should be expected that new tensions can occur and that they need to be dealt and coped with. In this coping strategy, an attempt can be made to resolve the tension by synthesizing the polar opposites at a higher level or by offering innovative solutions. An example of this strategy in practice would include integrating CSR practices into all HRM and line management processes. The tension between short-term economic rationale and resource sustenance would be managed by introducing HR regeneration policies and initiatives into all HRM processes (e.g. reward, selection and performance management). Organizations following this strategy would also dedicate resources to examine short- and long-term effects when taking any HRM decisions.

Balancing and *integrating*, represent higher level sustainable coping strategies. Spatially or temporally separating opposite poles (*layering* and *sequencing*) can be a tempting solution for organizations. However, these forms illustrate a delay in integration and a missed opportunity for taking a more advanced approach (Ehnert, 2014).

Other theories in the field of sustainable HRM

This chapter introduces key concepts and theories that form a foundation of sustainable HRM. However, the presented discussion is not exhaustive and there is a range of other approaches that could be used to study and explain sustainable HRM. Here is an outline of other notable theories.

Resource-based view (RBV) theory

According to RBV, organizations are defined by the resources they control. In order to gain a competitive advantage, companies need resources that are valuable, rare and costly to imitate (Barney, 1991). The theory emphasizes the role of employees in gaining a *sustainable* competitive advantage and is concerned with the enhancement of the human capital of the organization. RBV tends to be used to explain the value of resources. It can be adopted to examine more sustainable forms of developing and retaining human capital (Hronová and Špaček, 2021).

Organizational justice theory

Organizational justice can be explained as 'the extent to which employees perceive workplace procedures, interactions and outcomes to be fair in nature' (Baldwin, 2006). This theoretical framework highlights the significance of treating people in a fair and proper way, as well as considering employees' viewpoint and rewarding employees equitably.

Social exchange theory (SET)

According to SET, human relationships and social behaviour are rooted in an exchange process. This theory suggests that employees engage in reciprocal relationships. When staff believe that they receive assistance from their organization and managers, they can be motivated to remain loyal to the employer and show higher level of engagement in organizational goals. As Xu et al (2020) explains, 'More engagement brings more favorable supports from their supervisors and organization, leading to a virtuous cycle. Thus, employees are more likely to report more positive attitudes and intentions toward the organization when highly engaged.' The theory brings to the fore the issue of giving employees voice and noticing their concerns, opinions and ideas.

Gendered organizations theory

According to this theory, organizations present themselves as gender-neutral, but they are social structures where gender attributes are presumed and re-produced. Specifically, organizations operate with rules, procedures, rituals and expectations that typically tend to favour masculine traits (Acker, 1990). This theoretical framework can be key in exploring how unsustainable HRM practices affect employees differently depending on their gender.

Cognitive-affective system theory

The theory is used to describe the dynamics between individuals' personalities and related behaviours. From this perspective behaviour is not a result of a global personality trait but rather individuals' perceptions of themselves in a particular situation. Cognitive-affective system theory can be used to examine how employees' perception of green HRM influences staff's workplace green behaviours (Chen et al, 2021).

Summary

Even though the field of sustainable HRM is still relatively young, it is rapidly evolving and it draws on many established theoretical frameworks. CSR is one of the key concepts from which sustainable HRM has emerged. The chapter clarified the relationship between corporate social responsibility and people management. As indicated earlier in the discussion, organizations can take different approaches to connecting these two subjects. The HR function has the potential to support CSR initiatives and vice-versa. Similarly, the triple bottom line is an approach and terminology that many organizations may already be familiar with. The '3Ps' can be translated into the ROC model, which directly explains and expands the notion of sustainable HRM.

Following this, the chapter discussed stakeholder and institutional theories, which also form the theoretical foundations of sustainable HRM. Recognition of different groups of interest and the impact of HRM on them is at the heart of the sustainable approach. What's more, examining the environmental pressures allows us to understand the reasons why employers incorporate CSR into HRM or hold onto established institutionalized practices that are not sustainable in the long run.

Finally, the paradox theory can be used to examine tensions related to sustainable HRM. According to this framework, organizations can benefit from rejecting the 'either/or' logic and embracing the complexity of polar opposite values. Accepting and coping with the paradoxical tensions opens new opportunities for management practice and innovation.

Study questions

1 What is CSR? Explain why corporations may be required to show social responsibility.

2 According to Carroll's pyramid model of CSR, what are the four levels of corporate social responsibility and what implications do they have for the practice of sustainable HRM?

3 Explain what the triple bottom line is and how it is connected to the ROC model.

4 What is the main idea behind the stakeholder theory and why should HRM adopt a stakeholder perspective?

5 What is institutional isomorphism? What are the coercive, normative and mimetic forces that can lead to it?

6 Which model or theory do you think can be most useful for sustainable HRM practitioners? Support your answer with reasons explaining the choice.

Key reading

CIPD (2021) Corporate responsibility: an introduction, www.cipd.co.uk/knowledge/strategy/corporate-responsibility/factsheet (archived at https://perma.cc/RBA9-TP7Y)

Järlström, M, Saru, E and Vanhala, S (2018) Sustainable human resource management with salience of stakeholders: a top management perspective, *Journal of Business Ethics*, **152** (3), pp 703–24

References

Acker, J (1990) Hierarchies, jobs, bodies: a theory of gendered organizations, *Gender and Society*, **4** (2), pp 139–58

Baldwin, S (2006) *Organizational Justice*, Institute for Employment Studies, Brighton

Barney, J (1991) Firm resources and competitive advantage, *Journal of Management*, **17** (1), pp 99–120

Bolton, S C and Houlihan, M (eds.) (2007) *Searching for the Human in Human Resource Management: Theory, practice and workplace contexts*, Macmillan International Higher Education, New York

Brundtland, G (ed.) (1987) *Report of the World Commission on Environment and Development: our common future*, Oxford University Press, Oxford

Carroll, A B (1991) The pyramid of corporate social responsibility: toward the moral management of organizational stakeholders, *Business Horizons*, **34** (4), pp 39–48

Carroll, A B (2016) Carroll's pyramid of CSR: taking another look, *International Journal of Corporate Social Responsibility*, **1**, pp 1–8

Chen, S, Jiang, W, Li, X and Gao, H (2021) Effect of employees' perceived green HRM on their workplace green behaviors in oil and mining industries: based on cognitive-affective system theory, *International Journal of Environmental Research and Public Health*, **18** (8), p 4056.

CIPD (2003) *Corporate Social Responsibility and HR's Role*, CIPD, London

CIPD (2021) Corporate responsibility: an introduction, www.cipd.co.uk/ knowledge/strategy/corporate-responsibility/factsheet (archived at https://perma. cc/6D9N-CK7K)

Cleveland, J N, Byrne, Z S and Cavanagh, T,M (2015) The future of HR is RH: respect for humanity at work, *Human Resource Management Review*, **25**, pp 146–61

Crane, A, Matten, D, Glozer, S and Spence, L (2019) *Business Ethics: Managing corporate citizenship and sustainability in the age of globalization*, 5th edn, Oxford University Press, Oxford

De Lange, W and Koppens, J (2007) *De duurzame arbeidsorganizatie*, WEKA uitgeverij, Amsterdam

De Prins, P (2019) Bridging sustainable HRM theory and practice: the respect, openness and continuity model. In S Mariappanadar (ed.) *Sustainable Human Resource Management: Strategies, practices and challenges* (pp 188–215), Red Globe Press, London

De Prins, P, Van Beirendonck, L, De Vos, A and Segers, J (2014) Sustainable HRM: bridging theory and practice through the 'Respect Openness Continuity (ROC)'- model, *Management Revue*, **25** (4), pp 263–84

DiMaggio, P J and Powell, W W (1983) The iron cage revisited: institutional isomorphism and collective rationality in organizational fields, *American Sociological Review*, 48 (2), pp 147–60

DiMaggio, P J and Powell, W W (1991) Introduction. In W W Powell and P J DiMaggio (eds.) *The New Institutionalism in Organizational Analysis* (pp 1–38), University of Chicago Press, Chicago

Ehnert, I (2009) *Sustainable Human Resource Management: A conceptual and exploratory analysis from a paradox perspective*, Physica-Verlag, Berlin/Heidelberg, Germany

Ehnert, I (2014) Paradox as a lens for theorizing sustainable HRM. In I Ehnert, W Harry and K J Zink (eds.) *Sustainability and Human Resource Management: Developing sustainable business organizations* (pp 247–71), Springer Verlag, Berlin/Heidelberg, Germany

Elkington, J (1997) *Cannibals With Forks: The triple bottom line of twentieth century business*, Capstone, Oxford

Elkington, J (2018) 25 years ago I coined the phrase 'Triple Bottom Line.' Here's why it's time to rethink it, *Harvard Business Review*, https://hbr.org/2018/06/25-years-ago-i-coined-the-phrase-triple-bottom-line-heres-why-im-giving-up-on-it (archived at https://perma.cc/JP89-BE9N)

European Commission (2021) Corporate social responsibility and responsible business conduct, https://ec.europa.eu/growth/industry/sustainability/corporate-social-responsibility_en (archived at https://perma.cc/P79G-FMJK)

Ferrary, M (2009) A stakeholder's perspective on human resource management, *Journal of Business Ethics*, 87, pp 31–43

Financial Times (2021) Burnout: can investment banks cure their addiction to overwork?, www.ft.com/content/2f5d2587-d9a7-4cd5-ac84-e36d75b13a24#comments-anchor (archived at https://perma.cc/A3G8-E76E)

Freeman, R E (1984) *Strategic Management: A stakeholder perspective*, Prentice Hall, Englewood Cliffs, NJ

Godfrey, P C, Hatch, N W and Hansen, J M (2010) Toward a general theory of CSRs: the roles of beneficence, profitability, insurance, and industry heterogeneity, *Business and Society*, 49 (2), pp 316–44

Guerci, M, Shani, A B and Solari, L (2014) A stakeholder perspective for sustainable HRM. In I Ehnert, W Harry and K J Zink (eds.) *Sustainability and Human Resource Management: Developing sustainable business organizations* (pp 205–224), Springer Verlag, Berlin/Heidelberg, Germany

Hawrysz, L (2013) Patronage vs. implementation of the Corporate Social Responsibility (CSR) concept in the public sector, *Proceedings of Advanced Research in Scientific Areas, Zilina, The Slovak Republic*, pp 2–6

Health and Safety at Work etc. Act (1974) Commencement No.1, Order 1974, 1974/1439, art.2(a)/ Sch.1

Hronová, Š and Špaček, M (2021) Sustainable HRM practices in corporate reporting, *Economies*, **9** (2), p 75

HS1 (2022) Delivering the green gateway to Europe, our ESG report 2021/22, https://highspeed1.co.uk/media/34ll44us/hs1-esg-report-2021-22.pdf (archived at https://perma.cc/ASW7-FCZW)

Hughes, C P (2019) A paradox perspective for sustainable human resource management. In S Mariappanadar (ed.) *Sustainable Human Resource Management: Strategies, practices and challenges* (pp 61–77), Red Globe Press, London

Järlström, M, Saru, E and Vanhala, S (2018) Sustainable human resource management with salience of stakeholders: a top management perspective, *Journal of Business Ethics*, **152** (3), pp 703–24

Keynes, J M (1923) *A Tract on Monetary Reform*, Macmillan, London

Kobayashi, K and Eweje, G (2021) Barriers to gender equality in Japan: moving from myth to realities. In G Eweje, and S Nagano (eds.) *Corporate Social Responsibility and Gender Equality in Japan* (pp 13–30), Springer, Cham

Laplume, A O, Sonpar, K and Litz, R A (2008) Stakeholder theory: reviewing a theory that moves us, *Journal of Management*, **34** (6), pp 1152–89

Legge, K (1995) *Human Resource Management: Rhetoric and realities*, Macmillan, London

Lewis, M W (2000) Exploring paradox: toward a more comprehensive guide, *Academy of Management Review*, **25** (4), pp 760–76

Mariappanadar, S (2014) Stakeholder harm index: a framework to review work intensification from the critical HRM perspective, *Human Resource Management Review*, **24** (4), pp 313–29

Mariappanadar, S (2019) Institutional context for developing sustainable HRM. In S Mariappanadar (ed.) *Sustainable Human Resource Management: Strategies, practices and challenges* (pp 31–60), Red Globe Press, London

Matten, D and Moon, J (2008) 'Implicit' and 'explicit' CSR: a conceptual framework for a comparative understanding of corporate social responsibility, *Academy of Management Review*, **33** (2), pp 404–24

Meyer, J W and Rowan, B (1977) Institutionalized organizations: formal structure as myth and ceremony, *American Journal of Sociology*, **83** (2), pp 340–63

Mitchell, R K, Agle, B R and Wood, D J (1997) Toward a theory of stakeholder identification and salience: defining the principle of who and what really counts, *Academy of Management Review*, **22** (4), pp 853–86

Peters, B G (2020) *Institutional Theory in Political Science: The new institutionalism*, 3rd edn, Edward Elgar Publishing, Cheltenham

Poole, M S and Van de Ven, A H (1989) Using paradox to build management and organization theories, *Academy of Management Review*, 14 (4), pp 562–78

Poon, T S C and Law, K K (2020) Sustainable HRM: an extension of the paradox perspective, *Human Resource Management Review*, **32** (2), p 100818

Scott, W R (1995) *Institutions and organizations*, SAGE, Los Angeles

Smith, W K and Lewis, M W (2011) Toward a theory of paradox: a dynamic equilibrium model of organizing, *Academy of Management Review*, **36** (2), pp 381–403

Stankevičiūtė, Ž and Savanevičienė, A (2018) Raising the curtain in people management by exploring how sustainable HRM translates to practice: the case of Lithuanian organizations, *Sustainability*, 10 (12), p 4356

Tolbert, P S and Zucker, L G (1983) Institutional sources of change in the formal structure of organizations: the diffusion of civil service reform, 1880–1935, *Administrative Science Quarterly*, **28** (1), pp 22–39

Vince, R and Broussine, M (1996) Paradox, defense and attachment: accessing and working with emotions and relations underlying organizational change, *Organization Studies*, **17** (1), pp 1–21

Visser, W (2006) Revisiting Carroll's CSR pyramid: an African perspective. In M Huniche and E P Rahbek (eds.) *Corporate Citizenship in Developing Countries: New partnership perspectives* (pp 29–56), Copenhagen Business School Press, Copenhagen

Xu, F Z, Zhang, Y, Yang, H and Wu, B T (2020) Sustainable HRM through improving the measurement of employee work engagement: third-person rating method, *Sustainability*, **12** (17), p 7100

Harm caused by unsustainable HRM

3

LEARNING OBJECTIVES

After completing this chapter, you should be able to:

- Explain the meaning of negative externalities and their importance for HRM.
- Recognize different aspects of harm of work.
- Understand the risks of high-performance work systems and their potential harm.
- Explain how poor job design can lead to increased work-related stress.
- Explain why mass layoffs and downsizing represent an unsustainable approach to managing employees.
- Critically evaluate flexible HRM practices.
- Recognize that the harm caused by unsustainable HRM practices can have different impacts on various groups of employees.

Introduction

Academic and business interest in the subject of sustainability has significantly increased over the last few decades. Nevertheless, many organizations continue to use unsustainable business practices, which can harm the social and natural environments, as well as having a negative impact on the long-term productivity and profitability of the company. Many such practices have been 'institutionalized' and considered the norm within organizations and wider economic systems. Rethinking and challenging these business routines is essential for developing more sustainable organizations.

Consider a case of a sample corporation. There can be a number of unsustainable practices related to human resource management. It could be that the company expects its employees to work excessively long hours at the expense of their mental and physical well-being; or managers might take advantage of the fact that employees are able to check emails and work-related messages on their phones, and create pressure for staff to be on standby outside of office hours. If this company operates on a global scale, it can be even more difficult for employees to contain work within the boundaries of normal working hours or the working week. Additionally, it is important to consider employees' individual differences. We all have responsibilities outside of work and various degrees of tolerance for what constitutes an excessive amount of work. By intensifying workloads, organizations not only risk burning out their staff but also losing employees due to indirect discrimination. While some may be able and willing to put at stake their private time and even well-being to further their career, employees with caring responsibilities, disability or health problems may not be able to make such sacrifices.

In this chapter, we will look at the main ways in which organizations can cause harm with unsustainable human resource management. Our discussion centres around damage caused by irresponsible high-performance work systems (HPWS), poor job designs, mass layoffs and downsizing, as well as organizational flexibility that does not take into account the interests of key stakeholders. But before we start unpacking these practices, we need to explain what hides behind the term 'negative externalities', and what the main aspects of harm are, which we can identify when encountering unsustainable HRM.

Negative externalities

Mariappanadar (2012, 2019) is one of the leading scholars in the field of sustainable HRM and the bulk of their research focuses on understanding the negative impact caused by irresponsible people management practices. Mariappanadar proposed negative externality as a lens through which researchers and practitioners can examine the harm resulting from HRM practices on employees, their families and communities.

Externality is a concept that has been adopted from the field of economics. It was originally coined by Arthur Pigou in *The Economics of Welfare* (1920). *Externality* can be seen as a result of one agent's actions affecting the welfare of an uninvolved third party (Winterbotham, 2012). The concept captures the consequences (cost or benefit) of organizations' actions for third parties that did not choose to be subject to the cost or benefit. Externality is an effect that can be intended or unintended by the organization and is a result of producing goods and services (Mariappanadar, 2019). Positive externality occurs when actions of an organization benefit third parties. For example, a company that encourages employees to cycle and carpool to work benefits everyone in the society by reducing air pollution. Negative externality (NE) exists when an organization's action causes harm to third parties. In other words, stakeholders bear a portion of the cost associated with the production. For example, the public cost of healthcare increases because of the raised levels of work-related stress in the local economy. *Stress* is an adverse response to external stimuli that put excessive amounts of physical or psychological pressure on a person. The aim of sustainable HRM would be to retain the positive externalities of people management practices while reducing the negative externalities (NE) (Mariappanadar, 2014a). The NE concept helps practitioners and scholars explain and measure the social costs shouldered by stakeholders.

Mariappanadar (2014a) explained the harm of NE in the field of HRM as:

> The profound, incomprehensible and negative impact on employees and their family members' reduced personal outcomes, social and work-related health well-being that are caused by work practices used by organizations to extract maximum skills, abilities and motivation of employees to achieve highly effective and efficient performance.

According to Mariappanadar (2014a), we can identify four attributes of HRM NE:

1 Level of risk or severity of harm

2 Manifestation of harm

3 Impact of harm

4 Avoidability of harm

These attributes can be used as social indicators clarifying the repercussions of HRM negative externalities.

Level of risk or severity of harm

This is the employee's perceived level of harm of NE on themselves, their family or the community. The evaluation can be either *high* or *low*. When an employee sees the risk, or severity, of harm as high they can be more reluctant to take part in the activity. For example, if an employee believes that their current workload has negative consequences for their mental and physical well-being and has adverse effects on their family life, this employee may be avoiding engagement in some of the professional activities. When the level of risk, or severity, of harm is perceived by the stakeholders (e.g. employees, community) as high this could be an indicator of potential irreversible damage and should trigger an organization's efforts to lower the imprint of NE.

Manifestation of harm

Mariappanadar identifies two dimensions of this attribute: *instantaneous* and *time-lagged*. Put simply, we can differentiate between how quickly NE impinges employees, their family or community. NE that manifests within a short time frame (e.g. six months) after introducing a given managerial practice can be considered instantaneous. For example, employees who are hired on zero-hours contracts can experience fear of financial and social insecurity and strain on family relationships (Gheyoh Ndzi, 2021). Instantaneous manifestation of NE can take the form of employees experiencing mood swings or sleep disorders caused by work-related stress. In the case of time-lagged impact of NE, it could take one or more years after the introduction of the HRM practice for the costs to be borne by stakeholders. For example, a recent study conducted by Engelbrecht et al (2020) has demonstrated that work intensity was positively related to developing workaholism, which can lead to employees' burnout and musculoskeletal complaints (e.g. back pain).

Impact of harm

This represents the duration of the NE burden. Will the harm be *temporary* or *enduring*? Some negative effects of HRM practices can be reversible. For example, employees can recover from a temporary increase in work-related stress by taking intra-shift breaks, daily recovery after work, recovery at weekends and engaging in off-job activities (Fehrmann and Depenbrock,

2014). However, when organizations maintain a high level of work intensity without providing enough time for employees to recover, this could lead to development of prolonged stress, also known as chronic stress. This, in turn, can have a lasting impact on workers' physical and mental well-being including problems such as diabetes and even death. Indeed, stress is linked to six leading causes of death including heart disease, cancer, lung ailments, accidents, cirrhosis of the liver and suicide (Crum et al, 2013). Another example of enduring harm would be a decreased quality of romantic relationships. As explained by Debrot et al (2018), 'job stressors often elicit a sustained negative activation and, in these conditions, disengaging from work when leaving the professional setting is harder, impeding or delaying recovery (…) and resulting in higher strain at home.' A *stressor* is an external factor that impinges on a person and results in stress; at work it could be challenging deadlines, for example. Research has shown that partners who are in a relationship with an individual who is experiencing higher levels of stress report lower relationship quality, both on a daily basis and over extended periods of time. The extended exposure to stress and its impact on the quality of romantic relationships also increases the risk of divorce (Debrot et al, 2018; Neff and Karney, 2004).

Avoidability of harm

This parameter is concerned with the extent to which the harm of HRM NE is due to *avoidable* or *unavoidable* conditions in the internal or external environment. For example, consider a scenario where an organization acquires or merges with another company, with the hope of significant cost savings through workforce reduction. On average, when such an operation is made in the same industry, roughly 30 per cent of employees are deemed redundant after restructuring (Marks et al, 2017). What follows mergers and acquisitions is usually job losses, periods of uncertainty, increased workloads, pressure and stress. If the organizations engaged in the merger or acquisition to increase value for the shareholders, employees may perceive the harm caused by the subsequent reorganization and redundancies as avoidable. Conversely, if an organization took part in the merger or was acquired by another company because it was facing financial difficulties or even bankruptcy, then employees may be more likely to see the harm caused by the change in ownership as unavoidable.

Mariappanadar (2014a) acknowledged that, in a free-market economy, it may not be possible to completely eradicate the NE of HRM. However, a more sustainable approach would focus on understanding, containing and reducing the harm that HRM could cause to employees, their families and the wider community. NE attributes can be used to better recognize the different dimensions of negative externalities. These need to be taken into account when an organization is estimating efficiency and effectiveness of its strategic goals.

WORKSHOP DISCUSSION 2

Family Dollar

Family Dollar was founded in 1959 in North Carolina and became one of the fastest-growing retailers in the United States. Today it is a large chain of discount stores conveniently located in neighbourhood locations. The company has more than 15,000 shops across the US with approximately 60,000 employees. In 2015, the firm was acquired by Dollar Tree, another US chain of discount variety stores.

Since 2000, Family Dollar faced multiple lawsuits. In 2007, the company had to pay $35 million to a group of managers who accused Family Dollar of underpaying them. In 2008, the company had to pay $45 million to settle a gender-discrimination case. According to *Insider*, a US business news company, Family Dollar has updated its onboarding procedures and it now requires new employees to sign away their right to benefit from a large-scale lawsuit. What remains for employees is to solve disputes with the employer out of court through individual private arbitration.

Mandatory arbitration is an increasingly popular practice among large US companies. However, critics of this approach argue that arbitration in the US helps to keep employment disputes hidden from the public and makes it more difficult to keep companies accountable for malpractice. According to the American Association for Justice (AAJ), in 2020 workers received cash settlements in just 1.6 per cent of arbitration cases. Moreover, a 2015 study by the Economic Policy Institute found that even when workers are awarded money in arbitration cases, they receive significantly less compensation than they would have in court.

In 2020, Family Dollar and its parent company Dollar Tree arbitrated 1,135 cases. Reporters from *Insider* spoke with 32 former employees of Family Dollar, the majority of whom have received cash compensation from the company in arbitration.

From the group of former employees that *Insider* reporters spoke with, the largest paid settlement was $4,000. Some of the employees had worked for the company for several years and received less than $1,000. According to *Insider*, one of the former employees had worked for the company for 12 years with no holidays and no weekends and only received an $800 settlement.

Former employees reported that they had to work 80-hour weeks. Most of the workers interviewed by *Insider* had a manager role and were paid less than $50,000 a year before taxes, with no overtime. One of the former employees is a single parent with three children. She explained that she had a fixed salary, but when she worked 80 hours per week her compensation was equivalent to US $10 per hour. According to the former employees, Family Dollar gave them the position of manager because under US labour laws organizations usually do not have to pay overtime to managers. However, a large portion of these workers' tasks included menial work, such as stocking shelves, cleaning up the parking lot and working cash registers.

Insider found that some of the former employees had to sleep at work due to exhaustion, or because they did not have enough time to go home between shifts. For instance, one of the former managers said that he would sleep in the store on days when he had to do double or triple shifts.

Former employees also argued that their working conditions were unsanitary. They said that they encountered pests like snakes, lizards and large spiders in break rooms in the stores. In 2022, after a Food and Drug Administration (FDA) inspection, 404 Family Dollar stores had to be temporarily closed and a range of products had to be recalled because of rodent infestation and other unsanitary conditions.

A Family Dollar spokesman said in a statement that the company is committed to providing a safe environment for customers and workers. Referring to recalling products and temporary closure of stores, the spokesman said that the company takes 'this situation very seriously' and is 'in the process of remediating the issue'.

Former employees who discussed their work experience with *Insider* also raised the issue of support for staff. Employees mentioned that at work they often had to deal with robberies. The company trained them on how to handle a robbery, but allegedly the management did not provide substantial support after a store was robbed. One of the former employees explained that she had experienced two store robberies, and it was traumatizing for her to have to return to work.

In 2022, Dollar Tree received $1.5 million in penalties for more than 3,900 violations of the state's meal break laws in Family Dollar stores. Violations affected 620 employees from 100 locations in Worcester, Massachusetts. An investigation of Family Dollar found that in 2018 and 2019 the company routinely cut the necessary payroll hours. As a consequence, stores were understaffed and employees were not able to take meal breaks or leave the store during a break.

According to Massachusetts laws, employers have to provide employees with at least one 30-minute meal break when they have worked more than six hours in one day. Moreover, during the meal break employees should be allowed to leave the workplace. According to the investigation, Family Dollar failed to abide by the breaks and time-off laws.

In 2021, a Family Dollar store in Lincoln, Nebraska had to temporarily close because all employees walked out and quit. They left a sign on the store's front door which read, 'We all quit! Sorry for the inconvenience!'

Jared Austin, a local news reporter, spoke with a former employee who used to work in the store. The interviewee said, 'We got employees hired, they went through the onboarding process, they'd work for us for two days and they'd quit (...) It was just a never-ending cycle of training people and them quitting.'

Goldman Sachs

Goldman Sachs is a US multinational investment bank and financial services company. By revenue, it is the second-largest investment bank, right after JPMorgan Chase.

In 2021, a presentation with Goldman Sachs-branded slides was leaked to social media. The presentation allegedly reported results of an internal survey with 24 questions completed by 13 US-based first-year investment banking analysts. The presentation was titled 'Working Conditions Survey' and painted a bleak picture of burnout, sleep deprivation and declining mental and physical health.

According to the presentation, and the survey findings covered in it, on average 'first-year analysts are working over 95 hours per week and sleeping five hours per night'.

For the question 'How many hours have you worked this week (ending 13 February 2021)?' the average answer was 105 hours.

Respondents were asked to rate on a scale of 1 to 10 their well-being currently and before starting a job at Goldman Sachs. Junior analysts rated their mental health as a 2.8 and their physical well-being as a 2.1, compared with 8.8 and 9.0 respectively before starting their work at the investment bank.

Their personal relationships also suffered. All of the surveyed junior bankers said that the job had negatively affected their relationships with friends and family. Seventy-five per cent of respondents said that they had considered counselling due to the stress of the job.

A separate slide showed respondents' comments from open questions:

'I didn't come into this job expecting 9 am–5 pms, but I also didn't expect consistent 9 am–5 ams either.'

'The sleep deprivation, the treatment by senior bankers, the mental and physical stress... I've been through foster care and this is arguably worse.'

'I can't sleep anymore because my anxiety levels are through the roof.'

'My body physically hurts all the time and mentally I'm in a really dark place.'

'What is not ok to me is 110–120 hours over the course of a week! The math is simple, that leaves four hours a day for eating, sleeping, showering, bathroom and general transition time. This is beyond the level of "hard working", this is inhumane/abuse.'

In the presentation, which circulated on the internet, the alleged survey respondents also complained about mistreatment at work. Seventy-seven per cent said they had been victims of workplace abuse.

The survey was discussed by large news websites such as CNN, CNBC and Fox Business, to name a few. According to Yahoo Finance, a spokesperson for Goldman Sachs acknowledged the survey and report. The spokesperson explained that the poor working conditions were caused by surging business at the firm and Covid-19.

Due to the mounting media pressure David Solomon, the CEO of Goldman Sachs, also commented on the working hours of junior analysts, stating 'This is something that our leadership team and I take very seriously'. Solomon added that the company will better enforce the 'Saturday rule'. According to this rule, junior staff should not be expected in the office between 9 pm Friday and 9 am Sunday.

Solomon also recognized that one of the solutions to the issue would be to hire more junior staff across the investment banking division.

Questions

1   Read the section in this chapter dedicated to negative externalities. How would you use the concept of NE and the four attributes of HRM NE in the context of the management practices of Family Dollar Store and Goldman Sachs discussed above?

2   Critically discuss moral and business arguments for and against HRM practices described in the two companies.

3   What do you think are the main steps that Family Dollar Store and Goldman Sachs can take to improve their HRM practices?

Sources

www.businessinsider.com/how-family-dollar-kept-worker-lawsuits-hidden-
    arbitration-2021-12

www.telegram.com/story/business/2022/02/03/ag-sending-message-employers-why-
    family-dollar-hit-1-5-m-penalties-labor-laws-maura-healey/6649674001/

https://edition.cnn.com/2022/03/04/business/family-dollar-rat-infestation-memphis-
    dollar-tree/index.html

www.mass.gov/news/family-dollar-cited-15-million-for-thousands-of-meal-break-
    violations-at-massachusetts-locations

www.washingtonpost.com/business/2021/10/27/mandatory-arbitration-family-dollar/

www.epi.org/publication/the-arbitration-epidemic/

www.justice.org/resources/research/forced-arbitration-in-a-pandemic

https://topclassactions.com/lawsuit-settlements/lawsuit-news/family-dollar-class-action-alleges-company-sold-products-amid-massive-rat-infestation/

https://topclassactions.com/lawsuit-settlements/employment-labor/family-dollar-class-action-claims-workers-exposed-to-unsanitary-conditions-at-distribution-center/

www.entrepreneur.com/article/379981

www.independent.co.uk/news/world/americas/goldman-sachs-analyst-found-dead-hours-after-complaining-to-father-of-100-hour-weeks-10292977.html

www.bbc.com/news/business-56452494

www.theguardian.com/business/2021/mar/18/group-of-junior-bankers-at-goldman-sachs-claim-inhumane-work-conditions

www.fintechfutures.com/2021/03/goldman-sachs-analysts-reveal-abusive-working-conditions-in-leaked-survey/

www.fnlondon.com/articles/goldman-sachs-ceo-david-solomon-promises-to-beef-up-junior-ranks-after-scathing-survey-20210322

Aspects of harm of work

Mariappanadar (2012, 2019) highlights three general clusters that represent aspects of work harm and unsustainable HRM practices: 1) psychological, 2) social and 3) health. We will discuss each of these clusters proposed by Mariappanadar and expand the framework with the fourth category: 4) environmental harm of work. The forms of harm can be discussed in conjunction with the idea of NE but they can also be examined separately.

Psychological harm of work

Due to the psychological harm caused by unsustainable HRM practices, an employee can face reduced future rewards and career growth. For instance, consider a scenario where a manager increases employees' workload to the point where staff begin to struggle to manage their duties. They can experience high levels of stress, difficulties with concentration and even *occupational burnout*, which is a state of emotional exhaustion resulting from work demands consistently exceeding an employee's capacity to manage them. The psychological harm caused by unsustainable work can have an adverse impact on an employee's performance and subsequently prospects for maintaining employment or developing career opportunities. Employees who struggle with the aftermath of unsustainable work practices can be perceived by supervisors as lacking capabilities. In those cases, the burden of psychological harm is placed on employees themselves. Managers could play down organizational responsibility for supporting employees' mental well-being and perceive the reduced efficiency and effectiveness caused by psychological harm of work as a form of personal limitation. Thus, employees who experience the psychological harm of work may also receive reduced rewards and employment opportunities (Mariappanadar, 2019).

Social harm of work

This aspect of harm is related to the perception of how work restricts the social and family activities of the employee, leading to diminished social well-being of staff. As explained by Mariappanadar (2019),

> When workloads or work commitments restrict employees from spending quality time with their family members and friends, they will reduce their social well-being outcomes for employees and their families. The social harm of work highlights the unsustainable effect of work on employees' work–family adjustment.

Everyone has a finite amount of time and energy. Depleting them into one role, in this case work, means that the employee does not have time and energy available for other social roles such as family. This is sometimes referred to as *work–family conflict* or work–life conflict, with the latter being a broader term. Ilies et al (2007) found that both the objective amount of workload (in terms of the number of hours worked), as well as the subjective perception of workload, have a negative impact on employees' work–family balance. When employees are not working overtime, the strain or psychological distress caused by work can still cause work–family conflict. Moreover, employees report a work–family conflict when they have a permanently high level of workload, but also when they experience a high workload on specific days. Thus, managers need to understand that even when staff do not have chronically high workloads, but rather a high amount of work on certain days, this also can have a negative impact on their work–family balance. High work–family conflict negatively affects employees' social behaviour at home (Ilies et al, 2007) as well as their psychological well-being and job performance (Obrenovic et al, 2020).

Health harm of work

Unsustainable HRM practices can have a negative impact on employees' health. This is related to: a) 'employees' perception of restrictions for positive health' as well as b) 'work-related leading indicators for negative health' (Mariappanadar, 2019). Firstly, let's consider restrictions for positive health and unpack what that means. Positive health can be seen as 'well-being beyond the mere absence of disease' (Seligman et al, 2013). It is related to having *biological health assets* such as cardiorespiratory fitness; *subjective health assets* such as life satisfaction, sense of meaning and purpose; and *functional health assets* such as meaningful work and the ability to carry out work (Seligman et al, 2013). Even when work does not directly cause any illness or medical condition it may limit an employee's ability to achieve positive health and maintain health assets. Unsustainable practices such as work intensification can restrict employees from initiatives such as physical exercise, weight control initiatives or social activities, which can then negatively affect their health.

Secondly, we can look at the health harm caused by HRM through the lens of work-related leading indicators for negative health. Leading indicators is a concept adopted from the field of economics. Typically, it is a term used to determine measurable factors that, if monitored, could predict the ups and downs of the economy in the future. When applied to the practice of HRM, work-related leading indicators can help us predict what might happen to employees' health if management practices continue as they are. Each organization can develop its own system of leading indicators for HRM, but it can be useful to draw here on the body of literature dedicated to psychosocial risk factors in the workplace. For example, CCOHS (Canadian Centre for Occupational Health and Safety) identified 13 organizational factors 'that impact organizational health, the health of individual employees and the financial bottom line, including the way work is carried out and the context in which work occurs' (CCOHS, 2021). These are:

1 psychological support
2 organizational culture
3 clear leadership and expectations
4 civility and respect
5 psychological competencies and requirements

6 growth and development

7 recognition and reward

8 involvement and influence

9 workload management

10 engagement

11 balance

12 psychological protection

13 protection of physical safety

According to CCOHS, this list is based on extensive research and a review of empirical data from national and international best practices. The centre's websites includes a more detailed discussion of each of the factors (CCOHS, 2021).

Environmental harm of work

In addition to the points raised by Mariappanadar (2012, 2019), we should recognize that neglecting to use people management to protect the natural environment can have a detrimental impact on the ecosystem. Harm can be done to the environment by overlooking the role that the HRM plays in shaping organizational culture and implementing change. For example, without appropriate green induction and training, environmental policies may be unsuccessful in achieving their intended goals. Similarly, failing to introduce environmental targets or incentives (for individuals, teams or departments) in performance management systems could be seen as a lack of reasonable care for measures that are meant to prevent environmental harm. Chapter 5 discusses in more depth the role that HRM plays in helping organizations achieve environmental sustainability.

A significant amount of the discussion related to negative externalities and harm of work, which is presented by Mariappanadar (2019), centres around unsustainable practices of high-performance work systems (HPWS). The chapter now turns to this topic with the exploration of what HPWS are and why some scholars are concerned about the negative impact of these systems on stakeholders, such as employees and their families.

Skill check

Analysing harm of work. A key skill for any manager or HR professional. While navigating complex organizational policies and practices it is vital to recognize the potential harm that work can cause.

High-performance work systems

High-performance work systems (HPWS) can be explained as bundles of HRM practices that are strategically linked with one another, with the aim to advance employee abilities, motivation and provide cost-efficient results that will increase organizational profitability (Datta et al, 2005). 'HPWS' is sometimes interchangeably used with other similar acronyms and terms such as HPWP (high-performance work practices), HIWS (high-involvement work systems), HPWE (high-performance work environments), HCWS (high-commitment work systems) and HPMP (high-performance management practices). The academic literature shows a range of definitions for HPWS or its synonymous terms. However, what discussions on HPWS tend to have in common is that these are systems using interconnected human resource management practices to 'create value for an organization by reducing costs, improving productivity, as well as creating value for employees' (Mahdi et al, 2014, p 1). The challenge for sustainable HRM is how to ensure that organizations do not fixate on the first two elements and neglect the last part. As the name suggests, HPWS attempts to orient employees towards higher (or highest possible) levels of performance. Thus, it is pertinent to examine how sustainable HPWS are and how they are implemented in practice.

HPWS bundles include practices of (Appelbaum et al, 2000; Takeuchi et al, 2007):

- flexible job assignments
- rigorous and selective staffing
- extensive training and development
- developmental and merit-based performance appraisal
- competitive compensation
- extensive benefits

- participative decision making
- motivators, such as autonomy and teamwork

In theory, HPWS are meant to create a 'win-win' scenario where employers benefit from improved profitability and productivity while employees enjoy higher wages and job satisfaction. Indeed, many studies have demonstrated that HPWS can be mutually beneficial for both the organization and workers. For example, Giannikis and Nikandrou (2013) examined employees working in 22 manufacturing companies in Greece and found that HPWS positively impacted employees' level of job satisfaction and organizational commitment. The authors argued that, in a high-performance work environment, employees can experience positive outcomes as they 'believe that their organization is willing to invest in them, trusts them in decision-making processes and has a deep concern for their needs' (Giannikis and Nikandrou, 2013). However, other studies highlighted that HPWS can lead to positive experiences for employees only if their well-being is considered. There is a very thin line between HPWS and unsustainable work intensification or even exploitation.

Negative effects of HPWS

Without sufficient care for employees, HPWS can harm workers. This is a conclusion that Chang et al (2018) came to after analysing data from HR managers and employees working in the Chinese manufacturing and service industries. They found that, in the examined organizations, HPWS led to increased job demands and work intensification (working hours). Their findings support a more critical perspective on HPWS, in which they state that 'motivating greater involvement and participation – may lead to added responsibilities and extra workloads to attain organizational financial outcomes at the expense of employee well-being' (Chang et al, 2018). According to the authors, when HPWS are implemented they can coincide with a pursuit of cost-effectiveness, which consequently causes more workload, stress, lower job satisfaction, tensions between employees and management, and even experiences of labour exploitation.

Jensen et al (2013) conducted a survey on 1,592 Welsh government workers employed in 87 departments in the public sector. They found that when HPWS are introduced, and employees have little discretion over how they can implement work responsibilities, employees are likely to report anxiety, role overload and higher turnover intentions. In line with other academics taking a critical approach, Jensen et al (2013) ask: 'While HPWS may benefit organizational performance, what effect do they have on the lives of individual employees?'

Kroon et al (2009) surveyed 393 employees from 86 different Dutch organizations. The study found a slightly positive relationship between HPWP and burnout. The project contributed to a body of literature arguing that HPWP can lead to high levels of stress and intensification of job demands, potentially resulting in a state of emotional exhaustion. When introduced without care for employees, HPWS can lead to higher levels of:

- work intensification
- job demands/role overload
- work-related stress
- tensions between employees and management
- experiences of labour exploitation
- anxiety
- professional burnout
- turnover intentions

Work intensification refers to a substantial increase in work demands, and the amount of effort an employee needs to exercise. The easiest, but also imperfect, way to investigate it is through the number of working hours. Most research dedicated to this topic focuses on this measure, although there can be various reasons why a person works a longer shift. Thus, when examining work intensification in practice, or in academia, it may be useful to consider experiences of working at a heightened speed, performing different tasks simultaneously, an increased need to complete more tasks within one working day and/or reduced idle time (Bunner et al, 2018).

Intensified work puts greater demands on employees and is associated with physiological and psychological deterioration as well as increased risk of work–family conflict. Working 55 hours a week, compared to working 35–40 hours a week, is correlated with a 35 per cent higher risk of a stroke and a 17 per cent higher risk of dying from ischemic heart disease (Pega et al, 2021). Working long hours is also associated with depression, anxiety, short sleep and sleep disturbance, exhaustion, injuries, unhealthy behaviours (such as smoking, alcohol consumption) and decreases in physical activity (Wong et al, 2019). Unsurprisingly, the pressure to complete more tasks can contribute to a conflict between quality and quantity of work. However, work intensification also compromises individual safety behaviour and safety of the work environment. When performance targets are at risk, employees are often expected to work faster rather than safely. For example, Bunner et al (2018) found that work intensification negatively affects workers' safety compliance (following activities that maintain personal workplace safety, e.g. wearing protective equipment) and safety participation (contributing to the overall safety of the workplace). Moreover, as previously discussed in this chapter, working unsocial or long hours also creates challenges for balancing professional and out-of-work commitments.

When HPWS are introduced without suitable care for employees they can have a negative impact on employees' well-being. But what would employee care consist of? Some elements of it can be context specific, but in general, it is seen in terms of consideration of employees' health and safety beyond minimum statutory regulations, sincerely promoting good work–life balance, developing sustainable workloads and job designs, treating employees well as an end in itself, and listening to employee concerns. We explore further the ideas of employee care and regenerating human resources in Chapter 4.

Organizations need to be aware of the effects that HPWS have on employees. If the moral side of the discussion is not sufficient, then managers may need to remember that poor implementation of HPWS also can lead to higher intentions to leave the organization and poor safety performance.

As Mariappanadar (2014b) explained, 'All HPWPs are not intrinsically harmful but some HPWPs are harmful for employees; either the way those HPWPs are implemented in an organization or overuse of such practices by managers.' Sustainable HRM explains that HPWS can be introduced and improve organizational performance without harming employees and their families.

The above discussion raises issues such as high level of job demands and little control over how work can be performed. While these topics are related to HPWS they also fall into a discussion of job design.

Poor job design and its impact on work stress

Poor job design is another aspect that can cause harm to key stakeholders such as employees. Engaging in job design is one of the core functions of HRM.

According to CIPD (2021), job design is:

> A process of determining job roles and what a job involves, as well as how it relates to other relevant jobs and the organization's structure. It includes deciding on the duties and responsibilities of the job holder, the way the job is done, as well as what support and resources the job holder needs.

Job design plays a crucial role in managing performance. When conducted successfully it can improve employee motivation, job satisfaction and reduce turnover and absenteeism. It also has impact on employees' physical and mental well-being. When the task is inadequately designed, and/or procedures are ineffectively communicated, it can lead to additional mental or physical strain. For example, job design can have a direct impact on the level of stress that employees experience. A moderate amount of pressure can motivate employees to achieve their goals and may be necessary in an organizational setting. However, when it becomes excessive, it turns into stress, which is an adverse reaction to the environment in which we operate.

Job-Demand-Control-Support model

Job-Demand-Control-Support (JDCS) is a well-known model used to study job stress. When originally introduced by Robert Karasek in 1979 the model was focusing only on job demands and job control, but it was later expanded by the concept of social support (Johnson, 1986; Karasek and Theorell, 1990). The JDCS model explains how job characteristics influence employees' psychological well-being. The basic idea behind it is that job demands cause strain. However, the level of that strain depends also on the amount of control that the employee has over their work and on the extent of social support they receive in their role. Thus, the JDCS model consists of three main elements:

- **Job demands.** This focuses on the psychological rather than physical challenges of work. For example, it could be related to the time pressure, difficulty and workload that is required in a given role.
- **Job control** (also 'job decision latitude'). This represents the amount of autonomy an employee has over how they want to perform their tasks. For instance, to what extent they can influence the order, volume and content of their tasks.

- **Social support.** This describes the overall level of helpful social interaction available in the job. It captures support provided by co-workers and supervisors.

In the first version of the model, which focused only on the job demands and job control, Karasek (1979) identified four main types of job:

- **high-strain jobs** (high job demands and low job control)
- **active jobs** (high job demands and high job control)
- **low-strain jobs** (low job demands and high job control)
- **passive jobs** (low job demands and low job control)

Karasek argued that jobs characterized by high job demands and low control ('high-strain jobs') are expected to have a negative effect on workers' well-being. This type of job, if performed over a longer period of time, can cause mental strain and could be a risk for physical health. Then, in 'active jobs' the psychological strain caused by work is average and not excessive because the energy and challenges created by the job can be turned directly into action. These jobs are intense, but they do not imply negative psychological effects. Here high job demands are motivating to act, learn, make decisions and focus on personal growth at work. 'Low-strain jobs' tend to be self-paced occupations, for example as a self-employed maintenance person. Finally, 'passive jobs' tend to offer limited challenges and opportunities from work. The last two types of jobs are associated with lower health risks.

In the updated version of the model, Karasek and Theorell (1990) also considered social support and argued that high-isolation-strain jobs (high job demands, low job control and low social support) are related to the highest risk of chronic stress and stress-related physical illness.

The model has its limitations. One of the common critiques is that it oversimplifies complex work environment issues. However, researchers have been able to successfully use the model to make predictions about employees' physical conditions (cardiovascular and coronary heart disease), psychological disorders and harmful coping behaviours (e.g. smoking). For the field of management, the application of the model is straightforward. It highlights the importance of designing roles in a way that would balance high job demands with provision of autonomy and social support to employees.

Employers need to move beyond promoting mental well-being as a concept and focus on actually designing jobs that allow their employees to achieve good health. While in some high-demand jobs it can be difficult to increase the amount of control that employees have, e.g. because the work environment is volatile and dictated by other factors, it may still be possible to provide social support for employees working in this context.

Role conflict and ambiguity

Earlier in this chapter, the section dedicated to HPWS introduced a discussion of how work intensification and higher job demand can cause psychological stress. Subsequently, we explored how the JDCS model expanded this debate and introduced moderating factors of job control and social support. Now, we can move even further with the analysis of job design and work stress by considering 'role conflict' and 'role ambiguity'.

Role conflict

This occurs when employees receive incompatible work demands. For example, an employee may be holding two or more roles with competing requirements. In other cases, a person may have one main role but report to two or more supervisors who are expecting conflicting results. Role conflict has long been recognized as a work-related stressor. When we are in a position in which attending to one set of demands means disobeying others, we can feel frustrated and confused. These circumstances are often associated with (Rollinson, 2008; Kahn et al, 1964):

- high levels of interpersonal tension
- decreased job satisfaction
- poor interpersonal relations
- decreased confidence in the organization
- decreased commitment to the organization

Role conflict can also occur when the requirements of work and family are incompatible with each other. If employees experience these tensions, it may be beneficial for the organization to rethink and redesign roles to provide more flexibility in terms of scheduling or in terms of where the work can be carried out.

Finally, role conflict can also exist when a person is asked to perform tasks that are incongruent with their personal values. For example, someone who values excitement and social interactions is asked to perform desk-based tasks that require little contact with co-workers or clients. While this issue could be prevented by more effective job candidate selection and resource allocation, in some circumstances this form of role conflict can also be resolved through *job sculpting*, i.e. customizing the role to the needs of the employee.

Role ambiguity

This occurs when there is ambiguity or a lack of information concerning the role that a person is meant to be performing. For example, an employee may not know what is expected of them or how their performance is evaluated. They may not understand the scope and parameters of their job or what should be their priority. In other cases, employees may be uncertain about how they fit into the organization. When a worker experiences role ambiguity, they are unsure how to perform their job well or how to use available resources. As a result, they can psychologically withdraw from their tasks. The lack of direction and lack of clarity can cause stress and also has been linked to (McCormack and Cotter, 2013; Mañas et al, 2018):

- anxiety
- depression
- burnout
- lack of self-confidence
- dysfunction in dealing with social situations
- reduction of effort
- decreased satisfaction

Impact on work performance

Poor job design can cause stress, which in turn may have a negative impact on employees' work performance. When we are stressed, our decision-making skills suffer and we are more prone to make errors. Psychological research has demonstrated that stress impacts our cognitive processes such as attention, memory, problem-solving and judgment (Staal, 2004), all of which are key components of high-quality individual performance. It also has energy-depleting effects on our body and mind. When experienced over a longer period, stress makes it difficult to relax. Thus, it hinders recovery from work and makes it difficult to feel energetic and enthusiastic enough to face another day at work.

Stress can also affect employees' team performance. Impaired individual employee capabilities can translate into lower-quality communication, co-ordination and cooperation with team members. Staff who are stressed can also abandon their team-level focus and adopt more individualistic orientations. Stress can also shorten our tempers and make us more argumentative or irritable. When we are operating under excessive amounts of pressure, we can become snappier and show more emotional reactions, such as being more aggressive (or sensitive or tearful). Behaving out of character can further negatively affect our ability to work with others.

There is also a strong association between stress and staff turnover. Dissatisfied employees who have deteriorated in their health due to their job might be looking for alternative employment. Even when such employees stay in their roles, they may avoid work as the research has shown a link between stress and absenteeism (Davey et al, 2009).

Other factors affecting work-related stress

Work-related stress is a complex subject that goes beyond the discussion of job design or HPWS. We need to acknowledge that there can be a range of organizational stressors, including the culture of the organization (e.g. fear-based work culture), or organizational politics (employees engaging in different tactics to increase their personal or professional influence). In the UK the Health and Safety Executive (HSE, 2022) identifies six key areas that can lead to work-related stress:

- demands
- control
- support
- role
- relationships
- change

Even when organizations carefully design jobs, employees may experience stress, for example due to the relationships that they have with their colleagues, supervisors or customers. Repeated exposure to negative actions from colleagues or customers can be a major stressor. A substantial amount of stress can be caused directly by supervisors' or managers' behaviour towards the employee.

Moreover, organizations evolve and change, which could also be a source of stress. The anticipation and uncertainty related to change, or the frequency of organizational adjustments, can put excessive pressure on employees.

> **Skill check**
>
> **Job design.** To optimize work performance and protect employees' well-being, a good understanding of job design is essential.

Layoffs and downsizing

In the face of pressures created by global competition, technological advancements, economic cycles and changing customer demands, many organizations use layoffs as a tool to improve or maintain profitability. However, this is a high-risk strategy. Research shows that layoffs can have a significant negative impact not only on employees (both those who are removed and those who survive) but also on the overall performance of the organization.

The technical definitions of terms such as layoff, redundancy and downsizing would be determined by the legal framework and can vary between countries. To add to the confusion, there are also differences between legal definitions and how people use these terms in everyday life. For example, technically in the UK 'laying off' is an act of the employer asking an employee to stay at home or take unpaid leave because the employer does not have sufficient work for the employee (Gov.uk, 2022; ACAS, 2022). However, in practice people often use the term 'laying off' synonymously with making someone redundant, which is when someone loses their job because their employer does not need them anymore.

To clarify, in this book we use the term *laying off* as the act of terminating a worker for reasons other than their work performance. Laying employees off is one of the processes that organizations undertake when they downsize. *Downsizing* is a management strategy that involves intended, permanent and significant reductions of personnel. As part of downsizing, organizations terminate employees but also restructure, eliminate organizational layers, redesign jobs, merge units or combine functions in an attempt to improve efficiency and effectiveness (Wilkinson, 2005).

Downsizing is based on economic rationale and is an established management practice. It is introduced to avoid bankruptcy, or to boost profits. Downsizing is often performed during economic downturns or when an organization's revenue is declining, although it can also be caused by technological advancements and regulatory changes. Some organizations engage in it proactively without any apparent financial need (Love and Kraatz, 2009). The logic behind downsizing is simple and compelling: reducing operating costs. As explained by Cascio and Wynn (2004), 'It [downsizing] begins with the premise that there really are only two ways to make money in business: either you cut costs or you increase revenues. Which are more predictable, future costs or future revenues?'

Negative effects of downsizing

Despite its premise and popularity, it is questionable whether downsizing actually leads to organizational benefits. Let's first consider what harm downsizing can cause to the business side of organizations and then focus on the negative externalities.

Large-scale layoffs can have a negative impact on customer satisfaction. Reducing labour workforce means losing knowledge and experience that were retained by the lost staff. In consequence, some of the understanding of customer preferences, problem-solving methods or critical skillsets can be lost, thus leading to lower quality of service. Downsizing can also disturb the commitment and productivity of the remaining workforce. Employees who survive the layoffs are likely to become more disengaged with their work, which in turn can be noticed by customers. Organizations that rely on customer contact might be particularly affected by the lost talent and may therefore see a negative impact on their revenue (Mujtaba and Senathip, 2020).

Downsizing damages an organization's social networks, which consequently can significantly harm its learning capacity. When a company reduces the size of its personnel this not only shrinks the labour capacity but also diminishes the informal networks. Fewer links with the internal and external environment means that knowledge will be more difficult to spread across different units within an organization and with the external environment. That is to say that the ability of an organization and its members to generate new knowledge will be disrupted. According to estimates made by Fisher and White (2000), down-sizing by 20 per cent to 5 per cent would result in an estimated loss of 50 per cent up to 57.6 per cent in learning capacity. This is an issue that should be considered particularly carefully by companies that operate in turbulent industries and rely on innovation.

Downsizing can also harm an organization's reputation. This is especially true when such measures are introduced with the intention of increasing efficiency, as opposed to downsizing announced due to decline in demand. Schulz and Johann (2018) confirmed in their research that the motive for personnel reductions makes a significant difference to how badly the organization's reputation will suffer. First, shareholders can understand that efficiency-driven downsizing is risky and short-term gains can be overshadowed by long-term damages caused to learning and innovation capabilities. Second, over the years, downsizing has received a lot of criticism for its impact on employees' well-being and 'since firm performance is often tied to managers' compensation, cutting labor costs with the aim to improve firm performance can be seen as a selfish way of serving the managers' personal interests' (Schulz and Johann, 2018).

Indeed, the harm done to employees is significant. By looking at medically certified sickness absence, and other indicators of health, researchers found that employees were at least twice as likely to have health problems in organizations that underwent a major downsizing as opposed to organizations that did not undergo downsizing (Kivimäki et al, 2000). These findings can still underestimate the scale of health issues because employees in downsizing organizations may be reluctant to take leave, and due to work pressures attend work while being ill (Aronsson et al, 2000; Theorell et al, 2003). Longitudinal studies (Dragano et al, 2005) have shown that employees who 'survive' downsizing can experience a range of adverse health consequences such as:

- mortality risk
- musculoskeletal complaints
- hospital admission
- disability pension
- negative self-rated health
- depression

According to Frone and Blais (2020), downsizing has a broad impact on work conditions which then translates into consequences for employees' work experiences ('employee outcomes'). In a national study of US workers, Frone and Blais (2020) found that downsizing had a negative impact on nine work conditions, which can be broadly grouped into four categories:

- work role (work demands, role conflict)
- interpersonal conditions (supervisor aggression, friendship formation, dysfunctional leadership)
- rewards (**distributive justice**, promotion opportunities)
- security (job insecurity, employment insecurity)

In turn these adverse working conditions caused by downsizing have negative impact on a series of employees' work experiences:

- negative work rumination (e.g. replaying negative work events in your mind)
- inability to unwind
- physical, mental and emotional work fatigue
- depression
- anxiety
- anger
- decreased happiness, confidence and vigour
- negative general assessment of physical and mental health
- job satisfaction
- organizational commitment
- turnover intentions

Those who remain in employment after mass layoffs can develop a so-called *survivor syndrome* (also 'survivor sickness') (Sperry, 1996). The term describes feelings that employees experience after they remain in an organization that has had involuntary staff reductions. Studies suggest that 'survivors' can experience psychological burdens in the form of anger, depression, fear, distrust and guilt. Some may feel survivors' remorse as they are concerned about the future of co-workers and friends who have lost their jobs. These emotions can reduce employees' productivity, increase absenteeism and increase the risk of workers voluntarily leaving the organization. Due to lost trust in the employer and negative work experiences, many employees voluntarily leave the organization after they survive layoffs. Trevor and Nyberg (2008) found that, in an average company, even if just 1 per cent of the workforce is laid off this can lead to a 31 per cent increase in voluntary turnover after the process of downsizing. However, if the same organization lacks practices that promote fair procedures and employees are not strongly embedded in their jobs then 'the predicted increase in quitting becomes 112 per cent' (Trevor and Nyberg, 2008). Disillusioned with their employer, after surviving the layoff, employees may start exploring their options of working elsewhere.

On the other side of this discussion, we have workers who involuntarily lose their jobs due to downsizing. Studies show that they often experience poor physical and mental health. Job loss from downsizing is stressful and can lead to excessive alcohol use, sustained poor mental health (Junna et al, 2021; De Battisti et al, 2014; McKee-Ryan et al, 2005), and even higher risk of death by suicide (Classen and Dunn, 2012).

Downsizing can lead to significant harm at the individual and organizational levels. Not only does it affect well-being of 'survivors' and 'victims' but it can also lead to bankruptcy. Zorn et al (2017) examined data on 4,710 publicly traded US companies. They found that, *irrespective of companies' financial health*, organizations that downsized were twice as likely to declare bankruptcy than firms that did not downsize.

Flexibility gone wrong

The changing nature of work has created demand for organizations to adapt quickly to new environments. Social trends, market pressures, technological advancements as well as the complexity of contemporary business, force organizations to improve their flexibility, making it also a key subject for HRM.

Flexibility is a topic that has sparked heated debates among academics. On one hand, flexibility is seen as a strategic tool that can be utilized to achieve competitive advantage. On the other hand, the concept of organizational flexibility has been heavily criticized for its harm to workers and local communities (Kozica and Kaiser, 2012).

Kozica and Kaiser (2012) explained flexibility as 'the ability of organizations to cope with the dynamics and the uncertainty of their environments by rapidly changing their organizational routines or resource bases.' The term refers to a range of actions that organizations can take in order to proactively adjust to the environment. In order to critically evaluate flexibility practices that represent an unsustainable approach to HRM, we need to first differentiate between three main types of flexibility: functional, numerical and financial (Atkinson, 1984).

- **Functional flexibility.** This refers to the organization's ability to redeploy employees to different tasks as needed. Functional flexibility allows organizations to use employees' skills to meet the requirements of changing demands and methods of production. In practice, it often relies on employees' will to work outside of their job descriptions, ability to learn new tasks and roles, as well as readiness to work beyond traditional forms of Monday to Friday, 9 to 5. Functional flexibility uses full-time members of staff to multitask and perform similar responsibilities without the need to resource labour from outside of the organization.

- **Numerical flexibility.** This is an ability to adjust the amount of labour input depending on peaks and troughs in work or production schedule. When organizations achieve numerical flexibility, they are able to match the need for workers with the number of people who provide labour to the organization. It involves employing people on different contracts that will allow the organization to deploy workers when they are needed, but also easily dispose of them if they are no longer required. Numerical flexibility is attained through *atypical employment contracts* that do not conform to standard, open-ended and full-time employment arrangements (Eurofound, 2017). This includes, for example, part-time, fixed-term, temporary, casual and seasonal contracts. Atypical work, which helps to achieve flexibility, also includes consultants and self-employed workers, agency workers, subcontractors, apprentices and volunteers.

- **Financial flexibility.** Organizations can achieve flexibility through multiple payment and rewards strategies. Financial flexibility refers to the freedom to vary the pay individuals receive in ways that best allow the organization to meet its objectives. For example, it can be achieved through linking pay to individual performance, rather than paying everyone the same regardless of their results. Financial flexibility is interconnected with numerical and functional flexibility.

Flexibility helps organizations achieve their goals and minimize costs. It can also provide benefits for employees and the local community. For example, the provision of part-time contracts means that a wider population can engage in paid work. Non-standard employment contracts can be ideal for family-oriented individuals who have care responsibilities, or for students who want to make income while continuing education. However, some flexibility practices can cause harm to employees and local communities.

Critique of flexibility practices

One of the concerns raised by the critics is that **atypical contracts** can be used to undercut wages and avoid provision of employment benefits such as holiday pay, pension plans and insurance. Atypical contracts allow organizations to achieve numerical and financial flexibility, but when used irresponsibly they equate to unsustainable income for employees. Perhaps the most controversial form of non-standard form of employment is *zero-hours contracts* (ZHC), or in other words employment contracts whereby the employer is not obliged to provide any minimum working hours to the employee. While ZHC is a term used primarily in the UK, similar forms of employment arrangement also exist in other countries, such as Canada and Australia. If the local legal framework allows it, the employer can be tempted to replace someone's full-time, open-ended contract with a ZHC even when the person works regular shifts and is needed for day-to-day operations.

One of the companies that got into hot water due to unsustainable use of ZHCs was Sports Direct, the UK's largest sports goods retailer. Sports Direct's 'appalling working practices' led to a government investigation (Business, Innovation and Skills Committee, 2016). The chairman of the investigating committee said:

> Many of the agency workers at the Shirebrook warehouse have been working there for many years. The warehouse at Shirebrook is open 365 days a year, 24 hours a day, and the nature and flow of business activity in the warehouse can be forecast with some accuracy. We heard no convincing reason why Sports Direct engaged the workers through agencies on short-term, temporary contracts, other than to reduce costs and pass responsibility.

Sports Direct is just one example. Some of the other companies for which use of ZHCs has been publicly discussed include Amazon, McDonald's, Cineworld, Subway, JD Wetherspoon and even Buckingham Palace (see e.g. Neville et al, 2013). ZHCs are widely utilized by retailers, hospitality businesses, health and social work providers, transport, and education organizations. According to the Office for National Statistics, in 2021 approximately

996,000 people were hired on ZHCs in the UK (ONS, 2021). This number is no doubt underestimated because the survey requires participants to identify themselves as being on a ZHC. Some workers may not be certain which term would best describe their employment contract.

The data from the UK is concerning because many workers on ZHCs have no guarantee over a crucial part of their income. Their employment provides little security for being able to pay rent, bills or daily expenses. Advocates of atypical contracts would be quick to remind us that ZHCs are often used by people in full-time education (23 per cent of all people on ZHCs) or in semi-retirement (4.5 per cent of all people on ZHCs are aged 65+). Moreover, according to the national statistics, 61 per cent of those on ZHCs do not want more hours (ONS, 2021). Still, research shows that variable and zero-hours employment can lead to in-work poverty, where people work in more than one job and yet experience poverty (McBride and Smith, 2021). In-depth interviews with people on ZHCs reveal the impact that atypical employment has on workers. After examining experiences of people on ZHCs, Gheyoh Ndzi (2021) found that

> The uncertainty and insecurity of the contract affects workers' financial stability, social and family life, job quality and satisfaction, career progression and health. (…) issues such as the lack of opportunities for career progression, no/limited training provided where required, stress and anxiety relating to the insecurity and uncertainties remain a growing concern.

As Gheyoh Ndzi pointed out, employees on ZHCs may experience the additional work stress related to job insecurity and poor work–life balance whilst also missing out on workplace events such as training or being a part of decision-making groups.

Flexible HRM can be achieved by introducing atypical contracts or by overloading full-time staff (functional flexibility). These approaches to flexibility can provide short-term results by lowering costs and achieving resource efficiency. However, if introduced irresponsibly, in the long run flexible HRM can lead to a negative impact on stakeholders (e.g. employees, local community) and on organizations themselves. Businesses that abuse ZHCs and other forms of atypical contracts have staff who feel undervalued, unsupported and disengaged. If either party at any point can resolve the contract, and the employee's value to the organization is reduced to the number of hours they can provide, then it is hard to blame employees for not feeling connected to their organization and its success. Research has also shown that temporary employment has a negative impact on product innovation (Kleinknecht et al, 2014; Cetrulo et al, 2019).

Attempts to achieve organizational flexibility are not inherently negative or positive. However, a more sustainable approach to HRM would be to consider the short-term and long-term impacts that flexible HRM practices have on employees and other key stakeholders.

Employee individual differences

Mariappanadar (2014a) highlighted that when we discuss harm of unsustainable HRM practices, we should recognize the individual differences between employees. This is a broad subject that can be related to characteristics such as personality and abilities, as well as gender, age and/or disability. For example, Schaufeli and Enzmann (1998) reviewed more than 250 studies and found that the characteristic of neuroticism was one of the strongest personality dimensions correlated with burnout. In a longitudinal study, Udayar et al (2020) examined the correlation between personality traits, work-related stress and overall life satisfaction. They found that participants with an oversensitive profile had higher chances of work stress negatively affecting their life satisfaction, whereas participants with a resilient profile prevented the negative spillover of work stress from affecting their life satisfaction. Moreover, respondents with a resilient profile showed a positive spillover, where their life satisfaction was countering the adverse effects of negative experiences at work.

Understanding that individuals may be differently affected by harm of work is key to successful sustainable HRM practices. It is crucial to show empathy and understanding to our colleagues who may have different work experiences than us. Let's consider how gender, disability and age influence harm of unsustainable HRM practices.

Gender

According to Gascoigne et al (2015), when organizations raise the number of hours that employees are expected to dedicate to their job it can contribute to gender inequality. This is because role intensification increases the traditional division of roles between home and work. Societal gender norms, such as the emphasis on maternal parenting and women's domestic responsibilities, mean that longer working hours can have an adverse impact on women's careers.

When a person needs to dedicate more time to work at the expense of interacting with family, they may experience guilt and psychological distress. However, in a national survey of working Americans, Glavin et al (2011) found that this guilt and distress is felt more strongly by women. Family members can regularly remind their wives/mothers/daughters that they 'have family to look after' (Sommerlad, 2016). When women give in to the pressure of being the primary caretaker, they may not be able to subscribe to the culture of long working hours, which in turn affects their professional reputation and career opportunities.

Gender is also an important characteristic that may need to be considered during and after downsizing. Research conducted in Sweden found that, the year following either organizational downsizing or expansion, women show a reduced likelihood of taking medically certified sick leave (15 days or more) (Theorell et al, 2003). Moreover, women who had a *higher cardiovascular score* (higher risk of developing a heart or circulation problem) were *less likely* to take long-term sick leave, compared to women with a lower cardiovascular score (Theorell et al, 2003). These are puzzling and troubling results. Aronsson and Gustafsson (2005) presented a potential explanation:

> 'Medically vulnerable' employees in a downsizing situation feel that they have a reduced chance of finding a new job if they become unemployed. Accordingly, they refrain from exercising their right to stay away from work when they feel ill to a greater extent.

Findings related to the reduced likelihood of taking sick leave are especially noteworthy when we consider the fact that women are more susceptible than men to heart problems following stressful events (Bacon, 2018). Taking into account existing research, it is perhaps unsurprising that Ahammer et al (2020) found that women are at a higher risk of cardiac events due to mass layoffs.

While studies have found no consistent patterns in men's use of sick leave after downsizing (Theorell et al, 2003), research shows that men, compared to women, are at a significantly higher risk of death by suicide after becoming unemployed due to mass layoffs (Classen and Dunn, 2012).

Disability

Disabled people are more likely than non-disabled people to work on atypical contracts such as part-time, self-employed (Gov.uk, 2021) and zero-hours contracts (Roberts et al, 2021). However, on ZHCs it is easier for bad employers to dismiss their workers. As a consequence, employees on ZHCs may fear disclosing to their employers that they have an impairment because an employer could come to the conclusion that it is easier to terminate the contract than to make any work adjustments (Wales TUC, 2018).

High-performance work systems can also disproportionately impact disabled employees. HPWS include intense workloads and unrealistic targets, thereby increasing the level of work-related stress, often with limited support. Such work environments with rigid objectives and schedules can be particularly unhelpful to some disabled workers (Wales TUC, 2018). For example, in a workplace with short break times, it can be difficult for people with diabetes to eat as they need to (Bloodworth, 2018).

Age

Research suggests that younger and older workers can be differently affected by work intensification. For example, in a study of Finish upper-white-collar workers, Mauno et al (2019) found that older workers (50+ years) were more likely to report work intensification than their younger counterparts. Older workers also reported higher learning demands at work (intensification of knowledge- and skill-related demands). At the same time younger workers were more likely to report intensified demands related to career planning.

Organizations can easily fall into the trap of ignoring or excluding the experiences of older workers. According to Armstrong-Stassen and Cattaneo (2010), this can be the case for organizations that have downsized in particular. The authors conducted a broad cross-section examination of occupations and organizations across Canada and found that 'organizations that had downsized were significantly less likely to have human resource practices specifically tailored to the needs of older workers and to have a less supportive training and development climate for older workers' (Armstrong-Stassen and Cattaneo, 2010). This finding is particularly concerning if we take into account that older workers are more susceptible to adverse health shocks and they are one of the groups whose health is negatively affected by downsizing (Ahammer et al, 2020).

For the purposes of our discussion, we have looked at one trait at a time. However, in practice these and other characteristics can overlap, thereby creating intersecting experiences of disadvantage. Any form of discrimination and exclusionary workplace practice could be considered socially irresponsible and unsustainable. Thus, the discussion of how different groups of employees are affected by harm of work overlaps with the rich literature on equality, diversity and inclusion.

Summary

This chapter explained different ways in which HRM can cause harm. By now you should have a solid understanding of key themes related to unsustainable people management practices. Exploring the concept of negative externalities provides a good starting point in the study of this topic. NE draws our attention to the costs of producing goods and services that are shouldered by employees, their families and local communities. The chapter also introduced four attributes of HRM NE and then recognized the four main forms of harm of work: 1) psychological, 2) social, 3) health, and 4) environmental. Remember that these aspects of harm can occur separately but may also interconnect and influence each other. For example, the psychological harm of work in the form of high level of stress can, over time, have implications for an employee's physical health.

The main part of the chapter is dedicated to a critical discussion of high-performance work systems, poor job design, layoffs and downsizing, as well as negative effects of organizational flexibility. This is a collection of practices that have a particularly high risk of causing harm when HRM is managed in an irresponsible and unsustainable manner.

When examining the harm of work, it is crucial to bear in mind that not everyone is equally affected by initiatives such as increased workload. Employers should take steps to understand the full impact of their policies and practices and be proactive in communicating with their staff to better understand the experiences of their employees.

Study questions

1 What are negative externalities (NE) and what are the four attributes of HRM NE?

2 What are the four main aspects of harm of work?

3 Are high-performance work systems a 'win-win' scenario that leads to benefits for employers and employees? Discuss by presenting arguments for and against.

4 What aspects of job design can lead to increased work-related stress?

5 What harm can downsizing cause to organizations and their employees?

6 What are the common criticisms of practices that aim to improve organizational flexibility?

Key reading

Gheyoh Ndzi, E (2021) An investigation on the widespread use of zero hours contracts in the UK and the impact on workers, *International Journal of Law and Society*, **4** (2), pp 140–49

Zorn, M L, Norman, P M, Butler, F C and Bhussar, M S (2017) Cure or curse: does downsizing increase the likelihood of bankruptcy? *Journal of Business Research*, **76**, pp 24–33

References

ACAS (2022) Lay-offs and short-time working, www.acas.org.uk/lay-offs-and-short-time-working (archived at https://perma.cc/Y5SK-9TWM)

Ahammer, A, Grübl, D and Winter-Ebmer, R (2020) *The Health Externalities of Downsizing*, IZA Discussion Papers, no. 13984, Institute of Labor Economics (IZA), Bonn

Appelbaum, E, Bailey, T, Berg, P, Kalleberg, A L and Bailey, T A (2000) *Manufacturing Advantage: Why high-performance work systems pay off*, Cornell University Press, New York

Armstrong-Stassen, M and Cattaneo, J (2010) The effect of downsizing on organizational practices targeting older workers, *Journal of Management Development*, **29** (4), pp 344–63

Aronsson, G and Gustafsson, K (2005) Sickness presenteeism: prevalence, attendance-pressure factors and an outline of a model for research, *Journal of Occupational and Environmental Medicine*, **47** (9), pp 958–66

Aronsson, G, Gustafsson, K and Dallner, M (2000) Sick but yet at work. An empirical study of sickness presenteeism, *Journal of Epidemiology and Community Health*, **54** (7), pp 502–09

Atkinson, J (1984) Manpower strategies for flexible organizations, *Personnel Management*, **16** (8), pp 28–31

Bacon, S L (2018) The importance of sex in the stress–heart disease relationship and the potential contribution of gender to future research, *Arteriosclerosis, Thrombosis and Vascular Biology*, **38** (2), pp 290–91

Bloodworth, J (2018) *Hired*, Atlantic Books, London

Bunner, J, Prem, R and Korunka, C (2018) How work intensification relates to organization-level safety performance: the mediating roles of safety climate, safety motivation and safety knowledge, *Frontiers in Psychology*, **9**, p 2575

Business, Innovation and Skills Committee (2016) Employment practices at Sports Direct. Third report of the session 2016–2017. House of Commons, HC 219, https://publications.parliament.uk/pa/cm201617/cmselect/cmbis/219/219.pdf (archived at https://perma.cc/A2QH-CCXQ)

Cascio, W F and Wynn, P (2004) Managing a downsizing process, *Human Resource Management*, **43** (4), pp 425–36

CCOHS (2021) Mental health: psychosocial risk factors in the workplace, www.ccohs.ca/oshanswers/psychosocial/mentalhealth_risk.html (archived at https://perma.cc/AM4W-K7XM)

Cetrulo, A, Cirillo, V and Guarascio, D (2019) Weaker jobs, weaker innovation. Exploring the effects of temporary employment on new products, *Applied Economics*, **51** (59), pp 6350–75

Chang, P C, Wu, T and Liu, C L (2018) Do high-performance work systems really satisfy employees? Evidence from China, *Sustainability*, **10** (10), p 3360

CIPD (2021) Job Design, www.cipd.asia/knowledge/factsheets/job-design (archived at https://perma.cc/EUX4-PNXC)

Classen, T J and Dunn, R A (2012) The effect of job loss and unemployment duration on suicide risk in the United States: a new look using mass-layoffs and unemployment duration, *Health Economics*, **21** (3), pp 338–50

Crum, A J, Salovey, P and Achor, S (2013) Rethinking stress: the role of mindsets in determining the stress response, *Journal of Personality and Social Psychology*, **104** (4), pp 716–33

Datta, D, Guthrie, J and Wright, P (2005) Human resource management and labor productivity: does industry matter? *Academy of Management Journal*, **48** (1), pp 135–45

Davey, M M, Cummings, G, Newburn-Cook, C V and Lo, E A (2009) Predictors of nurse absenteeism in hospitals: a systematic review, *Journal of Nursing Management*, **17** (3), pp 312–30

De Battisti, F, Gilardi, S, Siletti, E and Solari, L (2014) Employability and mental health in dismissed workers: the contribution of lay-off justice and participation in outplacement services, *Quality and Quantity*, **48** (3), pp 1305–23

Debrot, A, Siegler, S, Klumb, P L and Schoebi, D (2018) Daily work stress and relationship satisfaction: detachment affects romantic couples' interactions quality, *Journal of Happiness Studies*, **19** (8), pp 2283–301

Dragano, N, Verde, P E and Siegrist, J (2005) Organizational downsizing and work stress: testing synergistic health effects in employed men and women, *Journal of Epidemiology and Community Health*, 59 (8), pp 694–99

Engelbrecht, G J, de Beer, L T and Schaufeli, W B (2020) The relationships between work intensity, workaholism, burnout and self-reported musculoskeletal complaints, *Human Factors and Ergonomics in Manufacturing and Service Industries*, **30** (1), pp 59–70

Eurofound (2017) EurWORK European observatory of working life, atypical contracts, www.eurofound.europa.eu/observatories/eurwork/industrial-relations-dictionary/atypical-contracts (archived at https://perma.cc/F4C5-KW9L)

Fehrmann, C and Depenbrock, F (2014) Recovery from work-related stress: a literature review, *Maastricht Student Journal of Psychology and Neuroscience*, 3, pp 85–96

Fisher, S R and White, M A (2000) Downsizing in a learning organization: are there hidden costs? *Academy of Management Review*, **25** (1), pp 244–51

Frone, M R and Blais, A R (2020) Organizational downsizing, work conditions and employee outcomes: identifying targets for workplace intervention among survivors, *International Journal of Environmental Research and Public Health*, **17** (3), p 719

Gascoigne, C, Parry, E and Buchanan, D (2015) Extreme work, gendered work? How extreme jobs and the discourse of 'personal choice' perpetuate gender inequality, *Organization*, **22** (4), pp 457–75

Gheyoh Ndzi, E (2021) An investigation on the widespread use of zero hours contracts in the UK and the impact on workers, *International Journal of Law and Society*, **4** (2), pp 140–49

Giannikis, S and Nikandrou, I (2013) The impact of corporate entrepreneurship and high-performance work systems on employees' job attitudes: empirical evidence from Greece during the economic downturn, *The International Journal of Human Resource Management*, **24** (19), pp 3644–66

Glavin, P, Schieman, S and Reid, S (2011) Boundary-spanning work demands and their consequences for guilt and psychological distress, *Journal of Health and Social Behavior*, **52** (1), pp 43–57

Gov.uk (2021) Official statistics. The employment of disabled people 2021, www.
gov.uk/government/statistics/the-employment-of-disabled-people-2021/the-
employment-of-disabled-people-2021 (archived at https://perma.cc/GE5X-
GDDS)

Gov.uk (2022) Making staff redundant, www.gov.uk/staff-redundant/layoffs-and-
shorttime-working (archived at https://perma.cc/84B9-MJWE)

HSE (2022) Work-related stress and how to manage it, causes of stress at work,
www.hse.gov.uk/stress/causes.htm (archived at https://perma.cc/3JUY-HT6N)

Ilies, R, Schwind, K M, Wagner, D T, Johnson, M D, DeRue, D S and Ilgen, D R
(2007) When can employees have a family life? The effects of daily workload
and effect on work–family conflict and social behaviors at home, *Journal of
Applied Psychology*, **92** (5), p 1368

Jensen, J M, Patel, P C and Messersmith, J G (2013) High-performance work
systems and job control: consequences for anxiety, role overload and turnover
intentions, *Journal of Management*, **39** (6), pp 1699–724

Johnson, J V (1986) The impact of workplace social support, job demands and
work control upon cardiovascular disease in Sweden, unpublished PhD thesis,
Department of Psychology, University of Stockholm

Junna, L, Moustgaard, H and Martikainen, P (2021) Unemployment from stable,
downsized and closed workplaces and alcohol-related mortality, *Addiction*,
116 (1), pp 74–82

Kahn, R L, Wolfe, D M, Quinn, R P, Snoek, J D and Rosenthal, R A (1964)
Organizational Stress: Studies in role conflict and ambiguity, John Wiley,
Hoboken, NJ

Karasek, R (1979) Job demands, job decision latitude and mental strain:
implications for job redesign, *Administrative Science Quarterly*, **24** (2),
pp 285–308

Karasek, R A and Theorell, T (1990) *Healthy Work: Stress, productivity and the
reconstruction of working life*, Basic Books, New York

Kivimäki, M, Vahtera, J, Pentti, J and Ferrie, J E (2000) Factors underlying the
effect of organizational downsizing on health of employees: longitudinal cohort
study, *BMJ*, **320** (7240), pp 971–75

Kleinknecht, A, van Schaik, F N and Zhou, H (2014) Is flexible labour good for
innovation? Evidence from firm-level data, *Cambridge Journal of Economics*, **38**
(5), pp 1207–19

Kozica, A and Kaiser, S (2012) A sustainability perspective on flexible HRM: how
to cope with paradoxes of contingent work, *Management Revue*, **23** (2),
pp 239–61

Kroon, B, Van de Voorde, K and Van Veldhoven, M J P M (2009) Cross-level
effects of high-performance work practices on burnout: two counteracting
mediating mechanisms compared, *Personnel Review*, **38** (5), pp 509–25

Love, E G and Kraatz, M (2009) Character, conformity, or the bottom line? How and why downsizing affected corporate reputation, *Academy of Management Journal*, **52** (2), pp 314–35

Mahdi, S M, Liao, J, Muhammad, S and Nader, H M (2014) The impact of high performance work system (HPWS) on employee productivity as related to organizational identity and job engagement, *European Journal of Business and Management*, **6** (39), pp 1–24

Mañas, M A, Díaz-Fúnez, P, Pecino, V, López-Liria, R, Padilla, D and Aguilar-Parra, J M (2018) Consequences of team job demands: role ambiguity climate, affective engagement and extra-role performance, *Frontiers in Psychology*, **8**, p 2292

Mariappanadar, S (2012) The harm indicators of negative externality of efficiency focused organizational practices, *International Journal of Social Economics*, **39** (3), pp 209–20

Mariappanadar, S (2014a) The model of negative externality for sustainable HRM. In I Ehnert, W Harry and K J Zink (eds.) *Sustainability and Human Resource Management: Developing sustainable business organizations* (pp 181–204), Springer Verlag, Berlin/Heidelberg, Germany

Mariappanadar, S (2014b) Stakeholder harm index: a framework to review work intensification from the critical HRM perspective, *Human Resource Management Review*, **24** (4), pp 313–29

Mariappanadar, S (2019) Sustainable HRM theories: simultaneous benefits for organizations and stakeholders. In S Mariappanadar (ed.) *Sustainable Human Resource Management: Strategies, practices and challenges* (pp 104–28), Red Globe Press, London

Marks, M L, Mirvis, P and Ashkenas, R (2017) Surviving M&A how to thrive amid the turmoil, *Harvard Business Review*, **95** (2), pp 145–50

Mauno, S, Minkkinen, J, Tsupari, H, Huhtala, M and Feldt, T (2019) Do older employees suffer more from work intensification and other intensified job demands? Evidence from upper white-collar workers, *Scandinavian Journal of Work and Organizational Psychology*, **4** (1), Article 3

McBride, J and Smith, A (2021) 'I feel like I'm in poverty. I don't do much outside of work other than survive': in-work poverty and multiple employment in the UK, *Economic and Industrial Democracy*, **43** (3), pp 1440–66

McCormack, N and Cotter, C (2013) *Managing Burnout in the Workplace: A guide for information professionals*, Elsevier, Amsterdam

McKee-Ryan, F, Song, Z, Wanberg, C R and Kinicki, A J (2005) Psychological and physical well-being during unemployment: a meta-analytic study, *Journal of Applied Psychology*, **90** (1), pp 53–76

Mujtaba, B G and Senathip, T (2020) Layoffs and downsizing implications for the leadership role of human resources, *Journal of Service Science and Management*, **13** (2), pp 209–28

Neff, L A and Karney, B R (2004) How does context affect intimate relationships? Linking external stress and cognitive processes within marriage, *Personality and Social Psychology Bulletin*, **30** (2), pp 134–48

Neville, S, Taylor, M and Inman, P (2013) Buckingham Palace uses zero-hours contracts for summer staff, *The Guardian*, 30 July

Obrenovic, B, Jianguo, D, Khudaykulov, A and Khan, M A S (2020) Work–family conflict impact on psychological safety and psychological well-being: a job performance model, *Frontiers in Psychology*, **11**, p 475

ONS (2021) EMP17: People in employment on zero hours contracts, www.ons.gov.uk/employmentandlabourmarket/peopleinwork/employmentandemployeetypes/datasets/emp17peopleinemploymentonzerohourscontracts (archived at https://perma.cc/T2S5-KE2C)

Pega, F, Náfrádi, B, Momen, N C, Ujita, Y, Streicher, K N, Prüss-Üstün, A M and Woodruff, T J (2021) Global, regional and national burdens of ischemic heart disease and stroke attributable to exposure to long working hours for 194 countries, 2000–2016: a systematic analysis from the WHO/ILO joint estimates of the work-related burden of disease and injury, *Environment International*, **154**, p 106595

Pigou, A C (1920) *The Economics of Welfare*, Macmillan, London

Roberts, J, Bryan, M, Bryce, A, Rice, N and Sechel, C (2021) Written evidence from Jennifer Roberts, Mark Bryan, Andrew Bryce, Nigel Rice, Cristina Sechel, University of Sheffield and University of York (DEG0132), disability employment gap, https://committees.parliament.uk/writtenevidence/19219/pdf/ (archived at https://perma.cc/NU34-KQRD)

Rollinson, D (2008) *Organizational Behaviour and Analysis: An integrated approach*, 4th edn, Pearson Education, New York

Salas, E, Driskell, J E and Hughes, S (1996) Introduction: the study of stress and human performance. In J E Driskell and E Salas (eds.) *Stress and Human Performance* (pp 1–45), Lawrence Erlbaum Associates, Mahwah, NJ

Schaufeli, W B and Enzmann, D (1998) *The Burnout Companion to Study and Practice: A critical analysis*, Taylor & Francis, London

Schulz, A C and Johann, S (2018) Downsizing and the fragility of corporate reputation: an analysis of the impact of contextual factors, *Scandinavian Journal of Management*, **34** (1), pp 40–50

Seligman, M E, Peterson, C, Barsky, A J, Boehm, J K, Kubzansky, L D, Park, N and Labarthe, D (2013) Positive health and health assets: re-analysis of longitudinal datasets [White paper], University of Pennsylvania and Robert Wood Johnson Foundation, https://ppc.sas.upenn.edu/sites/default/files/positivehealthassetspub.pdf (archived at https://perma.cc/T9UX-4PGR)

Sommerlad, H (2016) 'A pit to put women in': professionalism, work intensification, sexualisation and work–life balance in the legal profession in England and Wales, *International Journal of the Legal Profession*, **23** (1), pp 61–82

Sperry, L (ed.) (1996) *Corporate Therapy and Consulting*, Brunner/Mazel Publishers, New York

Staal, M A (2004) *Stress, Cognition and Human Performance: A literature review and conceptual framework*, National Aeronautics and Space Administration, Hanover, MD

Takeuchi, R, Lepak, D P, Wang, H and Takeuchi, K (2007) An empirical examination of the mechanisms mediating between high-performance work systems and the performance of Japanese organizations, *Journal of Applied Psychology*, **92** (4), p 1069

Theorell, T, Oxenstierna, G, Westerlund, H, Ferrie, J, Hagberg, J and Alfredsson, L (2003) Downsizing of staff is associated with lowered medically certified sick leave in female employees, *Occupational and Environmental Medicine*, **60** (9), pp 1–5

Trevor, C O and Nyberg, A J (2008) Keeping your headcount when all about you are losing theirs: downsizing, voluntary turnover rates and the moderating role of HR practices, *Academy of Management Journal*, **51** (2), pp 259–76

Udayar, S, Urbanaviciute, I, Massoudi, K and Rossier, J (2020) The role of personality profiles in the longitudinal relationship between work-related well-being and life satisfaction among working adults in Switzerland, *European Journal of Personality*, **34** (1), pp 77–92

van Engen, M, Vinkenburg, C and Dikkers, J (2012) Sustainability in combining career and care: challenging normative beliefs about parenting, *Journal of Social Issues*, **68** (4), pp 645–64

Wales TUC (2018) Disability and 'hidden' impairments in the workplace. A toolkit for trade unionists Wales TUC Cymru, www.tuc.org.uk/sites/default/files/DHIWtoolkitEng_1.pdf (archived at https://perma.cc/SDE6-SH33)

Wilkinson, A (2005) Downsizing, rightsizing or dumbsizing? Quality, human resources and the management of sustainability, *Total Quality Management and Business Excellence*, **16** (8–9), pp 1079–88

Winterbotham, A (2012) The solutions to externalities: from Pigou to Coase, *The Student Economic Review*, **26**, pp 172–80

Wong, K, Chan, A H and Ngan, S C (2019) The effect of long working hours and overtime on occupational health: a meta-analysis of evidence from 1998 to 2018, *International Journal of Environmental Research and Public Health*, **16** (12), p 2102

Zorn, M L, Norman, P M, Butler, F C and Bhussar, M S (2017) Cure or curse: does downsizing increase the likelihood of bankruptcy? *Journal of Business Research*, **76**, pp 24–33

Regenerating the human resource base

4

LEARNING OBJECTIVES

After completing this chapter, you should be able to:

- Explain what employee vitality is and what factors can improve it.
- Identify seven main aspects influencing employment quality.
- Discuss the impact of general working conditions on employment quality.
- Discuss the impact of mutually beneficial flexibility and work–life balance on employment quality.
- Discuss the impact of organizational justice on employment quality.
- Discuss the impact of stress management on employment quality.
- Discuss the impact of diversity and inclusion on employment quality.
- Discuss the impact of social relationships at work on employment quality.
- Discuss the impact of employee voice, and representative participation, on employment quality.

Introduction

One of the main objectives of sustainable HRM is to develop and regenerate an organization's human resources. This requires critical analysis of practices that harm employees and the wider community from which organizations draw their human resources. At the same time, the sustainable approach involves an application of proactive frameworks, practices and work designs that allow a balance between good work performance and energy recovery. Humans' capacity for being active, engaged and healthy is limited. When managed irresponsibly this capacity can be depleted on a daily basis. In Chapter 3 we discussed a range of unsustainable work practices that pass the negative effects of work onto employees, their families and local communities. This chapter focuses on positive practices that are pivotal for development and regeneration of the human resource base.

If handled conscientiously, human resources can provide sustained productivity by offering nurtured skills, knowledge, experience, creative thinking, social networks and commitment to the organization. Dorenbosch (2014) compares this process to building a perpetuum mobile. They ask, 'How can organizations and HRM ensure that employees themselves will "keep the ball rolling" now and in the future?' (Dorenbosch, 2014). The following discussion answers this question by focusing on two concepts: employee vitality and employment quality.

However, first we need to address an elephant in the room. By discussing a collection of best practices related to the regeneration of the HR base, our analysis can resemble the literature on high-performance work systems with its bundles of best methods (Kramar, 2014), which we have critically examined in Chapter 3. That is true. But, unlike the HPWS our debate focuses on a long-term sustainable and responsible approach to people management. The emphasis in our discussion is on the balance of good-quality performance and recovery of energy, instead of maximizing performance.

Employee vitality

A key element of sustainable HRM is fostering and maintaining 'employee vitality'. In recent years this term has become a buzzword in many organizations, and it is sometimes used as a synonym for 'employee wellness'. However, in line with existing academic literature we would argue that employee vitality represents more than just physical and mental well-being. Nix et al (1999) explained vitality as 'the positive feeling of having energy available to oneself'. According to De Jonge and Peeters (2019), 'a vital person is energetic and strong, and feels physically and mentally well'. *Employee vitality* represents a state where an employee is in a good physical and mental condition, shows resilience against work difficulties and is willing and able to invest effort into their work. One of the key characteristics of vital employees is turning energy and motivation into action.

By definition employee vitality represents a positive occurrence, and it may be in an organization's own best interest to develop a workforce that is healthy and reliable. Several studies have highlighted benefits of employee vitality. For example, a survey of employees working in Israel found that staff reporting vitality were more likely to get involved in creative work (Atwater and Carmeli, 2009) and show enhanced job performance (Carmeli, 2009). A survey of Dutch employees aged 45 and older found that respondents with higher levels of vitality were more likely to show career satisfaction and were less likely to go on early retirement. Older workers who had more vitality also reported higher job performance and achieved higher positions in their organizations (Hennekam, 2016).

With higher employee vitality comes higher stress resilience which in turn is associated with improved perceived health and immune functioning (Lantman et al, 2017). As has been demonstrated by the Covid-19 pandemic, having employees with strong mental and physical health can be of strategic importance. The question is how do we create a work environment where employees are in good health and spark energy in themselves and others?

Research points to several factors that can improve employee vitality. A study of a Dutch dairy company showed that an organizational culture that promotes self-determination and good work–life balance is particularly useful to promote vitality at work (van Scheppingen et al, 2015). The same project found that a healthy lifestyle and a high social capital within the workplace were also important for vitality at work. Organizational social capital represents networks, collaborations and shared values but also quality of relationships at work. In other words, the study found that employees who had a healthy social life at work were also likely to show vitality. Tummers et al (2015) examined which HRM practices are particularly effective in stimulating employee vitality. They surveyed large public healthcare organizations in the Netherlands and found that 1) high autonomy, 2) the possibility to participate in the decision-making process, and 3) high-quality teamwork are crucial. The researchers also found that increased task communication from leaders (Tummers et al, 2018) and a satisfaction of the need for competence (Graves and Luciano, 2013) were linked to improved employee vitality. By fulfilling basic psychological needs of employees, e.g. giving an opportunity to feel competent or providing some autonomy, we can energize our staff. A large survey of over 28,000 employees from 30 European countries found that, regardless of the type of working contract (permanent, temporary or temporary hired through agency), in order to have sustainably performing vital workers, employers need to focus on enabling job feedback and preventing excessive workload (Hakanen et al, 2019). Highly elevated amounts of work that need to be done leads to exhaustion, as well as decline in work performance and employee retention. Figure 4.1 provides an overview of the aspects linked with improved employee vitality.

Figure 4.1   Factors linked with improved employee vitality

- Organizational culture that meets basic psychological needs of employees.
- Promotion of self-determination.
- Good work–life balance.
- Healthy lifestyle.
- High social capital within the workplace.
- High autonomy.
- The possibility to participate in the decision-making process.
- High-quality teamwork.
- Increased task communication from leaders.
- Satisfaction of the need for competence.
- Job feedback.
- Sustainable workload.

Table 4.1   Framework of sustainable work performance

Categories of work performance	Vigour and proactivity	Characteristics of experience and performance
Vitality	High vigour High proactivity	– High energy levels – High resilience
'Forced' proactivity	Low vigour High proactivity	– Employee expands effort to meet targets – Risks health – Risks slipping into passivity
Passivity	Low vigour Low proactivity	– Precarious employment position – Risks withdrawal or dismissal
'Comfortable' energy	High vigour Low proactivity	– Energy available but preserved – An employee is limited by work opportunities

SOURCE Adapted from Dorenbosch (2014)

Dorenbosch (2014) argued that we can look at employee vitality as a combination of employee vigour and proactivity. This further emphasizes the idea that while providing care for employees' well-being is important, it is not sufficient. Healthy, satisfied employees could still show passive behaviour at work, e.g. by avoiding responsibilities or not pulling their weight in group projects. Dorenbosch (2014) drafted a framework for sustainable work performance (see Table 4.1) illustrating how a combination of employee high proactivity and vigour would be optimal for achieving employee vitality.

Skill check

Understanding employee vitality. Balancing work performance and vigour can be challenging for both managers and employees. Being able to break down this complex issue into more manageable parts will allow us to identify areas for improvement.

Employment quality

Another lens through which we can discuss the regeneration of the human resource base is employment quality. Here we need to recognize that there are many similar terms and frameworks concerned with the quality of work and its social sustainability, such as 'quality of working life', 'job quality', 'quality of work' and 'quality of employment' (Burchell et al, 2014) – or, recently initiated by the Scottish Government, the initiative of 'fair work' (Scottish Government, 2021). The International Labour Organization (ILO) also promotes 'decent work' practices. In 2015, ILO's four pillars of the Decent Work Agenda (rights at work, employment creation, social protection and social dialogue) became a part of the UN Sustainable Development Goal 8 (ILO, 2022; UN, 2015). Another key concept in this debate is the *quality of working life* (QWL, sometimes also QoWL). QWL is built on rich academic research going back to 1960s, with Elton Mayo being one of the first authors to use the term in research (Mayo, 1960). While there is no consensus in the academic community on the definition of QWL, Grote and Guest (2017) explained it as 'a coherent set of research-informed policies and practices that aim to enhance workers' emancipation and well-being'. Much of the work on QWL concentrates on researching favourable work conditions and identifying an employment environment that enhances employee well-being and satisfaction. For example, Mirvis and Lawler (1984) argued that the basic elements of a good quality of work are:

- a safe work environment
- equitable wages
- equal employment opportunities
- opportunities for advancement

Concepts such as decent work or QWL play an important role in the sustainable approach to HRM. They broaden our understanding of relevant work dimensions and aid us in measuring employment-related experiences. Drawing on the existing literature on this subject, the rest of the chapter discusses seven themes key for achieving social sustainability at work and good employment quality:

1 general working conditions

2 mutually beneficial flexibility and work–life balance

3 organizational justice

4 stress management

5 diversity and inclusion

6 social relationships at work

7 employee voice and representative participation

As you progress through the chapter, note how these themes relate to each other. For example, good work–life balance supports proactive stress management, and providing for employee voice can enhance each of the other elements of employment quality.

General working conditions

General working conditions, such as *wages*, *working time*, *job security* and *safe work environment*, represent a first set of factors that are necessary for good employment quality and improving employees' experience of work.

Wages

According to a study conducted by the American Psychological Association (APA, 2021), the number one factor causing workplace stress is low salaries.

Fifty-six per cent of the respondents reported that their low salary had a significant impact on their stress levels. This is 7 per cent higher than in 2019. During the Covid-19 pandemic, many organizations introduced well-being initiatives promoting an active lifestyle and educating staff about stress resilience. However, financial wellness of the workforce is equally important. As previously explained in Chapter 3, stress has a negative impact on the performance of individual employees and teams. There is a clear incentive for employers to provide financial and non-financial benefits that can help to retain and engage productive employees. In a survey of 1,600 full-time employed US adults, PwC (2021) found that the majority of workers, regardless of whether their financial stress increased due to the pandemic or not, would be attracted to another company that cares more about their financial well-being than their current employer. As explained by PwC (2021),

> Employers who invest in improving employee financial health can reap long-term benefits in metrics that matter to the organization, but it starts with a commitment to employee financial wellness as an integral piece of your organization's total wellness culture.

Working time

Another important field that affects general working conditions and quality of employment is working time. This includes, for example, management of overtime. In some organizations overtime may be necessary to respond to emergency situations or fluctuations in customer demand. It could even be good for employees when working beyond the regular schedule is compensated. However, excessive overtime has a negative impact on employees' work–life balance, health, morale, safety risk at work, work performance, and it can increase absenteeism and staff turnover rate. Where possible employers should avoid it. Where overtime cannot be prevented, information about performed additional hours should be recorded and capped. Management of overtime can be prone to malpractice. For instance, managers may attempt to operate without sufficient members of staff to save on wages. Organizations should be proactive, introduce clear policies on overtime and monitor workloads and staff experience (e.g. through third-party anonymous surveys).

Job security

Job security and safety are also key factors for developing decent work and high-quality working life (Leschke et al, 2008; Burchell et al, 2014). Developing a competitive level of job security may be important for attracting talent, encouraging loyalty among employees and keeping employee morale high. A 'hire fast and fire fast' approach can be expensive due to the hidden costs of training, time invested by management, HR and IT, as well as the lost productivity of a new employee. Guaranteeing job security is a difficult task. This is especially true during economic downturns. However, as explained by Allan (1997), there are many steps that organizations can take to minimize layoffs in a difficult market environment or during a technological revolution:

- freeze hiring and begin to decrease workforce size as employees quit or retire;
- larger organizations may be able to redeploy or transfer employees to other sites;
- encourage staff to take unpaid vacations or an unpaid voluntary leave of absence;
- encourage staff to take voluntary terminations with severance pay and benefits;
- encourage staff to take early voluntary retirement;
- introduce or expand work-sharing arrangements;
- freeze or reduce pay and benefits;
- perform work in-house that normally is contracted out;
- voluntarily or involuntarily retrain staff.

Safe work environment

Another key issue related to general working conditions is ensuring a healthy and safe work environment. Most industrialized countries have a range of regulations and policies that impose on organizations practices related to health and safety. However, the problems are enforcement and implementation of best practices promoted by the regulators.

Providing a safe work environment goes beyond preventing illnesses, injuries and deaths. A more sustainable approach helps employees achieve positive health (see Chapter 3), and prevents *presenteeism*, i.e. 'attending work while ill' (Johns, 2010). Employees who try to perform work when they are unwell are prone to make more errors, they can struggle to meet the organization's production and service standards and they show decreased on-the-job performance (Schultz and Edington, 2007). At the same time, working while not fully fit can be damaging for the employee's well-being. It increases the risk of future health problems and long-term sickness absence (Skagen and Collins, 2016). Presenteeism was also found to be associated with depression (Suzuki et al, 2015) and doubles the risk of serious coronary events (e.g. heart attack) (Kivimäki et al, 2005).

Mutually beneficial flexibility and work–life balance

Another dimension that is important for ensuring quality of employment is providing *mutually beneficial flexibility*. Good practices related to flexibility begin with a recognition that work arrangements should suit both the organization and the individual (Reilly, 2001). According to Reilly, mutual flexibility can reduce costs, improve quality and service, hedge against change and meet supply needs. When flexible work arrangements consider the interests of both the employer and employee they can also increase productivity and reduce staff turnover.

An important element of mutually beneficial flexibility is ensuring adequate terms and conditions for those who use alternative work arrangements. For example, CIPD (2021a) explained that atypical employees, including zero-hour contract workers, should have access to training, development, regular feedback and compensation comparable with those of other workers.

Work–life balance

Flexible work arrangements can help employees achieve better work–life balance. This can be supported with measures such as:

- 'Flexitime'. This is an arrangement for a flexible (within limits) start and finish of the working day – for instance, allowing an employee a schedule of 7 am to 3 pm on selected days of the week or all week.
- Compressed working hours. Instead of working the traditional eight hours for five days, an arrangement is made for longer shifts and a shorter work week. For example, an employee could do 10-hour days but work only Monday–Thursday.
- Shift and break arrangements. More flexibility regarding the shifts and breaks that employees can take.
- Remote and hybrid working. This allows employees to entirely or partially work outside of the traditional office environment.
- Part-time working and reduced hours schedule. This is an arrangement where a person works less than 35 hours per week.

- **Job-sharing.** This is an arrangement where two or more employees share duties of one full-time role, and are employed on a part-time or reduced-time basis.

- **Part-year work/term-time work.** This refers to an employee working only a certain number of months during the year, e.g. they work during the school term time with a break for eight weeks during the summer.

The Covid-19 pandemic further solidified and popularized the practice of providing mutually beneficial flexible work arrangements to acquire, retain and engage talent. A global study conducted by EY (2021) found that 90 per cent of surveyed employees want flexibility in where and when they work and 'more than half of employees globally would quit their jobs if not provided post-pandemic flexibility'.

For both parties to benefit from the flexible work arrangements, managers should ensure that employees are aware that such options are available. Furthermore, the work culture should not discourage employees from enquiring about flexible measures and using them.

In addition to flexible work arrangements, organizations can facilitate better work–life balance by setting clear boundaries between work and home. This includes having realistic expectations related to receiving and responding to work communication outside of office hours. On-the-clock managers should ensure their staff are taking breaks, during which they can psychologically detach themselves from work and allow recovery of energy levels (Sianoja et al, 2016).

Family-friendly policies

Family-friendly policies can help employees balance their care responsibilities with work. In a report dedicated to family-friendly policies, UNICEF (2019) presented a range of recommendations for both organizational and governmental policies. Figure 4.2 shows examples of UNICEF's suggestions for employers.

Finally, managers should listen to their employees' feedback on flexibility and work–life balance initiatives. Even well-intentioned measures may cause additional burden to staff. For example, Russell and Woods (2020) found that a strict email policy, such as banning workers from checking their emails outside of office hours, can be harmful to employees with 'high levels of anxiety and neuroticism'. The authors argued that one-size-fits-all email policies can be doing workers a disservice, and they propose to tailor work

Figure 4.2   Family-friendly policies recommended by UNICEF

– Minimum 18 weeks of paid maternity leave. – Additional 6 months or more of paid maternity, paternity, parental leave.	– Provision of safe, clean, hygienic and culturally appropriate space for breastfeeding and expressing milk. – Provision of safe, clean, hygienic and culturally appropriate space for refrigeration and storage of expressed milk.
– Effective protection of employees against discrimination on the basis of pregnancy, breastfeeding or family status.	– Provision of training to managers on family-friendly practices and the benefits of employees breastfeeding (e.g. lower absenteeism, higher employee retention).

SOURCE Based on UNICEF (2019)

email use to individual goals. In addition to informal feedback gathered through daily interactions, organizations can conduct surveys and audits related to flexibility, work–life balance and turnover intentions. *Exit interviews* with employees who are about to leave the organization can also be a good opportunity for an honest conversation on these topics.

Organizational justice

According to Lambert et al (2020), *organizational justice* refers to 'the perception that the employing organization treats employees in a fair and just manner'. This is another important dimension that indicates the quality of work. We can differentiate two main types of organizational justice: *distributive justice* and *procedural justice*.

Distributive justice

This concept addresses whether the resources we receive and outcomes of our actions (e.g. pay, promotion, bigger office, workplace discipline) are distributed in a just manner according to our own perception. Employees tend to make this judgment by looking at what they have and what they did to receive those outcomes, then comparing it with others and their inputs/outputs ratios. For managers, distributive justice means that employees should receive resources and opportunities that are provided equitably and in accordance with their contributions (Armstrong and Taylor, 2020).

The subject of distributive justice is crucial for ensuring sustainable quality of employment. Employees' perception of distributive justice has an impact on their job satisfaction (Lambert et al, 2020), organizational commitment (Kassahun, 2005) and enabling trust during organizational change (Saunders and Thornhill, 2003). It also has an impact on employees' **organizational citizenship behaviours** (OCB). OCBs are employees' voluntary contributions that go beyond what is normally expected and bring benefit to the organization (Ertürk et al, 2004). An example of OCB would be helping co-workers with their workload. As explained by Ertürk et al (2004), 'Fairness should be one of the foremost thoughts of top management to maintain and increase the extra-role behaviours of the employees.'

Moreover, low levels of perceived distributive fairness lead to negative outcomes such as higher stress and increased intentions to leave the employer (Yang et al, 2021). Employees reporting negative perceptions of distributive justice are also more likely to engage in **counterproductive work behaviour** (CBW) (Chernyak-Hai and Tziner, 2014). This means intentionally behaving in ways that are contrary to the organization's interests. Examples of CBW include wasting resources, destroying employer's property or stealing something from the organization.

The perception of how fairly resources and outcomes are distributed in the organization can be improved by employers fulfilling the psychological contract with the employees and by empowering staff (Zhang and Agarwal, 2009). **Psychological contract** describes employees' and employers' perceptions of their employment agreement, including implied work-related promises and obligations. When employees believe that their employer has not delivered on their promises (i.e. when the psychological contract was breached) they may also feel that they have been deprived of desired outcomes, and they are more likely to perceive their organization as unjust. Careful management and fulfilment of the psychological contract can make employees feel more equitably treated. Empowerment of employees is also important. When employees have an opportunity to express their views and participate in the decision-making process, they have a feeling of control, which increases the chances of seeing organizational decisions as fair (Zhang and Agarwal, 2009).

Procedural justice

This concept captures whether our employees perceive organizational procedures, policies and decision-making processes as fair. The believed fairness of the decision-making *process* can be as important as, or in some cases even more important than, the *outcome*. For example, employees are more likely to accept a negative outcome if they believe that the decisions that led to the conclusion were based on fair organizational principles (Greenberg, 1994).

Similar to distributive justice, procedural justice also has an impact on job satisfaction (Lambert et al, 2020), organizational commitment (Kassahun, 2005), trust and organizational citizenship behaviour (Dolan et al, 2005), job stress (Lambert et al, 2007), turnover intent (Lambert et al, 2010) and counterproductive work behaviours (Devonish and Greenidge, 2010).

Enhanced organizational communication and fulfilling the psychological contract can improve employees' perception of how just procedures are (Zhang and Agarwal, 2009). Most employees want organizational processes to be consistent, transparent and considerate of their views. Listed below are factors that can help improve perception of procedural justice (Workplace Health and Safety QLD, 2022):

- design of procedures that allows consistent application to all workers and in the same way;
- impartial decision making with awareness and suppression of personal biases;
- consideration of views of employees who are/will be impacted by a procedure;
- providing employees with an appeal procedure and not obstructing the appeal;
- familiarizing workers with organizational policies and procedures;
- encouraging employees' involvement in the development of procedures;
- communicating to employees the reason for a change in policy or procedure;
- communicating to employees explanations of made decisions.

Stress management

The extent to which organizations support employees in reducing work-related stress can be another sign of employment quality. Employers should be proactive in monitoring workers' levels of stress, as well as preventing and minimizing the effects of job-related stressors on employees' well-being. Line managers play a key role here, because they may be able to *recognize signs* of their colleagues facing excessive pressure and be in a position to do something about it. We can identify a range of emotional, cognitive, physical, behavioural and performance-related signs of stress. Examples of symptoms include:

- **Emotional:** anxiety, depression, nervousness, moodiness, feeling angry, feeling irritated, having mood swings (e.g. being more tearful, sensitive or aggressive), losing sense of humour, losing confidence, feeling powerless or helpless.

- **Cognitive:** inability to make decisions, poor concentration and memory, decreased attention, difficulty in getting things done, less creative problem solving.

- **Physical:** high blood pressure, back pains, muscle tension, headaches, insomnia, dizziness, feeling nauseous or breathless, change in appetite, ringing in the ears, frequent infections, asthma, ulcers, skin complaints, gastrointestinal upsets (e.g. diarrhoea or constipation).

- **Behavioural:** impatience, impulsiveness, having accidents and making mistakes, eating/sleeping problems, hyperactivity, substance abuse (e.g. tobacco, alcohol), avoiding difficult situations, overworking.

- **Work performance:** an increase in sick days or absenteeism, work avoidance (e.g. arriving for work later), a drop in work performance, loss of motivation and commitment, more complaints and grievances.

Supervisors should be alert for signs of stress among their co-workers. Moreover, organizations can use tools to systematically monitor levels of pressure experienced by employees. For example, an anonymous annual staff survey could include questions related to common stressors such as role clarity or workload.

In informal conversations managers could ask their employees if they are experiencing excessive levels of pressure. However, in direct encounters staff will often hide signs of stress and discomfort from their employers, in fear of coming across as someone who struggles with their work. This highlights the importance of *developing supportive organizational culture*. In a supportive work environment, employees are encouraged to openly communicate about their well-being with supervisors. Staff know that it is alright for them to talk about work-related stress with their peers and to ask for assistance when needed. In a supportive workplace managers recognize issues such as stress and deal with them with respect and understanding. In order to prevent or reduce work-place stress, managers also need to pay attention to the common stressors (see Chapter 3) and regularly *review and realistically manage workloads and expectations*.

Employee training can also be helpful. It raises awareness of stress symptoms and explains the impact of prolonged stress on well-being and work performance. Every individual varies in how well they cope with different levels of pressure. However, training may help employees reflect on what is causing their work stress, what coping mechanisms are available to them and how they can develop a plan to lower the pressure. At the same time, the training cannot be used as an opportunity for the employer to pass on the responsibility for managing stress to employees. Without wider organizational support and managers' participation, the employee training would be counterproductive. In cases where the employer maintains a work environment with many stressors, additional training or coaching may be seen by staff as more of a burden than a help.

WORKSHOP DISCUSSION 3

Singer Instruments

Singer Instruments (from here on Singer) is a family-owned business located outside of Watchet, England. The company has 60 employees and specializes in developing and manufacturing scientific equipment for research laboratories.

In 2012, when the company had only 20 employees, two staff members had to take sick leave because of work-related stress. The managing director asked Adrian Huxley, who was at the time a quality manager, to look into the matter. This is how Adrian's role started to evolve. He took on additional responsibilities of health and safety management and became the Champion for Prevention of Stress in the organization.

One of the first steps that Adrian took was to bring in a consultant who would expand his and all employees' understanding of work-related stress and its management. In a podcast for IOM3 (Institute of Materials, Minerals and Mining), Adrian also explained that he wanted to improve communication between staff and employees to help the organization support its employees. Adrian said, 'It's clear that when someone is in a situation like that, they feel like they cannot go to work, it's all about communication. As much communication as possible, and understanding.'

Adrian arranged individual meetings with the staff members who took sick leave because of work-related stress. The aim was to understand what the problem was and how the company could support its employees. From these conversations it became clear that both colleagues were overloaded workwise. To address this Singer hired extra staff.

The company also discussed with the two employees their gradual return to work. First, they started to do half a day a week, then one and two days a week. They slowly eased themselves into work. Moreover, the company made changes to their roles to ensure that they did not encounter the same problems as before. Both colleagues successfully returned to work.

Singer also used the 'Management Standards Indicator Tool', which is a 35-question questionnaire developed by Health and Safety Executive. This survey tool helps to keep track of employees' well-being and identifies their work-related worries. After using it at the company it turned out that colleagues' biggest concern was lack of management support. Feeling isolated and not being able to discuss their work challenges were major issues.

To address these issues the company promoted the practice of reaching out to Adrian and confidentially discussing any concerns. Adrian took training as a counsellor and made himself available to anyone in the company. He soon became a go-to person for colleagues who needed to discuss their work-related and sometimes private worries.

Together with the managing director, Adrian also promoted the idea that 'It's OK not to be OK'. Admitting and having a conversation about feeling overwhelmed or unwell is not a sign of weakness. Employees face different mental well-being challenges and that is understandable. The key is to get to a position where colleagues are not afraid to seek help when they need it.

To support the message behind their project, the managing director and Adrian had individual conversations with each member of staff to remove the stigma related to stress and mental health. In the podcast for IOM3, Adrian highlighted how important it is to have the support of senior management. 'With matters like this it has to start at the top of the company and trickle down. If it does not start at the top, then people won't believe it, and it will almost certainly fail', Adrian said.

Adrian's and the senior management's initiative brought visible results. More employees became comfortable with discussing and addressing their concerns. It allowed the company to be proactive and resolve staff problems more quickly before they become worse.

Singer continued to grow in size and expand its operations. This created new obstacles for staff. Two years after Adrian became the Champion for Prevention of Stress, the company saw slightly lower results in the Management Standards survey, specifically in the assembly department. Adrian conducted confidential interviews with everyone in that part of the organization to get a clear picture of what concerned them. It turned out that the assembly team were worried they would not be able to meet the demands of additional workload as the company was expanding. The company decided to act on this feedback. 'We have addressed this by increasing the number of staff and implementing, with their support, an ongoing training programme which aims to train everybody in the assembly department to do every job', said a company representative. The training, which Singer developed as a part of the intervention, gave assembly employees new skills and knowledge. This meant that they now were able to switch jobs and better deal with repetitive elements of their work.

After the intervention Adrian conducted follow-up interviews with staff responsible for product assembly. Employees who were previously stressed about the company's expansion were now happy that their concerns had been addressed, and they became confident that the department would be able to cope with future growth.

Adrian admitted that when his company first used the Management Standards survey his colleagues were unsure of the process and why it was important. However, after several years of using the survey it became an accepted practice. During this time staff became more accustomed with the idea of openly discussing and addressing issues related to stress and mental health.

Questions

1 What were the causes of Singer employees' work-related stress?

2 What steps did Singer take to manage work-related stress?

3 What do you think were the benefits of Singer's stress management?

Sources

www.iom3.org/resource/iom3-investigates-mental-health.html

www.hse.gov.uk/stress/casestudies/singer-instruments.htm

www.hse.gov.uk/stress/standards/downloads.htm

www.hse.gov.uk/stress/assets/docs/indicatortool.pdf

Diversity and inclusion

In 2020 CIPD consulted HR professionals from across the world and attempted to identify key future trends that will impact the people profession (CIPD, 2020). According to the CIPD's findings, one of the trends that is expected to continue to influence the world of work is 'Diversity of employment relationships'. CIPD (2020) explained:

> The people profession needs to support a shift in thinking around inclusion, individuality and the value of diversity. This is all the more important in the wake of political and societal change in the next decade. (…) People management practices need to support all employees to thrive and take an individualized approach to do this.

Diversity and inclusion (D&I) is one of the main dimensions of sustainable HRM. D&I as an organizational strategy recognizes, accepts and values differences among employees while striving to integrate the perspectives of different groups of people into the work environment. D&I improves employers' legitimacy and credibility with diverse communities, helps with the recruitment and retention of talent and reduces the level of discrimination and harassment in an organization.

One of the common practices for promoting D&I in a workplace is *diversity training* (DT). This is a programme that raises awareness about diversity issues in the workplace, and how to approach individual differences at work with understanding. DT is often seen as an essential tool for creating diverse and inclusive workplaces, although studies show mixed results of its effects. Schoen and Rost (2021) found that diversity practices such as family-friendly policies increase the proportion of women in management positions, but their research did not find any effects of diversity training. In fact, according to Dobbin and Kalev (2016), mandatory diversity training can do more harm than good by activating bias or sparking a backlash. Managers may see the compulsory DT as a form of coercion and in an attempt to prove their autonomy they may do the opposite to the intended effect of the training. Dobbin and Kalev (2016) found that:

> Five years after instituting required training for managers, companies saw no improvement in the proportion of white women, black men, and Hispanics in management, and the share of black women actually decreased by 9 per cent, on average, while the ranks of Asian-American men and women shrank by 4 per cent to 5 per cent.

Dobbin and Kalev (2016) argued that unlike mandatory training, voluntary training tends to produce positive results. In organizations with voluntary DT, the scholars reported 'increases of 9 per cent to 13 per cent in black men, Hispanic men, and Asian-American men and women in management five years out (with no decline in white or black women).'

Instead of strong-arming and policing managers, a few more systemic changes can lead to more meaningful and persistent improvement of D&I. These initiatives include *engagement* (recruitment programmes, mentoring), *contact* (self-managed teams, cross-training) and *social accounting* (diversity managers, diversity task forces) (Dobbin and Kalev, 2016).

Managers are vital to the implementation of D&I. Dobbin and Kalev found that one of the effective methods of engaging managers in D&I is asking them to participate in university recruitment programmes targeting a group that is underrepresented in the workplace (e.g. women or minorities). If participation in the initiative is voluntary, managers can personally connect with the initiative and become determined to find good candidates, while furthering organizational D&I.

Another way to engage managers in D&I is through mentoring. Employees who belong to underrepresented groups can face more challenges in progressing in their careers. Mentoring is crucial for retaining and developing talent and is particularly important for minimizing obstacles faced by employees from underrepresented backgrounds. Mentoring aids cultivation of professional relationships across an organization.

Contact between groups, where employees are working as equals and aim to achieve the same goals, also furthers D&I. Dobbin and Kalev (2016) explained that self-managed teams bringing employees together from different roles help to remove barriers and build relationships between employees with different backgrounds. This is because organizations may have employees of a certain demographic profile predominating a specific function, e.g. women may make up the majority of the HR division. By organizing teams with colleagues from different roles we can create more opportunities for diverse teams to work together, share experiences and confront biases. In a similar fashion, cross-training can also create meaningful interactions that support D&I. *Cross-training* is a development initiative where employees train how to do work in different roles. In addition to giving people an opportunity to gain new skills and better understand other areas of the organization, cross-training 'has a positive impact on diversity, because it exposes both department heads and trainees to a wider variety of people' (Dobbin and Kalev, 2016).

Finally, organizations can make employees more accountable for the success of D&I. This can be done by appointing a diversity manager. A diversity professional helps different areas of the organization stay in line with the D&I strategy. Employers may also assemble diversity task forces. Such teams could include senior managers and employees who belong to underrepresented groups or who want to support D&I. A task force can look at the data behind recruitment, development and retention of staff, investigate if there are any areas of improvement and put forward potential solutions.

Dobbin and Kalev found in their research that each of the above-mentioned practices, related to engagement, contact and social accountability, significantly increase representation of women and ethnic minorities in management positions.

> **Skill check**
>
> **Diversity and inclusion.** The ability to sustainably manage diversity and inclusion is key to attract, retain, develop and motivate a wide pool of talent.

Social relationships at work

Employment by its nature involves social interaction. However, building positive and harmonious relationships at work can be challenging. Interpersonal factors such as *social cohesion, psychological safety* and *management support* are important dimensions of employment quality (CIPD, 2021b).

Social cohesion is a complex phenomenon which can be examined at multiple levels (e.g. organizational or task-group level). In general, **social cohesion** can be defined as a shared sense of solidarity among group members, and the motivation to build and maintain social relationships within the group (Carless and De Paola, 2000). At the organizational level, social cohesion generates a sense of unity in the workplace. It represents harmonious relationships and lowers the risk of conflicts. The concept of social cohesion also forces us to think about developing a workplace atmosphere that would cultivate all employees' feelings of belonging and being a part of the organization. As explained by Jahanbani et al (2018), social cohesion 'teaches the staff how to effectively participate in the activities of the organization and with the other members of organization'. Fostering social cohesion and a sense of community in the workplace can be an important goal for sustainable HRM (Stankevičiūtė and Savanevičienė, 2018).

At the level of teams, and groups oriented towards specific organizational goals, social cohesion has been linked to several improved outcomes such as:

Communication. Greater cohesion in a team can enhance communication between group members. Cohesiveness can lead to faster sharing of resources, such as information (Smith et al, 1994).

Cooperation. Cohesive groups can show improved cooperation among members. This could be because cohesion is linked with trust between group members. In cohesive groups teammates are more willing to use shared resources and act on agreed goals, thus enhancing collaboration (Vissa and Chacar, 2009).

Satisfaction. Members of cohesive groups tend to report higher satisfaction with their jobs and organization (Ahronson and Cameron, 2007).

Well-being. Higher group cohesion is associated with lower job stress (Steinhardt et al, 2003) and an improved general sense of psychological well-being (Bliese and Halverson, 1996).

Performance. Higher levels of team cohesion have been associated with higher productivity rates, better schedule performance, improved safety performance and higher quality of services and outcomes (Pandit et al, 2019).

Although most of the research has demonstrated positive effects of social cohesion, high cohesiveness has also been associated with the phenomenon of *groupthink*. Janis (1972) defines groupthink as a 'mode of thinking that people engage in when they are deeply involved in a cohesive in-group, when the members' strivings for unanimity override their motivation to realistically appraise alternative courses of action'. When groupthink occurs, individual members of the group may fail to speak out against poor decisions. Due to strong pressure on group members to reach agreement, minority or unpopular views are suppressed. Fortunately, there are practices that make groupthink less likely to occur while maintaining high cohesion. Managers should encourage ethical thinking, consider the risk of groupthink when making a decision and encourage expression of dissenting opinions (Riordan and Riordan, 2013).

Establishing good social cohesion can be especially important when managing virtual groups of employees. With staff spatially separated, and coordinated mainly through technology rather than physical proximity, members of virtual teams can find it more challenging to achieve mutual understanding. Compared to face-to-face teams, 'virtual team members report lower levels of trust, cohesion, outcome satisfaction, and process satisfaction' (Furumo and Pearson, 2006). This means that in virtual teams it is especially important to build positive interpersonal relationships between team members, and to do it ideally from the beginning of team development (Lin et al, 2008).

Another social factor that is important for quality of employment is psychological safety. According to Kahn (1990), *psychological safety* is 'feeling able to show and employ one's self without fear of negative consequences to self-image, status, or career'. Psychological safety affects how colleagues feel about and interact with each other. When employees feel psychological safety this creates a climate at work where interpersonal risks are minimized and colleagues are encouraged to speak up with suggestions, concerns or mistakes. Employees who experience psychological safety are more likely to engage with their work and show higher task performance. Furthermore, psychological safety leads to positive behaviours at work such as (Frazier et al, 2017):

- information sharing
- citizenship behaviours
- creativity
- learning behaviours

In a fast-evolving work environment, psychological safety may play a particularly important role. Due to social and technological changes employees are often expected to undertake new tasks and responsibilities. In these circumstances employees' perceptions of whether they can ask for help or make a suggestion matter. But how do we foster a psychologically safe workplace?

According to Frazier et al (2017), the following factors have been linked with psychological safety:

- positive relations with the leader
- entrusting employees with important decisions (work autonomy)
- providing employees with a clear understanding of their role (role clarity)
- engaging in interdependent work
- supportive work context

This brings us to the third key social factor. Management support, and particularly top management support, is one of the necessary conditions for good quality of employment (see e.g. Mosadeghrad, 2013). *Management support* refers to managers providing their employees with the necessary resources, time or attention. This could be related to tangible help, for instance, in the form of finding budget for certain projects. However, it can also be intangible assistance, e.g. in the form of managers' enthusiasm or personal commitment to specific initiatives, such as maintaining a good work–life balance. Management support can be provided at different organizational levels, by immediate supervisors, middle management, directors or even the CEO. Although once top management shows involvement with a given idea, this puts additional pressure on middle and lower levels of management to also follow suit.

Employee voice and representative participation

Workers' sense of being represented, and having a say in matters of concern, are also important aspects of employment quality. As defined by Paulet et al (2021, emphasis added), '*Employee voice* refers to the mechanisms through which employees attempt to have a say about aspects of their work, be it formal and/or informal channels, or individually and/or collectively.' Employee voice is the means through which workers can engage in a two-way communication with their employer and express their concerns or put forward interests and opinions. According to the CIPD (2022), there are three main purposes for employee voice:

- to protect employees' right to have good working conditions and give them an opportunity to shape their work arrangements;
- to express employees' ideas and collaborate with co-workers on how to improve organizational functions and performance;
- to highlight organizational failures and issues which have or could have damaging consequences.

Employee voice can be categorized into five main forms of representative participation (CIPD, 2021c):

Collective representation. In these arrangements, representatives of trade unions, or other forms of staff association, negotiate with senior management to discuss issues such as remuneration and other work conditions.

Partnership schemes. This represents agreements between trade unions, or other forms of staff association, and senior management to build relationships based on collaboration rather than adversity.

Joint consultation. This is a formal mechanism that provides communication between an organization's management and the employees' representatives, discussing issues affecting the workforce. Usually this is carried out by a Joint Consultation Committee (JCC). As explained by CIPD (2021c), 'In unionized organizations, the trade unions typically provide the employee representatives, but JCCs also run with non-union employee representatives.'

Employee forums. This is a means for the management to seek employees' views and opinions, which can help achieve organizational goals. These groups provide a way for organizations to proactively seek feedback from employees on different areas of business and also an opportunity for employees, and their representatives, to gain insight into the business strategy and goals of the organization.

Other structures provided for by specific legislation. There can be other bodies of representative participation. For example, employees working in large companies in the European Economic Area can ask for a European Works Council (EWC) to be set up, which will bring together senior managers and workforce representatives.

Employee participation and voice lie at the centre of sustainable HRM (Richards, 2022). Improving the quality of working life requires representation of employees' interests in a two-way communication between the employer and the workforce. Thus, trade unions play a paramount role in supporting social sustainability due to their concern with the general conditions of work as well as health and safety (Mayer, 2011). In a literature review related to sustainable HRM, Richards (2022) pointed out that trade union activities have been linked to organizational benefits of:

- lower employee turnover
- lower sickness absence
- improved effectiveness of CSR initiatives
- supporting organizations in their expansions into growing markets
- improved organizational productivity
- provision of more sustainable remuneration for staff (e.g. paying *living wage*, challenging wage stagnation)
- protecting employees' pension rights
- development of occupational pension systems
- greater equality in the distribution of training

Many of these positive outcomes are achieved through employer-trade union partnership agreements.

Paulet et al (2021) highlight that organizations can draw on formal or informal channels through which employees can voice their opinions. However, the quality of these channels is more important than quantity. This is because the mere existence, or plurality of channels, does not guarantee employees will use them, or that the employer will listen to the provided feedback. As explained by Paulet et al (2021), situations can occur where:

> management builds voice channels but, either intentionally or unintentionally due to time, resource and/or skills constraints, creates a culture of employee silence through institutional structures which place constraints on employee voice, supported by pseudo or lip-service voice mechanisms or 'deaf ear'.

The participation in available channels for employee-employer communication is likely to have an impact on the success of sustainable HRM.

Employee voice and representative participation in organizational decisions supports not only social and economic goals but also environmental sustainability. ILO (1999) has cited case studies from all over the world where environmentally sustainable development issues have been integrated into trade union work. In a similar vein, a report to the United Nations Environment Programme (Heins et al, 2004) emphasizes the pivotal role that trade unions play in influencing sustainable consumption and production. For instance, Britain's Trade Union Council (TUC) has produced and shared a significant number of materials on climate adaptation and environmental sustainability. This includes training resources aimed at workers and trade unions, educating on the upsides of sustainability, and producing guides with information and sample arguments that can be used to explain to management why the company should embrace green solutions (see e.g. TUC, 2021). In their statement linking social and environmental sustainability, TUC explained (2021):

> There are no climate deniers in the trade union movement, but workers are much more enthusiastic about the drive to a 'net-zero' carbon economy if it is something done in partnership with them than if it is implemented by politicians and managers above their heads, with unions having no say in the process.

In the next chapter we will discuss in more depth environmental sustainability and how it can be achieved through HRM practices.

Summary

It is challenging to manage organizations in ways that provide optimal use of employees' energy. The key to regenerating and maintaining a successful human resource base may be considering employee vitality and employment quality. Vital employees show mental resilience when working and demonstrate higher organizational commitment. At the same time, when vitality is low, employees are susceptible to the negative impact of stress and are at a higher risk of getting sick. Staff with decreased well-being can lead to increased absenteeism, higher workforce turnover and lost productivity. The chapter outlined key factors linked to improved employee vitality and explained how the concept fits in the framework of sustainable work performance.

Another perspective, facilitating a more sustainable management of human resources, comes from the literature dedicated to employment quality. Academic and professional debates led to the development of numerous similar concepts, frameworks and initiatives discussing the quality of work life. Moreover, employment quality is a multifaceted phenomenon, and each framework covers several sub-themes. The chapter attempted to summarize key information related to employment quality by focusing on seven key aspects:

1 general working conditions

2 mutually beneficial flexibility and work–life balance

3 organizational justice

4 stress management

5 diversity and inclusion

6 social relationships at work

7 employee voice and representative participation

Study questions

1 What is employee vitality and how does it fit in Dorenbosch's framework of sustainable work performance?

2 How can general working conditions impact employment quality?

3 What is mutually beneficial flexibility and how it can be achieved?

4 What are distributive and procedural justice? Explain their impact on quality of employment.

5 Is managing stress employees' responsibility? Discuss and explain the steps that organizations can take to prevent and minimize the effect of work-related stress.

6 Critically discuss to what extent traditional diversity training helps organizations achieve a diverse and inclusive workforce.

7 What are social cohesion, psychological safety and management support, and how can they impact employment quality?

8 Define the term 'employee voice' and explain how it is related to sustainable HRM.

Key reading

Burchell, B, Sehnbruch, K, Piasna, A and Agloni, N (2014) The quality of employment and decent work: definitions, methodologies, and ongoing debates, *Cambridge Journal of Economics*, **38** (2), pp 459–77.

Dobbin, F and Kalev, A (2016) Why diversity programs fail, *Harvard Business Review*, July–August, pp 1–10

Dorenbosch, L (2014) Striking a balance between work effort and resource regeneration. In I Ehnert, W Harry and K J Zink (eds.) *Sustainability and Human Resource Management: Developing sustainable business organizations* (pp 155–80), Springer, Berlin/Heidelberg, Germany

References

Ahronson, A and Cameron, J E (2007) The nature and consequences of group cohesion in a military sample, *Military Psychology*, **19** (1), pp 9–25

Allan, P (1997) Minimizing employee layoffs while downsizing: employer practices that work, *International Journal of Manpower*, **18** (7), pp 576–96

APA (2021) The American workforce faces compounding pressure, APA's 2021 Work and Well-being Survey results, www.apa.org/pubs/reports/work-well-being/compounding-pressure-2021.html (archived at https://perma.cc/QX6J-27RY)

Armstrong, M and Taylor, S (2020) *Armstrong's Handbook of Human Resource Management Practice*, 15th edn, Kogan Page, London

Atwater, L and Carmeli, A (2009) Leader–member exchange, feelings of energy and involvement in creative work, *The Leadership Quarterly*, **20** (3), pp 264–75

Bliese, P D and Halverson, R R (1996) Individual and nomothetic models of job stress: an examination of work hours, cohesion and well-being, *Journal of Applied Social Psychology*, **26** (13), pp 1171–89

Burchell, B, Sehnbruch, K, Piasna, A and Agloni, N (2014) The quality of employment and decent work: definitions, methodologies and ongoing debates, *Cambridge Journal of Economics*, **38** (2), pp 459–77

Carless, S A and De Paola, C (2000) The measurement of cohesion in work teams, *Small Group Research*, **31** (1), pp 71–88

Carmeli, A (2009) Chapter 3 Positive work relationships, vitality and job performance. In C E J Härtel, N M Ashkanasy and W J Zerbe (eds.) *Emotions in Groups, Organizations and Cultures (Research on Emotion in Organizations, Vol. 5)* (pp 45–71), Emerald Group Publishing Limited, Bingley

Chernyak-Hai, L and Tziner, A (2014) Relationships between counterproductive work behavior, perceived justice and climate, occupational status and leader-member exchange, *Revista de Psicología del Trabajo y de las Organizaciones*, 30 (1), pp 1–12

CIPD (2020) People profession 2030 a collective view of future trends, www.cipd.co.uk/Images/people-profession-2030-report-compressed_tcm18-86095.pdf (archived at https://perma.cc/UEL9-9AAB)

CIPD (2021a) Zero-hours contracts. Understand the advantages and disadvantages of zero-hours contracts, recent UK legislative changes and good practices to follow, www.cipd.co.uk/knowledge/fundamentals/emp-law/terms-conditions/zero-hours-factsheet#6083 (archived at https://perma.cc/YXQ9-G52K)

CIPD (2021b) CIPD Good Work Index, www.cipd.co.uk/knowledge/work/trends/goodwork (archived at https://perma.cc/4YW5-8YM4)

CIPD (2021c) Employee voice – learn about employee voice, its purposes and use and the benefits it can bring to an organization and its workforce, www.cipd.co.uk/knowledge/fundamentals/relations/communication/voice-factsheet (archived at https://perma.cc/R6YY-AZ6S)

CIPD (2022) Employee voice – explore the CIPD's point of view on employee voice, including actions for Government and recommendations for employers, www.cipd.co.uk/news-views/viewpoint/employee-voice#66500 (archived at https://perma.cc/6ZGD-FYYY)

De Jonge, J and Peeters, M C W (2019) The vital worker: towards sustainable performance at work, *International Journal of Environmental Research and Public Health,* **16** (6), p 910

Devonish, D and Greenidge, D (2010) The effect of organizational justice on contextual performance, counterproductive work behaviors and task performance: investigating the moderating role of ability-based emotional intelligence, *International Journal of Selection and Assessment*, **18** (1), pp 75–86

Dobbin, F and Kalev, A (2016) Why diversity programs fail, *Harvard Business Review*, July–August, pp 1–10

Dolan, S L, Tzafrir, S S and Baruch, Y (2005) Testing the causal relationships between procedural justice, trust and organizational citizenship behavior, *Revue de gestion des Resources Humaines*, **57**, pp 79–89

Dorenbosch, L (2014) Striking a balance between work effort and resource regeneration. In I Ehnert, W Harry and K J Zink (eds.) *Sustainability and Human Resource Management: Developing sustainable business organizations* (pp 155–180), Springer, Berlin/Heidelberg, Germany

Ertürk, A, Yılmaz, C and Ceylan, A (2004) Promoting organizational citizenship behaviors: relative effects of job satisfaction, organizational commitment and perceived managerial fairness, *METU Studies in Development*, **31**, pp 189–210.

EY (2021) More than half of employees globally would quit their jobs if not provided post-pandemic flexibility, EY survey finds, www.ey.com/en_gl/ news/2021/05/more-than-half-of-employees-globally-would-quit-their-jobs-if-not-provided-post-pandemic-flexibility-ey-survey-finds (archived at https:// perma.cc/7H2N-H6XT)

Frazier, M L, Fainshmidt, S, Klinger, R L, Pezeshkan, A and Vracheva, V (2017) Psychological safety: a meta-analytic review and extension, *Personnel Psychology*, **70** (1), pp 113–65

Furumo, K and Pearson, J M (2006) An empirical investigation of how trust, cohesion and performance vary in virtual and face-to-face teams. In *Proceedings of the 39th Annual Hawaii International Conference on System Sciences (HICSS'06)*, **1**

Graves, L M and Luciano, M M (2013) Self-determination at work: understanding the role of leader-member exchange, *Motivation and Emotion*, **37** (3), pp 518–36

Greenberg, J (1994) Using socially fair treatment to promote acceptance of a work site smoking ban, *Journal of Applied Psychology*, **79** (2), pp 288–97

Grote, G and Guest, D (2017) The case for reinvigorating quality of working life research, *Human Relations*, **70** (2), pp 149–67

Hakanen J J, Ropponen A, De Witte H and Schaufeli W B (2019) Testing demands and resources as determinants of vitality among different employment contract groups. A study in 30 European countries, *International Journal of Environmental Research and Public Health*, **16** (24), p 4951

Heins, B, Knigge, M, Kranz, N and von Bieberstein, A (2004) The role of labour unions in the process towards sustainable consumption and production, *Final report to the United Nations Environment Programme (UNEP)*, Division of Technology, Industry and Economics (DTIE), Paris, France

Hennekam, S (2016) Vitality of older workers and its relationship with performance, career satisfaction and career success, *Management Avenir*, **1**, pp 15–32

ILO (1999) Trade Union Actions to Promote Environmentally Sustainable Development, www.ilo.org/wcmsp5/groups/public/@ed_dialogue/@actrav/documents/publication/wcms_122116.pdf (archived at https://perma.cc/6VFJ-Q4PW)

ILO (2022) Decent Work, www.ilo.org/global/topics/decent-work/lang--en/index.htm (archived at https://perma.cc/MX5B-FHNW)

Jahanbani, E, Mohammadi, M, Noori Noruzi, N and Bahrami, F (2018) Quality of work life and job satisfaction among employees of health centers in Ahvaz, Iran, *Jundishapur Journal of Health Sciences*, **10** (1), pp 1–7

Janis, I L (1972) *Victims of groupthink*, Houghton-Mifflin, Boston

Johns, G (2010) Presenteeism in the workplace: a review and research agenda, *Journal of Organizational Behavior*, **31** (4), pp 519–42

Kahn, W A (1990) Psychological conditions of personal engagement and disengagement at work, *Academy of Management Journal*, **33** (4), pp 692–724

Kassahun, T (2005) Level of organizational commitment: its correlates and predictors, *Indian Journal of Industrial Relations*, **41** (1), pp 29–63

Kivimäki, M, Head, J, Ferrie, J E, Hemingway, H, Shipley, M J, Vahtera, J and Marmot, M G (2005) Working while ill as a risk factor for serious coronary events: the Whitehall II study, *American Journal of Public Health*, **95** (1), pp 98–102

Kramar, R (2014) Beyond strategic human resource management: is sustainable human resource management the next approach?, *The International Journal of Human Resource Management*, **25** (8), pp 1069–89

Lambert, E G, Hogan, N L and Griffin, M L (2007) The impact of distributive and procedural justice on correctional staff job stress, job satisfaction and organizational commitment, *Journal of Criminal Justice*, **35** (6), pp 644–56

Lambert, E G, Hogan, N L, Jiang, S, Elechi, O O, Benjamin, B, Morris, A and Dupuy, P (2010) The relationship among distributive and procedural justice and correctional life satisfaction, burnout and turnover intent: An exploratory study, *Journal of Criminal Justice*, **38** (1), pp 7–16

Lambert, E G, Keena, L D, Leone, M, May, D and Haynes, S H (2020) The effects of distributive and procedural justice on job satisfaction and organizational commitment of correctional staff, *The Social Science Journal*, **57** (4), pp 405–16

Lantman, M V S, Mackus, M, Otten, L S, de Kruijff, D, van de Loo, A J, Kraneveld, A D and Verster, J C (2017) Mental resilience, perceived immune functioning and health, *Journal of Multidisciplinary Healthcare*, **10**, pp 107–112

Leschke, J, Watt, A and Finn, M (2008) Putting a number on job quality? Constructing a European job quality index, The European Trade Union Institute, www.etui.org/publications/working-papers/putting-a-number-on-job-quality (archived at https://perma.cc/K7V2-TVWS)

Lin, C, Standing, C and Liu, Y C (2008) A model to develop effective virtual teams, *Decision Support Systems*, **45** (4), pp 1031–45

Mayer, B (2011) *Blue-Green Coalitions: Fighting for safe workplaces and healthy communities*, Cornell University Press, Ithaca, NY

Mayo, E (1960) *The Human Problems of an Industrial Civilisation*, Viking Press, New York

Mirvis, P H and Lawler III, E E (1984) Accounting for the quality of work life, *Journal of Organizational Behavior*, **5** (3), pp 197–212

Mosadeghrad, A M (2013) Quality of working life: an antecedent to employee turnover intention, *International Journal of Health Policy and Management*, **1** (1), pp 43–50

Nix, G A, Ryan, R M, Manly, J B and Deci, E L (1999) Revitalization through self-regulation: the effects of autonomous and controlled motivation on happiness and vitality, *Journal of Experimental Social Psychology*, **35** (3), pp 266–84

Pandit, B, Albert, A, Patil, Y and Al-Bayati, A J (2019) Fostering safety communication among construction workers: Role of safety climate and crew-level cohesion, *International Journal of Environmental Research and Public Health*, **16** (1), p 71

Paulet, R, Holland, P and Bratton, A (2021) Employee voice: the missing factor in sustainable HRM?, *Sustainability*, **13** (17), p 9732

PwC (2021) 2021 PwC employee financial wellness survey, four steps employers should take to strengthen workforce financial wellness, www.pwc.com/us/en/services/consulting/workforce-of-the-future/library/employee-financial-wellness-survey.html (archived at https://perma.cc/28WP-7LDD)

Reilly, P A (2001) *Flexibility at Work: Balancing the interests of employer and employee*, Gower Publishing Ltd, Aldershot

Richards, J (2022) Putting employees at the centre of sustainable HRM: a review, map and research agenda, *Employee Relations*, **44** (3), pp 533–54

Riordan, D and Riordan, M (2013) Guarding against groupthink in the professional work environment: a checklist, *Journal of Academic and Business Ethics*, **7**, pp 1–8

Russell, E and Woods, S A (2020) Personality differences as predictors of action-goal relationships in work-email activity, *Computers in Human Behavior*, **103**, pp 67–79

Saunders, M N and Thornhill, A (2003) Organizational justice, trust and the management of change: an exploration, *Personnel Review*, **32** (3), pp 360–75

Schoen, C and Rost, K (2021) What really works?! Evaluating the effectiveness of practices to increase the managerial diversity of women and minorities, *European Management Journal*, **39** (1), pp 95–108

Schultz, A B and Edington, D W (2007) Employee health and presenteeism: a systematic review, *Journal of Occupational Rehabilitation*, **17** (3), pp 547–79

Scottish Government (2021) Fair Work: action plan, www.gov.scot/publications/fair-work-action-plan/ (archived at https://perma.cc/P58P-NVKA)

Sianoja, M, Kinnunen, U, Bloom, J D, Korpela, K and Geurts, S A E (2016) Recovery during lunch breaks: testing long-term relations with energy levels at work, *Scandinavian Journal of Work and Organizational Psychology*, **1** (7), pp 1–12

Skagen, J and Collins, A M (2016) The consequences of sickness presenteeism on health and wellbeing over time: a systematic review, *Social Science & Medicine*, **161**, pp 169–77

Smith, K G, Smith, K A, Olian, J D, Sims Jr, H P, O'Bannon, D P and Scully, J A (1994) Top management team demography and process: the role of social integration and communication, *Administrative Science Quarterly*, **39** (3), pp 412–38

Stankevičiūtė, Ž and Savanevičienė, A (2018) Raising the curtain in people management by exploring how sustainable HRM translates to practice: the case of Lithuanian organizations, *Sustainability*, **10** (12), p 4356

Steinhardt, M A, Dolbier, C L, Gottlieb, N H and McCalister, K T (2003) The relationship between hardiness, supervisor support, group cohesion and job stress as predictors of job satisfaction, *American Journal of Health Promotion*, **17** (6), pp 382–89

Suzuki, T, Miyaki, K, Song, Y, Tsutsumi, A, Kawakami, N, Shimazu, A, Takahashi, M, Inoue, A and Kurioka, S (2015) Relationship between sickness presenteeism (WHO–HPQ) with depression and sickness absence due to mental disease in a cohort of Japanese workers, *Journal of Affective Disorders*, **180**, pp 14–20

TUC (2021) Go green at work: the union effect, From TUC Workplace Manual, www.tuc.org.uk/resource/go-green-work-union-effect (archived at https://perma.cc/87M9-2E92)

Tummers, L, Kruyen, P M, Vijverberg, D M and Voesenek, T J (2015) Connecting HRM and change management: the importance of proactivity and vitality, *Journal of Organizational Change Management*, **28** (4), pp 627–40

Tummers, L, Steijn, B, Nevicka, B and Heerema, M (2018) The effects of leadership and job autonomy on vitality: survey and experimental evidence, *Review of Public Personnel Administration*, **38** (3), pp 355–77

UN (2015) Resolution adopted by the General Assembly on 25 September 2015, transforming our world: the 2030 agenda for sustainable development, https://sdgs.un.org/2030agenda (archived at https://perma.cc/5FTH-NMFW)

UNICEF (2019) Family-friendly policies, redesigning the workplace of the future, a policy brief, www.unicef.org/sites/default/files/2019-07/UNICEF-policy-brief-family-friendly-policies-2019.pdf (archived at https://perma.cc/TZ7Q-SQ6N)

van Scheppingen, A R, de Vroome, E M, Ten Have, K C, Zwetsloot, G I, Wiezer, N and van Mechelen, W (2015) Vitality at work and its associations with lifestyle, self-determination, organizational culture and with employees' performance and sustainable employability, *Work*, **52** (1), pp 45–55

Vissa, B and Chacar, A S (2009) Leveraging ties: the contingent value of entrepreneurial teams' external advice networks on Indian software venture performance, *Strategic Management Journal*, **30** (11), pp 1179–91

Workplace Health and Safety QLD (2022) Organizational justice and work-related stress: tip sheet 12, www.safework.nsw.gov.au/resource-library/mental-health/mental-health-strategy-research/stress-tip-sheets/organisational-justice-and-work-related-stress (archived at https://perma.cc/C7GW-Q5AJ)

Yang, T, Jin, X, Shi, H, Liu, Y, Guo, Y, Gao, Y and Deng, J (2021) Occupational stress, distributive justice and turnover intention among public hospital nurses in China: a cross-sectional study, *Applied Nursing Research*, **61**, p 151481

Zhang, H and Agarwal, N C (2009) The mediating roles of organizational justice on the relationships between HR practices and workplace outcomes: an investigation in China, *The International Journal of Human Resource Management*, **20** (3), pp 676–93

Green HRM 5

LEARNING OBJECTIVES

After completing this chapter, you should be able to:

- Describe the origin and definition of green HRM.
- Recognize outcomes of GHRM at the organizational, team and individual levels.
- Understand the theoretical underpinnings of GHRM.
- Explain the practice of green recruitment and selection
- Explain the practice of green induction and training.
- Explain the practice of green performance management.
- Explain the use of the green reward systems.
- Explain green behaviour and discipline management.
- Explain the practice of green empowerment.
- Explain the phenomenon of the green employee commitment.
- Identify internal and external factors affecting GHRM adoption.

Introduction

With the growing concern about climate change, organizations are urged to act, and limit environmental degradation. Many businesses are facing legal, ethical and societal pressures to tackle issues such as waste management, energy efficiency and carbon emissions. The public is paying attention to environmental challenges, and this translates into additional organizational responsibilities. Progressive employers who adjust to the new market forces can gain competitive advantage by meeting customers' and investors' preferences for products and services produced in an environmentally sustainable manner. At the same time organizations ignoring societal trends can face customer boycotts and negative brand perception.

This chapter explores what role HRM can play in achieving environmental sustainability. The discussion begins with an explanation of what 'green HRM' (GHRM) is and what its origins are. We then highlight the importance of GHRM by describing its benefits at the organizational, team and individual levels. The section that follows introduces two theories commonly used in the field of GHRM, namely the AMO and social identity theories. The remainder of the chapter focuses on practices that can be tied to pro-environmental goals, such as recruitment and selection, induction and training, performance management, reward systems, discipline management, and developing employee empowerment and commitment. The penultimate section reviews internal and external factors affecting GHRM adoption, for instance, involvement of executive management and the influence of government regulations. The chapter closes with a summary revising key arguments.

Origins of GHRM

The systematic discussion of the role people management plays in achieving environmental goals began in the 1990s (Paulet et al, 2021). Early research in this domain focused on the *environmental management* (EM) perspective. In the organizational context EM can be seen as an umbrella term for processes, practices, policies and application of tools addressing various ecological issues and improving organizations' impact on the natural environment. As organizations started to adopt EM, they initially concentrated on technical solutions, e.g. equipment and processes needed to reduce, reuse and recycle materials. However, with time more attention was paid to the human side of the equation and how employees initiate, shape and implement environmental activities. Wehrmeyer (1996) is often cited as the main author merging EM with HRM. Wehrmeyer argued that 'if a company is to adopt an environmentally aware approach to its activities, the employees are the key to its success or failure'.

This conceptual marriage of HRM and EM led to the emergence of *green HRM*, which Wagner (2013) defined as 'those parts of sustainable HR management dealing with the needs that relate to environmental sustainability'.

The GHRM concept represents the idea that HRM is necessary to ensure employees perform green behaviours and implement green policies. This can be achieved by embedding environmental objectives in processes such as recruitment or training and clear communication of organizational values. According to Ren et al (2018), GHRM is concerned with:

- development of the overall HRM philosophy that embraces green values;
- the promotion of HRM policies that clarify the organization's position on environmental protection and guide employees' green performance;
- actively managing and appraising green HRM practice;
- using green technological solutions for development, implementation and evaluation of GHRM and its evolving practices.

Outcomes of GHRM

Ren and colleagues (2018) observed that 'designing and implementing GHRM practices requires major investments in organizational resources, likely leading managers to question whether such investments are worthwhile'. Therefore, it is imperative to review potential outcomes of successful GHRM. The discussion below breaks down GHRM's impact into three levels: organizational, team and individual. However, we should recognize that in practice these levels are not rigid – they can to some extent blur and overlap.

Role of GHRM for organizations

Green HRM has positive effects on organizational *reputation and attractiveness*. Chaudhary (2018) conducted a study on final-year students from various departments of a well-reputed engineering institute in India. Prospective applicants reported higher *job pursuit intention* and higher *organizational prestige* for employers with information about GHRM. Similar results were identified in research on US undergraduate and postgraduate students (Behrend et al, 2009). These findings are also consistent with studies in the field of CSR where researchers learned that organizations committed to environmental values are seen as more prestigious and tend to attract higher-quality job applicants (Behrend et al, 2009; Gully et al, 2013). As concluded by Muisyo et al (2021), 'the adoption of GHRM is an ideal way for firms to stay distinct and unique from their rivals'.

These claims are further supported by research on GHRM impact on *turn-over intention*. Islam et al (2020) examined millennial employees working in three-, four- and five-star hotels in Malaysia and found that green involvement and green rewards reduce turnover intention of millennials. **Green involvement** is a practice of presenting employees with opportunities to participate in environmental management. It includes, for example, allowing employees to take part in quality improvement and problem solving on environmental issues, or providing formal or informal communication channels to spread green culture at work. Whereas **green rewards** represent financial or non-financial benefits used to motivate and recognize employees' green performance and their contribution to the organizational green goals.

GHRM enhances employers' *environmental performance* which in turn has positive influence on overall *organizational performance*. This was found, for example, by Obeidat et al (2020) in a study of the Qatari oil and gas industry. The researchers surveyed 144 managers and asked them to report on: a) the degree to which their businesses use green HR practices; b) the extent to which their businesses are able to achieve a set of environmental performance indicators; and c) a range of organizational performance indicators. Based on their findings, the researchers found a link between GHRM practices, environmental performance and general organizational performance (Obeidat et al, 2020). In a similar study O'Donohue and Torugsa (2016) illustrated how green HRM enables environmental management and increases *financial benefits deriving from EM*. The researchers examined over 1,200 small firms from the Australian machinery and equipment manufacturing sector and concluded:

> This study presents empirical evidence that adoption of practices associated with green HRM in the management of a small firm's human resources (…) is a significant contributor to the enhancement of the business and financial benefits a small firm can derive from the implementation of a proactive approach to environmental management (O'Donohue and Torugsa, 2016).

GHRM supports wider pro-environmental efforts in the organization. For instance, there is a growing body of academic research examining the impact of GHRM on *green supply chain management* (GSCM). GHRM practices (e.g. green recruitment, selection and rewards) help organizations reduce the barriers to implementing GSCM. As Zaid et al (2018) explained, integrating GHRM and GSCM is indispensable in building a holistic green organization. They examined 121 firms functioning in the most polluting manufacturing sectors in Palestine and, in line with other similar studies, found a significant positive influence of GHRM bundle practices on GSCM. For example, green training for managerial and non-managerial staff disseminated better understanding of GSCM within the organization.

According to Song et al (2020), GHRM can also spark *green innovation* and develop *green human capital*. The researchers came to such a conclusion after collecting data from 143 companies from the regions of Zhejiang and Guangzhou in China. As the name of the concept suggests, **green innovation** is a form of innovation that helps to achieve environmental goals, such as minimizing environmental damage. GHRM plays an important role in developing employees' knowledge, skills and abilities in the field of environmental practices. Green induction and training are instrumental in giving employees the means to identify green products, processes and solutions. Green rewards can incentivize employees to create novel ideas for achieving environmental goals. Song and their colleagues also looked at **green human capital**, which represents 'the summation of employees' knowledge, skills, capabilities, experience, attitude, wisdom, creativities, and commitments, etc. about environmental protection or green innovation' (Chen, 2008). Recruiting and selecting employees who value environmental sustainability, and have some level of understanding in this area, increases organizations' pool of talent with green attributes. Furthermore, green training develops employees' core capabilities necessary for achieving environmental goals. These and other GHRM practices (e.g. performance management, enhancing employees' commitment) increase organizations' green human capital (Song et al, 2020).

Role of GHRM for employee teams and groups

Studies suggest that at the group level GHRM facilitates employees' collective engagement in *organizational citizenship behaviours towards the environment* (OCBE). Pinzone et al (2016) examined National Health Service (NHS) organizations in England and found that a) green competence building, b) green performance management, and c) green employee involvement practices positively influence collective OCBE. The idea here is that employers who invest in green practices such as GHRM are likely to see their employees reciprocate these efforts by 'going the extra mile' and collaboratively engaging in OCBEs.

Ogbeibu et al (2020) found that GHRM has an impact on **green team creativity**, which the authors defined as 'conception, improvement, and advancement of environmentally sustainable and innovative ideas among teams in an organization'. Ogbeibu et al (2020) conducted a study on 31 manufacturing organizations in Malaysia and further highlighted the link between GHRM and green innovation. However, this time the researchers examined it at the team level. The study found that green recruitment, selection and training are positive predictors of green team creativity. But interestingly, green performance and compensation were found to negatively predict green team creativity. One of the reasons for the negative correlation can be that too high or poorly defined green targets may stifle creativity. Ineffective communication of green performance and rewards or poor implementation of environmental compensation policies can provoke fewer creative efforts of team members (Ogbeibu et al, 2020). The authors argued that when it comes to using green performance and compensation practices, organizations should show flexibility and not use excessive force and control, to allow teams to show more initiative.

Role of GHRM for individual employees

At the individual level GHRM boosts employees' behaviours and attitudes related to environmental issues, as well as non-green workplace outcomes. For example, Pinzone and their colleagues (2019) collected data from a survey of 260 healthcare professionals working in an Italian hospital and found that green training improves employees' *job satisfaction*. Being a part of sustainability initiatives can have a positive spill-over effect onto overall satisfaction with the work that we do. Employees who feel that their actions make a difference can be more satisfied with their jobs. Additionally, if staff members personally value environmental protection, then green training is an opportunity for the employer to highlight that their interests align. Training can also increase job satisfaction when employees are equipped with skills and abilities that are useful in different contexts. Learning behaviours that help to protect the environment in some cases could be beneficial for employees in their private lives (Pinzone et al, 2019).

Shen et al (2018) conducted a study on a food packaging manufacturer in China and found that employees' perceptions of green HRM, mediated by organizational identification, affect employees' *task performance*. In other words, employees' perceptions of green HRM indirectly have a beneficial impact on how employees perform their tasks. This is because green HRM first enhances **organizational identification**, which is the degree to which an employee identifies with their organization and believes they belong to it. When an employer is engaged in social goals, e.g. protection of the natural environment, employees are more likely to feel proud to be members of such an establishment and can identify themselves with it. Organizational identification then creates positive outcomes including increased task performance.

This brings us to a discussion of how GHRM shapes employees' green behaviours and attitudes. Studies found that green training has a strong and positive impact on a range of employees' *green competencies* such as green awareness, abilities, skills, knowledge, attitudes and behaviours (see e.g. Gull and Idrees, 2022; Cabral and Dhar, 2020). These pro-environment competencies in turn have an impact on organizational efficiency. Gull and Idrees (2022) conducted a survey on ISO-14001 certified textile manufacturing organizations in Pakistan. Companies that are 'ISO-14001 certified' meet international standards for designing and implementing plans for managing environmental impact. Gull and Idrees surveyed 235 managerial-level employees and found a link between GHRM, green competencies and organizational efficiency. Understanding how to responsibly use natural resources and being able to apply environmental knowledge can aid staff in performing tasks in an efficient manner. With successful green training employees feel involved and motivated to look for innovative ecological solutions and enhanced ways to achieve organizational goals (Gull and Idrees, 2022).

Unsurprisingly, GHRM also leads to better employee *green performance*. For example, Chaudhary (2019) surveyed employees from the automobile sector in India and found that GHRM has a significant and positive impact on employees' green performance. This included a) pro-environmental performance related to one's job duties, as well as b) voluntary green performance involving personal initiative and exceeding organizational expectations.

One of the areas where GHRM can advance employees' *pro-environmental performance* is information technology (IT). Ojo et al (2020) surveyed IT professionals from 88 Malaysian companies that are ISO-14001 certified. The authors found that 'through GHRM practices, a firm can enhance its environmental IT performance when the employees take discretionary actions on the production and usage of IT' (Ojo et al, 2020). The study found employees' green IT performance was correlated with environmental training, development, performance management and empowerment.

GHRM can lead to a range of desirable work outcomes. Some of them are directly related to environmental sustainability. For example, GHRM can boost environmental performance of the organization or enhance green supply chain management. However, we also should highlight that GHRM can improve social sustainability (e.g. staff turnover and attracting candidates) and financial sustainability (e.g. increasing financial benefits related to environmental management). With its versatile utility GHRM has the potential to be an important source of competitive advantage (Yong et al, 2019a).

The research demonstrates that for certain outcomes specific elements of GHRM may be more effective than others. Nevertheless, overall GHRM has the potential to bring the following positive outcomes (see also Pham et al, 2019).

Outcomes for organizations:

- organizational reputation
- attracting job candidates
- staff turnover
- environmental performance
- organizational performance
- financial benefits related to environmental management
- green supply chain management
- green innovation
- green human capital

Outcomes for employee teams and groups:

- organizational citizenship behaviours towards the environment
- green team creativity

Outcomes for individual employees:

- job satisfaction
- job performance
- organizational identification and commitment
- green competencies (green awareness, abilities, skills, knowledge, attitudes and behaviours)
- green employee performance

Skill check

Analysing benefits of GHRM. This is a key skill because it helps you consider how GHRM could support your organization.

Theoretical underpinnings of GHRM

In Chapter 2 we discussed several theoretical frameworks that can be applied to sustainable HRM in general, e.g. stakeholder theory and institutional theory. However, there are two theories we have not mentioned yet, and they are commonly used specifically to examine GHRM. These are AMO (ability, motivation and opportunity) theory and social identity theory.

AMO theory

The AMO framework was initially proposed by Bailey (1993) and then further developed by Appelbaum et al (2000). AMO suggests that employees' performance is affected by their abilities (A), motivation (M) and opportunities to participate (O). When all three elements of the equation are available, we are more likely to perform well and increase organizational outcomes, such as profitability. The theory has been adopted extensively to examine how different HRM practices can affect AMO and subsequently employees' performance. Employees' abilities can be improved through attracting qualified staff to begin with and then further training and developing them. The second element, motivation, can be stimulated through reward and performance management. Finally, we can provide employees with opportunities to participate and perform by engaging in careful job design, organizing self-directed work teams and creating employee involvement activities (Renwick et al, 2013).

The AMO theory can also be used to examine the relationship between GRHM practices and employees' behaviours or performance. The theory provides a framework for planning what GHRM practices may be necessary to achieve organizational goals. AMO can also be used to explain the impact of specific concepts and practices such as green training (Gull and Idrees, 2022).

In the context of GHRM the key argument of the AMO theory would be that by a) fostering employees' green abilities, b) enhancing their motivation for green behaviour and c) giving them opportunities to participate in green initiatives we can improve individual employees' ecological performance and consequently contribute to the achievement of various organizational goals.

Social identity theory

Social identity theory (SIT) has its roots in early studies of social psychology from the beginning of the 20th century but the term itself was coined in the 1970s by Tajfel and Turner (Tajfel, 1978; Tajfel and Turner, 1979). SIT starts with a premise that individuals develop their sense of who they are not only on the grounds of their own characteristics (e.g. personality), but also on the basis of social groups to which they belong. This identification with a collective could be related, for example, to demographic groups (e.g. gender, sexuality, nationality, etc.) but also to organizational membership. By exploring people's self-identification with social groups, the theory sheds light on intra- and inter-group relations. SIT helps us understand under what circumstances people identify with social groups and what could be the consequences of individuals perceiving themselves as group members.

When applied to the context of organizations, SIT suggests that the workplace can be an important environment from which employees derive their identity. Through the perspective of SIT, Tyler (1999) argued that the employees' need to construct their identities becomes one of the driving forces for joining organizations and abiding by their rules. Moreover, the social identity of organizational membership influences our behaviours at work and affects how motivated we are to participate in formal goals or discretionary tasks. Our perceived categorization as a member of an organization could be a source of pride and increased self-esteem if we belong to a high-status company or institution. Our opinion of the organization will have an impact on the extent to which we want to identify with that group and consequently it will shape our support for the employer.

SIT provides a theoretical framework that helps us understand why is it that GHRM can enhance employees' self-esteem. When an organization displays dedication to social goals, such as environmental protection, this increases the chances of workers feeling proud to be associated with the organization. As a result, employees are expected to demonstrate desirable outcomes such as stronger organizational commitment and willingness to engage in extra-role behaviours.

Having explained key theoretical underpinnings, the following discussion focuses on different elements of GHRM, starting with green recruitment and selection.

Green recruitment and selection

Even though the terms 'recruitment' and 'selection' are often used interchangeably, it is useful to clarify the difference between them. **Recruitment** can be explained as 'the process of generating a pool of qualified applicants for organizational jobs' (Mathis and Jackson, 2010). It is a deliberate task where an organization is trying to get people interested in a vacancy and make them apply for it. On the other hand, **selection** is a process of choosing the best candidates for the job from the pool of applicants. If this is the case, then **green recruitment and selection** represents a process of recruiting and selecting candidates who have personal qualities and attributes considered useful for an organization's environmental goals. This is one of the crucial elements of GHRM. In order to develop employees' green competencies, and leverage effective environmental management, the organization needs to first attract and select employees with the right potential.

The recruitment strategy should be clear, with a message that is attractive to the target audience, and in line with organizational goals. If the organization is committed to the cause of the environment this should be reflected in recruitment efforts. Green recruitment may come naturally to organizations that already have an established sustainable organizational culture and reputation. In these cases, the employer can simply be open about the environmental achievements and practices that are already embedded in the organizational fabric. However, green recruitment and selection can also be a driver for change. Organizations that are still learning how to embrace environmental sustainability can use 'new blood' to produce new thoughts, a fresh perspective and commitment towards recently founded green goals. If an organization is still developing its environment-friendly practices, it is crucial that new employees who are brought into the organization support and reinforce this cultural change.

Employers should match their recruitment strategies in accordance with the needs of the talent they want to attract. The global annual survey conducted by Deloitte (2022) found that Millennials and Gen Zs strongly value the idea of environmental sustainability. In 2022, 'climate change' was the second-greatest concern for Millennials and Gen Zs, right behind the 'cost of living'. More respondents were concerned with environmental issues than 'healthcare/disease prevention', 'unemployment', 'crime/personal safety' or 'mental health'.

When an organization communicates in the recruitment process that it is looking for employees who value protection of the natural environment, it helps to attract candidates (Behrend et al, 2009) and contributes to the promotion of the organization (Muisyo et al, 2021). Recruitment efforts (e.g. job adverts, word of mouth), then become messages reinforcing the positive, socially responsible image of the organization. However, it is crucial that the recruitment rhetoric matches the actual organizational practice.

In terms of selection, organizations that are looking for employees who are going to fit their sustainable culture could add *additional desirable criteria* for the job. For example, during interviews the panel could check how aware job candidates are of sustainable practices in their profession, and to what extent they understand or show interest in initiatives such as conserving resources. The organization could develop evaluation tools that will help candidates demonstrate, in the application process, their knowledge, skills and experiences in protecting the environment. The items used in selection methods can examine the green values of the candidates and ensure that they are aligned with those of the organization (Adjei-Bamfo et al, 2020). Once the most suitable person is selected for the role, it is time to introduce them to their new working environment.

Skill check

Green recruitment and selection. This is a key skill for organizations that are concerned with environmental protection. When correctly managed it allows them to reinforce existing sustainability values or support a cultural change by hiring employees with new fresh ideas.

Green induction and training

Induction, sometimes also referred to as onboarding, is 'the process through which employees adjust or acclimatise to their new jobs and working environment' (CIPD, 2021a). Employers can adopt two main approaches to green induction: general green induction and job-specific green induction (Arulrajah et al, 2015). The general green induction:

- gives consistent messages about sustainability and its role in the organization's values and culture;

- makes new employees familiar with the pro-environmental efforts of the organization (e.g. investment in eco-friendly equipment);

- provides key information about environmental policies, practices and systems (e.g. issues related to energy management, reducing resource use and waste, encouraging greener forms of transport, responsible procurement);

- enables new recruits to socialize with each other and share information about their own sustainability efforts;

- encourages recruits' engagement in green citizenship behaviour.

Additionally, in some instances, organizations may choose to also provide a green induction for particular roles. This would involve instructing job-specific green practices and explaining the implications that environmental sustainability has for that role, team or department.

Beyond induction it is still important to provide environmental training and development for employees in both managerial and non-managerial roles. Organizations should analyse needs for green training, then develop the necessary programmes. For example, as part of its commitment to sustainability and environmental education the Fujifilm Group has developed its 'Expert Training Curriculum'. This programme is available to 'employees who are engaged in the relevant operations and recommended by their supervisor, or who voluntarily wish to participate in the curriculum.' The expert programme covers seminars on the management of chemical substances, design for environment, industrial waste management and product safety. The expert programme is offered in addition to the general e-leaning-based environmental education available for all employees of the company (FUJIFILM, 2022).

Green competency development can be used to build a workforce that is better equipped to deal with ecological issues. Trained staff can 'enable an organization to develop innovative ways of increasing organizational performance without creating negative a footprint of their business operations on the natural environment' (Gull and Idrees, 2022).

Training plays a pivotal role in changing employees' behaviours and attitudes. If an organization is going through a cultural change into a more sustainable workplace, new skills, knowledge and habits need to be established.

HRM has the capacity to bring together all internal stakeholders and through training establish understanding of organizational goals. Particularly during the early phases of introducing new environmental initiatives it is important to develop the necessary competencies and educate members of the organization on the link between their roles, environmental sustainability and organizational objectives. Separate training programmes may also be necessary for managerial staff to ensure effective green recruitment, selection and supervision of employees' environmental behaviours. In order for sustainability and environmental protection to be firmly embedded in organizational culture and values, the green perspective needs to become a permanent element of the organizational knowledge-sharing processes (Staffelbach et al, 2012). Well-designed training will link green education with employees' everyday activities and with the system of goals and targets that is used to manage staff performance.

Green performance management

The role of *performance management* (PM) is to identify, measure and develop the performance of individuals and teams in line with the needs of the organization (Aguinis, 2005). PM is about coordinating actions in order to achieve desirable outcomes. It is a systematic and continuous process that makes employees accountable for achieving their objectives and sets targets for the future.

In light of the above explanation, *green performance management* (GPM) can be defined as the process of establishing goals, measuring performance and providing feedback on how employees, departments and the organization as a whole achieve environmental results. By integrating green performance standards into the existing PM system the HR team can significantly support the environment management efforts of the employer (Epstein and Roy, 1997).

GPM should be aligned with the organization's strategy and environmental plan. Green objectives can be established for the organization and then 'cascaded' down through different levels of management all the way to individual employees. On the basis of the performance objectives identified for a given function or department the managers would then set goals and responsibilities for their subordinates. Managers should also regularly provide feedback to their employees or teams on how to improve environmental performance.

However, organizations can also introduce elements of the 'bottom-up' approach for GPM. Front-line staff, who understand details of everyday operations, can be encouraged to identify one-off green tasks to be completed by specified dates or indicators of green performance standards that will need to be met on a regular basis. Ideas for new or updated green performance targets could be developed individually or in teams, and can be tied to the green training that employees receive.

Arulrajah et al (2016) and their colleagues highlight that 'Every employee is responsible for the environmental performance of an organization. Each employee can reduce the negative environmental impact of [their] job and also can improve the positive environmental impact of [their] job.'

It is easy to imagine a scenario where our colleague agrees with us that environmental sustainability is important but it's 'not their job'. One of the tasks for GPM is to make members of the organization aware that environmental performance is a shared responsibility, which includes everyone in the organization. Staff have influence over the amount of energy, fuel and resources used in organizations. Thus, it is logical to engage all employees and install environmental performance standards across the organization. This needs to be done with a clear communication of the rationale for green schemes and an explanation of green performance indicators.

Green performance management at the individual and group levels can evaluate quantitatively and qualitatively elements such as:

1 Progress towards specific environmental targets (e.g. decreased energy and water wastage).

2 Development of environmental ideas, initiatives, problem solutions and practices:
   a. collaboration with key stakeholders to find and introduce environmentally friendly solutions and practices;
   b. development of resource efficiency and monitoring standards;
   c. internal promotion and sharing of environmentally friendly actions and behaviours.

3 Other steps taken to support and implement environmental strategy:
   a. participation in relevant training;
   b. community engagement.

Guerci et al (2016) surveyed employees working at 74 Italian manufacturing and service companies. They found that practices of green performance management combined with green rewards are significantly and positively related to the organization's overall environmental performance.

Green reward system

One of the most important aspects in any organization is how employees are rewarded for their efforts. Well-designed work benefits are aligned with the needs of the organization and employees' expectations. Incentives provided by the employer should reflect organizational values, strategic objectives and performance.

A *green reward system* is a combination of policies, practices and standards used to allocate financial and non-financial benefits, which are meant to motivate and recognize employees' green performance. As explained by Guerci et al (2016), rewards and incentives for green behaviours play a vital role in achieving environmental goals of the organization. They show that employees' and employers' values for sustainability are relevant and related to staff's everyday work.

Employers can use a combination of intrinsic and extrinsic rewards to encourage and incentivize pro-environmental behaviours. *Intrinsic rewards* are psychological rewards that employees achieve from performing well or engaging in meaningful work. For example, the act itself, of participating in pro-environmental behaviour, can provide positive emotional experience. By giving the employees an opportunity to engage in tasks that highlight that their work is meaningful not only for the organization but also the wider community, the employer stimulates intrinsic motivation. The challenge here is for managers to set green responsibilities and performance objectives that will be intrinsically rewarding. *Extrinsic rewards* are rewards that come from an external source. These are incentives we receive from the employer, e.g. financial bonuses, vouchers or titles. It is worth recognizing that some rewards, such as announcing an employee as the 'green employee of the month', can represent a mix of extrinsic and intrinsic reward and can be a useful tool for encouraging green behaviours.

Due to scarcity of financial resources recognition rewards have been an established practice used to incentivize environmental performance. Awards, special recognitions and honours can be used to acknowledge employees' green achievements and increase staff awareness of environmental efforts. Awards can be presented during important meetings or events (Arulrajah et al, 2015).

Green rewards can also include non-financial prizes in the form of workplace and lifestyle benefits. For example, a US company, Christopher B. Burke Engineering, offers employees who bike to work a free breakfast. The firm also has quarterly giveaways of bike gear and once a year they hold a competition for the employee who logs the most miles. The winner of the annual contest gets a free bike (Perman, 2011). Individuals, teams or departments that achieve green milestones can be rewarded with energy-efficient merchandise or appliances.

Researchers tend to agree that a combination of monetary and non-monetary incentives may be particularly effective in motivating employees. Green awards and recognition rewards can be accompanied by paid vacations or gift certificates (Saeed et al, 2019). In order to make the green compensation system successful, rewards may also have to be introduced at different levels of the organizational structure. Rewards can be used not just for meeting performance targets but also when employees and project teams are showing initiative for identifying innovative environmental practices. Strategic use of rewards can stimulate staff creativity (Arulrajah et al, 2015).

Finally, employers should remember that when they focus on environmental protection the rewards they provide should also reflect that sustainability commitment. For example, it may be inappropriate for a green company to reward employees for meeting performance goals with a bigger car that has a high carbon footprint (CIPD, 2021b).

WORKSHOP DISCUSSION 4

Royal Bank of Scotland

The Royal Bank of Scotland (RBS) was established in 1724 and has approximately 70,000 employees. It is one of the major retail and commercial banks in Scotland.

In 2015 RBS publicly announced a range of environmental targets related to issues such as saving energy, recycling and sustainable travel. As a part of this initiative, the bank wanted to engage its employees in sustainable behaviours. From December 2015 until December 2016 the company trailed a new method to incentivize green practices at work – an award-winning app and platform called 'JUMP'. Through JUMP, RBS employees could access custom-made online modules covering themes such as: engagement, energy, water, waste, paper and travel. Each theme gave five possible actions through which colleagues earned points.

The trial report published by JUMP gave examples of positive actions included in the app:

- learning more about a particular issue
- promoting the JUMP platform
- creating a last-person-out checklist with their team
- claiming a Keep Cup (reusable coffee cup), shower timer, switch-off sticker or wall socket timer

Every month, top performers would collect rewards such as Marks & Spencer, iTunes and high street vouchers.

When the programme was at the planning stage RBS worked closely with the JUMP team to identify what elements would be most suitable for bank employees. Focus groups with colleagues were organized to find suitable green actions and rewards.

RBS also commissioned a company called Acclaro Advisory to create an awareness and training programme that would guide the content and the approach of the JUMP programme.

To further motivate its users JUMP allows staff to compete in teams. In the trial, employees formed groups based on their departments and locations. The platform showed leader boards with best-performing teams and individuals.

The pilot was introduced in 52 locations, including branches, offices and cash centres. The app was released in the middle of the trial period and 80 per cent of staff (1,200 employees) from the selected locations took part in the trial. The app recorded more than 2,600 sustainable actions.

During the trial active locations saw on average 5 per cent reduction in energy consumption. This included 10 per cent lower electricity usage out of hours, implying that staff were more conscious of switching off devices when leaving work. Retail sites saw a 10 to 30 per cent reduction in electricity usage. Estimates suggest that just through the reduced energy consumption the bank was able to save £3 million.

In a survey conducted after the pilot, 87 per cent of participating employees felt that JUMP helped the company to protect the environment and reduce cost.

Thanks to the successful roll-out of the JUMP programme, RBS won the 'Bank of the Year' award in the 2017 Better Society Awards. The company came ahead of competitors HSBC, Liberum, Barclays and Société Générale.

Michael Lynch, Head of Sustainable Workplace Culture at RBS, said, 'We are delighted to have won this award and be recognized for our innovative JUMP programme which is making significant savings in costs, energy and other resources by engaging colleagues in simple, positive steps.'

Another organization that used JUMP is the Scottish Courts and Tribunals Service (SCTS). SCTC is an independent public body responsible for management of the courts and tribunals in Scotland. SCTC and its facilities management company, Atalian Servest, collaborated with JUMP to create a custom-made programme for the 200 staff at the Sherriff Court in Glasgow.

The programme was launched in November 2018 and as of June 2022 JUMP has helped employees at the Court in Glasgow to:

- save more than 25,000 kg of CO_2
- motivated staff to reduce waste by over 6,000 kg
- record more than 4,500 active journeys on a bike
- keep track of over 125,000 calories burned through exercise
- keep track of over 20,000 positive actions taken by colleagues.

Questions

1 What actions did RBS take to promote green behaviours at work?

2 What were the positive outcomes of the JUMP programme at RBS and SCTS?

3 Could the programme used at RBS be expanded to different CSR activities and goals? Discuss.

Sources

Adapted from Lynch, M (2017) Innovation Trial Report, https://teamjump.co.uk/wp-content/uploads/2022/05/RBS-Natwest-Case-Study.pdf

Adapted from Jump (2022) SCTS Case Study Q2 2022, https://teamjump.co.uk/wp-content/uploads/2022/07/SCTS-Case-Study-Q2-2022.pdf

www.acclaro-advisory.com/case-studies/entry/environmental-awareness-learning-programme/

www.environmenttimes.co.uk/marketplace/item/522-green-rewards

Employee green behaviour and discipline management

Let's take a step back and unpack what *employee green behaviour* (EGB) is. Ones and Dilchert (2012) defined EGB as 'scalable actions and behaviours that employees engage in that are linked with and contribute to or detract from environmental sustainability'. They considered EGB as any actions made by members of the organization that conserve resources, contribute to working sustainably, avoid environmental harm, influence others to behave sustainably or take initiative to act sustainably. The focus here is on the behaviours that employees can and do influence. The concept does not focus on employee actions that might have environmental consequences but are beyond the control of the worker. Thus, EGB is synonymous with employee green performance. Ones and Dilchert (2012) also reiterate the importance of measuring employees' contributions to an organization's sustainability goals. EGB refers to both beneficial and harmful behaviours. The employers should encourage employees' proactive eco-friendly actions, such as identifying more resource-efficient practices, and deter behaviours that harm the environment, for example polluting.

In some cases, managing EGB may require discipline. Wehrmeyer (1996) argued that a set of rules about environmental standards in the organization can be used as a tool for employees to self-regulate their own habits and behaviours. According to Wehrmeyer, companies that use this approach introduce environmental policies and take disciplinary actions (e.g. warning, fining, suspension, etc.) in instances where employees do not comply with the regulations. In a similar vein, Renwick et al (2008) argued that using negative reinforcements (criticism, reminders) can be another means through which organizations can ensure that environmental standards are met. Financial and non-financial rewards are important for creating positive attitudes towards pro-environmental initiatives; however, additionally, environmental obligations can be added to job descriptions and to the list of employees' responsibilities (Khan et al, 2021).

The same best practices that are followed in other disciplinary procedures adhere to the regulation of EGB (see e.g. Armstrong and Taylor, 2020). Organizations that take a more disciplined approach should formulate and communicate rules of conduct related to environmental management. The policy should clarify potential penalties for non-compliance with regulations. No disciplinary actions should be taken against employees who were not aware of environmental rules that they were expected to follow, or who were not aware of environmental performance standards they were expected to meet. The disciplinary system should progress from the least to most severe penalties with actions taken that are approximate to the nature of the offence.

Setting disciplinary practices and procedures is an important element of people management. Nevertheless, it is worth noting that the majority of academic discussion focuses on green positive reinforcement and empowering employees.

Green empowerment

Green empowerment refers to giving employees the autonomy, resources and support they need to act independently towards environmental goals, as well as providing a degree of freedom to tackle and solve green work-related problems. According to Tariq et al (2016), for employees to pursue green functions they must be empowered, encouraged and eco-conscious. To meet versatile demands of stakeholders, employees need to be able to take responsibility for green goals. Staff should be able to give voice on environmental solutions and take part in the decision-making process. Typical activities that are used for employee empowerment can be adopted in the context of an environmental agenda, for example interactive skill building, improving feedback channels, benchmark setting, team formation exercises, providing necessary resources and brainstorming. These practices can help employees reach their full potential in green performance (Tariq et al, 2016).

Empowerment is a sign of recognizing employees' abilities and trusting their judgement, which can be motivating for staff. Employees who feel empowered can report higher job satisfaction and commitment. These factors are necessary to increase the likelihood of success for environmental management. Moreover, Ercantan and Eyupoglu (2022) argue that green empowerment 'creates eco-intrapreneurs that continue the organization's environmental initiatives'. *Intrapreneurs* are employees who develop innovative ideas and solutions within an organization. By giving subordinates a degree of autonomy managers can tap into employees' creativity for new environmental practices. To stimulate innovative thinking, training may be necessary. Successful empowerment is closely connected with employee development. It should be introduced in combination with mentoring, coaching and training programmes to help employees step up to the challenge of environmental goals. The efforts to empower staff can be explicitly communicated in an organization's strategy or it can be implicitly integrated into the existing practices. Either way, green empowerment helps to translate organizational rhetoric of organizational sustainability into practice (Van Velsor and Quinn, 2012).

Green employee commitment

Commitment has been identified as one of the major dimensions in HRM, because it leads to improved employee loyalty and willingness to make extra efforts beyond their duties. As explained by Guest (1987), HRM policies and practices are designed to 'maximize organizational integration, employee commitment, flexibility and quality of work'. Thus, this subject also deserves a discussion in the context of GHRM.

Mesmer-Magnus et al (2012) suggest that we break down the discussion about green commitment into three main parts:

- employee commitment (to the organization)
- individual environmental commitment
- organizational commitment to environmental sustainability

Employee commitment to the organization/organizational commitment

The general concept of *employee commitment* refers to the degree to which an employee identifies with their organization and demonstrates involvement with it (Mowday et al, 1979). The term is also sometimes used interchangeably with 'organizational commitment'. They both represent workers' attachment to the organization. Employee commitment is important because it can be used to obtain support for organizational ends and interests. Committed employees plan to stay with their employer, identify with the organization and want to be involved in its affairs, whereas individuals with low organizational commitment are primarily interested in pursuing self-interest.

Research suggests that GHRM practices improve employees' commitment to their organization (Kim et al, 2019). This is in line with studies that found that general environmental management has a positive impact on employees' commitment to the organization.

Individual environmental commitment

Individual environmental commitment is explained by Mesmer-Magnus et al (2012) as the 'extent to which an individual is dedicated to environmental sustainability and is willing to engage in pro-environmental behaviors'. The concept helps us understand employees' *intent* to engage in green behaviour, meet environmental performance standards or engage in green extra-role tasks. It is related to the amount of *personal attachment* a person has towards the environmental goals of the organization. Research suggests that it can be relatively difficult to increase an employee's personal conviction in this context. Pham et al (2020) surveyed 220 employees from three- to five-star hotels in Vietnam and examined the link between the staff's environmental commitment and:

- green training (GT), e.g. frequent and efficient use of green training, chance to apply green training in practice;
- green performance management (GPM), e.g. setting specific green targets, providing feedback on environmental targets;
- green employee involvement (GEI), e.g. giving employees a chance to make decisions and suggest improvement related to environmental protection.

Pham et al (2020) found that neither GPM nor GEI practices had a significant impact on employees' environmental commitment. However, the study also showed that GT has a significant and positive impact on an individual's green commitment.

Organizational commitment to environmental sustainability

Is an organization committed to environmental sustainability or does it simply use different environmental policies and statements as a form of greenwashing? *Greenwashing* is a practice where an organization releases false or misleading information to present itself as environmentally responsible (Tahir et al, 2020). Some organizations overstate their environmental efforts in an attempt to appeal to socially conscious stakeholders. Marrucci and Daddi (2021) found that many organizations that adopt environmental management systems (EMS) struggle to produce results in environmental performance. The authors explained: 'Some organizations may use EMSs just to obtain the certification, which can be used as a tool to increase the organization's environmental reputation, instead of developing green practices and improving environmental performance' (Marrucci and Daddi, 2021).

Organizational commitment to environmental sustainability is the degree to which an organization is dedicated to reducing its environmental impacts (Mesmer-Magnus et al, 2012). It affects an organization's willingness to engage in meaningful environmental initiatives and promotion of employee green behaviours. When organizations show low commitment to green goals this denies or undermines GHRM efforts.

Factors affecting GHRM adoption

In previous sections we focused on different areas of GHRM. However, we should also review some of the factors that affect the adoption and effectiveness of GHRM and employees' green behaviours. These can be organized into two main categories – internal and external factors.

Internal factors

Commitment of senior organizational leaders is vital to a successful roll-out of green initiatives such as GHRM. Top management support for sustainability is particularly important to set the example for the rest of the organization (CIPD, 2021b). Employees can be initially sceptical about the organization's claims to engage in green initiatives. One way to persuade and engage staff is to demonstrate that the intentions are sincere. Senior managers leading the way can be more convincing than words.

This brings us to another point that general resistance to change is one of the forces affecting adoption of GHRM practices, such as green recruitment and selection (Nejati et al, 2017). This can be a substantial barrier because GHRM is meant to be one of the tools used to facilitate wider transition in the organization and green recruitment and selection is one of the steps needed to change organizational culture. According to Jabbour et al (2010), unless the organization is already environmentally proactive we may expect some resistance to the introduction of GHRM and the change that it represents.

Internal economic conditions of the organization can also be a barrier to GHRM adoption. Kodua et al (2022) examined Ghanaian firms and found that financial resources available internally and the cost of GHRM implementation are factors that limited green people management.

Also worth mentioning is that employees' individual characteristics, such as gender or age, do not make a particularly big difference to adoption of green behaviours in the workplace. In light of a growing number of research on employees' green behaviours, Katz et al (2022) conducted a meta-analysis of the literature on EGB. They examined insights from 135 projects which together surveyed over 47,000 workers. They found that gender was not significantly related to EGB and characteristics such as age, tenure and education were only slightly connected with EGB. Older workers, employees with longer tenure or employees with higher educational levels were found to be only somewhat more likely to engage in EGB.

External factors

Legal frameworks and regulations have an evident impact on the adoption of GHRM. Guerci and Carollo (2016) studied six Italian companies and found that the examined firms implemented green HRM practices because they were fulfilling explicit commercial requirements enforced by public regulators. The companies were also taking the opportunity to access available public resources dedicated to green training. Good regulation can incentivize green initiatives.

Clients can also influence GHRM adoption. This applies to both individual customers and business partners. Retail customers' expectations have changed, and now, in addition to attractive price and good product quality, many urge organizations to adopt green practices. Similarly, business clients, especially from the global market, can request that the organization complies with international best practices and standards in environment protection and green policies. These trends and competition for customers pressure organizations to adopt solutions such as GHRM (Guerci et al, 2016; Yong et al 2019b). For example, Masri and Jaaron (2017) discussed in their research how Palestinian chemical manufacturers face fierce competition from Israeli companies. This puts pressure on Palestinian businesses to invest more in green employee training, to keep up with the market or even try to achieve competitive advantage.

Summary

The chapter discussed green elements of sustainable HRM. Pro-environmental people management serves many purposes. On the one hand, it is necessary to support green efforts of different organizational functions. For example, it plays a pivotal role in enhancing green supply chain management. On the other hand, GHRM in itself can be a source of desirable outcomes, such as attracting job candidates and improving staff turnover. At the beginning of the chapter we reviewed a series of studies that illustrate how GHRM is connected to a range of positive effects at the organizational, team and individual levels. GHRM is a multifaceted subject. Thus, the chapter also introduced theories of AMO (ability, motivation and opportunity) and social identity, to further explain how and why GHRM can benefit organizations. While different theoretical perspectives can be used to explore the subject, these two are among the most commonly adopted.

The main part of the chapter was dedicated to a more detailed discussion of green practices in recruitment and selection, induction and training, performance management, reward systems, discipline management, as well as managing employee empowerment and commitment. Weaving a green agenda into HRM practices is often a response to stakeholders' expectations. Government regulations are one of the most significant factors affecting GHRM adaption. Many organizations implement environmental solutions and GHRM to avoid any legal implications or to take advantage of available public funding of sustainability programmes. Market competition is also an important force driving adoption of GHRM. Due to customer pressure, employers may incorporate sustainable HRM as an element of their organizational goals. The strategic nature of sustainable HRM is a topic we explore in depth in the next chapter.

Study questions

1 Explain what green HRM is and what its origins are.

2 Describe examples of different organizational, team and individual outcomes that can arise from GHRM practices.

3 Explain what the theories of AMO and social identity are. How would you apply these theories in the context of GHRM?

4 Can organizational recruitment and selection be used for furthering environmental sustainability? Justify your answer by referring to specific practices.

5 What are the two main approaches to green induction? Does staff green training end after employees are introduced to the organization?

6 Explain how a combination of financial and non-financial rewards can be used to encourage green employee behaviours.

7 What is green employee behaviour? Can disciplinary actions be taken if an employee does not follow environmental policies?

8 Describe two internal and two external factors that can affect GHRM adoption.

Key reading

CIPD (2021b) Embedding environmental sustainability in your organization, a guide for HR professionals, www.cipd.co.uk/Images/sustainability-guide_tcm18-98576.pdf

Jackson, S E, Ones, D S and Dilchert, S (eds.) (2012) *Managing Human Resources for Environmental Sustainability*, Jossey-Bass/Wiley, San Francisco

Ren, S, Tang, G and E Jackson, S (2018) Green human resource management research in emergence: a review and future directions, *Asia Pacific Journal of Management,* **35** (3), pp 769–803

References

Adjei-Bamfo, P, Bempong, B, Osei, J and Kusi-Sarpong, S (2020) Green candidate selection for organizational environmental management, *International Journal of Manpower*, **41** (7), pp 1081–96

Aguinis, H (2005) *Performance Management*, Pearson Education, Upper Saddle River, NJ

Appelbaum, E, Bailey, T, Berg, P and Kalleberg, A L (2000) *Manufacturing Advantage: Why high performance work systems pay off*, ILR Press, London

Armstrong, M and Taylor, S (2020) *Armstrong's Handbook of Human Resource Management Practice*, 15th edn, Kogan Page, London

Arulrajah, A A, Opatha, H H D N P and Nawaratne, N N J (2015) Green human resource management practices: a review, *Sri Lankan Journal of Human Resource Management*, **5** (1), pp 1–16

Arulrajah, A A, Opatha, H H D N P and Nawaratne, N N J (2016) Employee green performance of job: a systematic attempt towards measurement, *Sri Lankan Journal of Human Resource Management*, **6** (1), pp 37–62

Bailey, T (1993) *Discretionary Effort and the Organization of Work: Employee participation and work reform since Hawthorne*, Teachers College and Conservation of Human Resources, Columbia University

Behrend, T S, Baker, B A and Thompson, L F (2009) Effects of pro-environmental recruiting messages: the role of organizational reputation, *Journal of Business and Psychology*, **24** (3), pp 341–50

Cabral, C and Dhar, R L (2020) Green competencies: insights and recommendations from a systematic literature review, *Benchmarking: An International Journal*, **28** (1), pp 66–105

Chaudhary, R (2018) Can green human resource management attract young talent? An empirical analysis, *Evidence-Based HRM*, **6** (3), pp 305–19

Chaudhary, R (2019) Green human resource management and employee green behavior: an empirical analysis, *Corporate Social Responsibility and Environmental Management*, **27** (2), pp 630–41

Chen, Y S (2008) The positive effect of green intellectual capital on competitive advantages of firms, *Journal of Business Ethics*, **77** (3), pp 271–86

CIPD (2021a) Induction, www.cipd.co.uk/knowledge/fundamentals/people/recruitment/induction-factsheet (archived at https://perma.cc/2XK7-9PNP)

CIPD (2021b) Embedding environmental sustainability in your organization, a guide for HR professionals, www.cipd.co.uk/Images/sustainability-guide_tcm18-98576.pdf (archived at https://perma.cc/AW5Q-3F4)

Deloitte (2022) The Deloitte Global 2022 Gen Z and Millennial Survey, www2.deloitte.com/global/en/pages/about-deloitte/articles/genzmillennialsurvey.html (archived at https://perma.cc/UBB6-6K7B)

Epstein, M and Roy, M (1997) Using ISO 14000 for improved organizational learning and environmental management, *Environmental Quality Management*, **7** (1), pp 21–30

Ercantan, O and Eyupoglu, S (2022) How do green human resource management practices encourage employees to engage in green behavior? Perceptions of university students as prospective employees, *Sustainability*, **14** (3), p 1718

FUJIFILM (2022) Environmental education, https://holdings.fujifilm.com/en/sustainability/activity/environment/education (archived at https://perma.cc/PK5B-WAN8)

Guerci, M and Carollo, L (2016) A paradox view on green human resource management: insights from the Italian context, *The International Journal of Human Resource Management*, **27** (2), pp 212–38

Guerci, M, Longoni, A and Luzzini, D (2016) Translating stakeholder pressures into environmental performance – the mediating role of green HRM practices, *The International Journal of Human Resource Management*, **27** (2), pp 262–89

Guest, D E (1987) Human resource management and industrial relations, *Journal of Management Studies*, **24** (5), pp 503–21

Gull, S and Idrees, H (2022) Green training and organizational efficiency: mediating role of green competencies, *European Journal of Training and Development*, **46** (1/2), pp 105–11

Gully, S M, Phillips, J M, Castellano, W G, Han, K and Kim, A (2013) A mediated moderation model of recruiting socially and environmentally responsible job applicants, *Personnel Psychology*, **66** (4), pp 935–73

Islam, M A, Jantan, A H, Yusoff, Y M, Chong, C W and Hossain, M S (2020) Green Human Resource Management (GHRM) practices and millennial employees' turnover intentions in tourism industry in Malaysia: moderating role of work environment, *Global Business Review*, pp 1–21

Jabbour, C J C, Santos, F C A and Nagano, M S (2010) Contributions of HRM throughout the stages of environmental management: methodological triangulation applied to companies in Brazil, *The International Journal of Human Resource Management*, **21** (7), pp 1049–89

Katz, I M, Rauvola, R S, Rudolph, C W and Zacher, H (2022) Employee green behavior: a meta-analysis, *Corporate Social Responsibility and Environmental Management*, pp 1–12

Khan, A, Ullah, H, Khattak, A A, Khattak, A, Hussain, A, Nadir, F, Nasir, M and Khan, M (2021) The mediating role of proactive environmental behavior between environmental knowledge and green discipline management, *International Journal of Innovation, Creativity and Change*, 15 (2), pp 470–91

Kim, Y J, Kim, W G, Choi, H M and Phetvaroon, K (2019) The effect of green human resource management on hotel employees' eco-friendly behavior and environmental performance, *International Journal of Hospitality Management*, 76, pp 83–93

Kodua, L T, Xiao, Y, Adjei, N O, Asante, D, Ofosu, B O and Amankona, D (2022) Barriers to green human resources management (GHRM) implementation in developing countries. Evidence from Ghana, *Journal of Cleaner Production*, **340**, p 130671

Marrucci, L and Daddi, T (2021) The contribution of the eco-management and audit scheme to the environmental performance of manufacturing organizations, *Business Strategy and the Environment*, **31** (4), pp 1347–57

Masri, H A and Jaaron, A A (2017) Assessing green human resources management practices in Palestinian manufacturing context: an empirical study, *Journal of Cleaner Production*, **143** (1), pp 474–89

Mathis, R L and Jackson, J H (2010) *Human Resource Management*, South-Western College, California

Mesmer–Magnus, J, Viswesvaran, C and Wiernik, B M (2012) The role of commitment in bridging the gap between organizational sustainability and environmental sustainability. In S E Jackson, D S Ones and S Dilchert (eds.) *Managing Human Resources for Environmental Sustainability* (pp 155–86), Jossey-Bass/Wiley, San Francisco

Mowday, R T, Steers, R M and Porter, L W (1979) The measurement of organizational commitment, *Journal of Vocational Behavior*, **14** (2), pp 224–47

Muisyo, P K, Qin, S, Julius, M M, Ho, T H and Ho, T H (2021) Green HRM and employer branding: the role of collective affective commitment to environmental management change and environmental reputation, *Journal of Sustainable Tourism*, **30** (8), pp 1897–914

Nejati, M, Rabiei, S and Jabbour, C J C (2017) Envisioning the invisible: understanding the synergy between green human resource management and green supply chain management in manufacturing firms in Iran in light of the moderating effect of employees' resistance to change, *Journal of Cleaner Production*, **168** (1), pp 163–72

Obeidat, S M, Al Bakri, A A and Elbanna, S (2020) Leveraging 'green' human resource practices to enable environmental and organizational performance: evidence from the Qatari oil and gas industry, *Journal of Business Ethics*, **164** (2), pp 371–88

O'Donohue, W and Torugsa, N (2016) The moderating effect of 'green' HRM on the association between proactive environmental management and financial performance in small firms, *The International Journal of Human Resource Management*, **27** (2), pp 239–61

Ogbeibu, S, Emelifeonwu, J, Senadjki, A, Gaskin, J and Kaivo-oja, J (2020) Technological turbulence and greening of team creativity, product innovation and human resource management: implications for sustainability, *Journal of Cleaner Production*, **244**, p 118703

Ojo, A O, Tan, C N L and Alias, M. (2020) Linking green HRM practices to environmental performance through pro-environment behaviour in the information technology sector, *Social Responsibility Journal*, **18** (1), pp 1–18

Ones, D S and Dilchert, S (2012) Employee green behaviors. In S E Jackson, D S Ones and S Dilchert (eds.) *Managing Human Resources for Environmental Sustainability* (pp 85–116), Jossey-Bass/Wiley, San Francisco

Paulet, R, Holland, P and Morgan, D (2021) A meta-review of 10 years of green human resource management: is green HRM headed towards a roadblock or a revitalisation? *Asia Pacific Journal of Human Resources*, **59** (2), pp 159–83

Perman (2011) Cool perks for going green, CNBC, www.cnbc.com/2011/01/27/Cool-Perks-for-Going-Green.html (archived at https://perma.cc/KNM9-WAZ4)

Pham, N T, Hoang, H T and Phan, Q P T (2019) Green human resource management: a comprehensive review and future research agenda, *International Journal of Manpower*, **41** (7), pp 845–78

Pham, N T, Thanh, T V, Tučková, Z and Thuy, V T N (2020) The role of green human resource management in driving hotel's environmental performance: interaction and mediation analysis, *International Journal of Hospitality Management*, **88**, p 102392

Pinzone, M, Guerci, M, Lettieri, E and Huisingh, D (2019) Effects of 'green' training on pro-environmental behaviors and job satisfaction: evidence from the Italian healthcare sector, *Journal of Cleaner Production*, **226**, pp 221–32

Pinzone, M, Guerci, M, Lettieri, E and Redman, T (2016) Progressing in the change journey towards sustainability in healthcare: the role of 'green' HRM, *Journal of Cleaner Production*, **122**, pp 201–11

Ren, S, Tang, G and Jackson, S E (2018) Green human resource management research in emergence: a review and future directions, *Asia Pacific Journal of Management*, **35** (3), pp 769–803

Renwick, D W, Redman, T and Maguire, S (2008) *Green HRM: A review, process model and research agenda*, University of Sheffield Working Paper

Renwick, D W, Redman, T and Maguire, S (2013) Green human resource management: a review and research agenda, *International Journal of Management Reviews*, **15** (1), pp 1–14

Saeed, B B, Afsar, B, Hafeez, S, Khan, I, Tahir, M and Afridi, M A (2019) Promoting employee's proenvironmental behavior through green human resource management practices, *Corporate Social Responsibility and Environmental Management*, **26** (2), pp 424–38

Shen, J, Dumont, J and Deng, X (2018) Employees' perceptions of green HRM and non-green employee work outcomes: the social identity and stakeholder perspectives, *Group & Organization Management*, **43** (4), pp 594–622

Song, W, Yu, H and Xu, H (2020) Effects of green human resource management and managerial environmental concern on green innovation, *European Journal of Innovation Management*, **24** (3), pp 951–67

Staffelbach, B, Brugger, E A and Bäbler, S, (2012) The role of strategic context in environmental sustainability initiatives: three case studies. In S E Jackson, D S Ones and S Dilchert (eds.) *Managing Human Resources for Environmental Sustainability* (pp 36–60), Jossey-Bass/Wiley, San Francisco

Tahir, R, Athar, M R and Afzal, A (2020) The impact of greenwashing practices on green employee behaviour: mediating role of employee value orientation and green psychological climate, *Cogent Business & Management*, 7 (1), p 1781996

Tajfel, H (1978) The achievement of inter-group differentiation. In H Tajfel (ed.) *Differentiation Between Social Groups* (pp 77–100), Academic Press, London

Tajfel, H and Turner, J C (1979) An integrative theory of inter-group conflict. In W. G. Austin and S Worchel (eds.) *The Social Psychology of Inter-group Relations* (pp 33–47), Brooks/Cole, Monterey, CA

Tariq, S, Jan, F A and Ahmad, M S (2016) Green employee empowerment: a systematic literature review on state-of-art in green human resource management, *Quality & Quantity*, **50** (1), pp 237–69

Tyler, T R (1999) Why people cooperate with organizations: an identity-based perspective. In R I Sutton and B M Staw (eds.) *Research in Organizational Behavior* (pp 201–47), JAI Press, Greenwich, CT

Van Velsor, E and Quinn, L (2012) Leadership and environmental sustainability. In S E Jackson, D S Ones and S Dilchert (eds.) *Managing Human Resources for Environmental Sustainability* (pp 241–261), Jossey-Bass/Wiley, San Francisco

Wagner, M (2013) 'Green' human resource benefits: do they matter as determinants of environmental management system implementation? *Journal of Business Ethics*, **114**, pp 443–56

Wehrmeyer, W (1996) *Greening People: Human resources and environmental management*, Greenleaf Publishing, Sheffield

Yong, J Y, Yusliza, M Y and Fawehinmi, O O (2019a) Green human resource management: a systematic literature review from 2007 to 2019, *Benchmarking: An International Journal*, **27** (7), pp 2005–27

Yong, J Y, Yusliza, M Y, Jabbour, C J C and Ahmad, N H (2019b) Exploratory cases on the interplay between green human resource management and advanced green manufacturing in light of the Ability-Motivation-Opportunity theory, *Journal of Management Development*, **39** (1), pp 31–49

Zaid, A A, Jaaron, A A and Bon, A T (2018) The impact of green human resource management and green supply chain management practices on sustainable performance: an empirical study, *Journal of Cleaner Production*, 204, pp 965–79

Sustainable HRM as a business strategy   6

LEARNING OBJECTIVES

After completing this chapter, you should be able to:

- Explain the strategic nature of sustainable HRM.
- Identify six characteristics of sustainable HRM that expand traditional strategic HRM.
- Understand what the resource-based view is and how it is applicable to sustainable HRM.
- Understand what strategic fit is and how it is applicable to sustainable HRM.
- Identify four strategic positionings in relation to sustainable HRM.
- Describe organizational culture and how it affects sustainable HRM strategies.
- Recognize seven sustainable organizational values and how they are linked to sustainable HRM strategies.
- Explain what the Great Resignation, lying flat movement and antiwork community have in common.

Introduction

In Chapter 1 we explained that sustainable people management is concerned with the use of HRM to achieve long-term social, environmental and business goals. These three pillars are closely interlocked. For example, in Chapters 3 and 4, the conversation about *social sustainability* was also connected to best practices for the economic longevity of organizations. We recognized that downsizing has a detrimental impact on employees, and is linked with lower customer satisfaction and damaged reputation. In Chapter 5 our review showed that GHRM not only leads to *environmental sustainability*, but it also supports social elements (e.g. reduced staff turnover intention) and business benefits (e.g. increased financial results related to environmental management). In this chapter our focus turns more towards *business sustainability*, although similar to the previous parts of the book, you will notice that the discussion here remains interconnected with the other two forms of sustainability.

The chapter commences by explaining what strategic HRM is, and how it is related to sustainable HRM. Then, by examining six characteristics of sustainable HRM we will see how the new approach expands strategic HRM. The next topics to be explored are the resource-based view and strategic fit. Both perspectives are well established in the literature on strategic HRM and in this chapter we will discuss why they are also vital for sustainable HRM. This is followed by an analysis of four strategic positionings that organizations can take in relation to sustainable HRM: under-sustainability (under-investment), quasi-spot sustainability, mutual sustainability and over-sustainability. The choice of these strategic arrangements is influenced by an organization's culture and its values. Thus, the chapter proceeds to explain what organizational culture is, and how it is related to strategic decisions about sustainable HRM.

When an organization embraces a move towards a regenerative and more sustainable future this can be a source of competitive advantage. Likewise, when employers develop a toxic culture and focus only on short-term benefits this can lead to employees resigning en masse and people joining anti-work communities openly criticizing their workplaces. This is something we explore in the final sections of the chapter.

Strategic nature of sustainable HRM

One of the key concepts demonstrating how HRM can be used to achieve organizations' business goals is *strategic HRM*. Wright and McMahan (1992) explained strategic HRM as 'the pattern of planned human resource deployments and activities intended to enable the firm to achieve its goals'. Baird and Meshoulam (1988) argued that business objectives are accomplished when human resources are used to meet organizations' needs, i.e. when they are utilized strategically. People management practices need to be integrated internally, correspond with the external environment and, most importantly, linked to organizational strategic objectives. The concept of strategic HRM is not inherently designed to zero in on delivering financial outcomes, but if an organization measures success only in terms of finances this determines a narrow application of strategic HRM.

Sustainable HRM represents an expansion of strategic HRM practice by adopting activities and policies that 'enable the achievement of financial, social and ecological goals, with an impact inside and outside of the organization' (Ehnert et al, 2016). Sustainable HRM can and should be strategic. In other words, the practice of sustainable HRM needs to be systematically connected to the objectives of the organization. As the organization identifies the importance of various internal and external stakeholders, sustainable HRM becomes key to achieving strategic goals.

The business (economic), environmental and social challenges and opportunities are multifaceted and require a systematic and strategic approach. On the one hand, the sustainability approach brings in a strategic way the discussion of larger systems in which the organization attempts to be successful. On the other hand, sustainable HRM emphasizes the maintenance of the long-term viability of an organization by paying attention to the short- and long-term effects of HRM practices (Ehnert, 2009).

By its nature the concept of *strategy* represents something that is forward-looking. Chandler (1962) defines strategy as 'the determination of the long-term goals and objectives of an enterprise, and the adoption of courses of action and the allocation of resources necessary for carrying out those goals.' A strategy is meant to set the vision or plan for the direction of the organization. Yet HRM practices have often been criticized for maximization of short-term profits at the expense of the long-term benefits for the organization and its employees (Collings et al, 2019). In these cases, HRM is not as strategic as it could be, or the strategic approach has a restricted focus.

Six characteristics of sustainable HRM

As previously mentioned, sustainable HRM represents a new, extended approach to the strategic position that HRM takes in organizations. This is emphasized by the following six characteristics of sustainable HRM identified by Ehnert (2014).

1 **Long-term-oriented.** The short-term efforts to resolve current challenges need to be balanced with the long-run requirements of maintaining and developing human resources of knowledge, skills, passion, motivation, energy and health which employees *choose* to dedicate to their organization. The long-term view is necessary to prevent future short-term crises. Some of the immediate problems call for more substantial permanent adjustments. For example, the issue of staff shortage may require urgent action by hiring suitable employees as soon as possible, but it may also need improvement of overall employment quality to minimize voluntary turnover.

2 **Impact-control-oriented.** Sustainable HRM represents an approach that considers the impact of people management practices and strategies on the organization, employees, society and HRM itself. This is related to minimizing the unintended effect of HRM embodied by, for example, psychological or social harm. Ehnert (2014) emphasized that organizations and their HRM should control negative externalities being a) passed on to employees, and b) handed down to the environment from which critical resources come (e.g. local communities, wider society, natural habitat).

3 **Substance and self-sustaining-oriented.** This highlights the need for proactive frameworks and work designs that will strike a balance between regeneration and deployment of human resources. The sustainable approach contributes to the strategic debate concerned with resource 'reproduction'. In practice this translates, for example, into supporting employees in their efforts to have a good work–life balance. Conversations about good performance need to include a discussion of how to sustain energy and allow recovery. The HRM needs to reflect on and deal with self-substance of social, ecological and economic environments.

4 **Partnership-oriented.** The sustainable approach suggests an expansion of collaborations for HRM. In addition to being a partner with different organizational functions (e.g. marketing), HRM should develop alliances with a wider range of stakeholders, for instance the education system, corporate partners, NGOs (non-governmental organizations) or trade unions. Creating meaningful mutual relationships can support business

objectives and solve HRM challenges of attracting, maintaining and motivating skilled employees. HRM relies on the wider environment and its provision of human resources which can then be turned into competitive advantage. Sustainable HRM has at its disposal practices of supporting lifelong learning, cooperation with universities, coverage of training expenses or provision of grants (Stankevičiūtė and Savanevičienė 2018). Stankevičiūtė and Savanevičienė recognized that the emphasis on partnerships is also linked with the idea that HRM practices offered within the organization need to match expectations of stakeholders outside the organization.

5 **Multiple bottom lines-oriented.** Sustainable HRM addresses multiple bottom lines representing wider trends for socially responsible organizations. Attention to social and environmental goals in addition to economic targets changes the notion of success. This means a renewed and reinforced emphasis on social resources, placing employee voice at the centre of the debate (Richards, 2022). Moreover, it embraces the HRM capacity for supporting environmental efforts within the organization. Multiple bottom lines can be incorporated into a performance management system and other forms of HRM control.

6 **Paradox-oriented.** As explained in Chapter 2, HRM practice faces paradoxical tensions in the form of short-term economic rationale contrasting with the regeneration of the HR base, maintenance of social legitimacy and recognition of long-term economic rationale. The sustainable approach identifies different strategies that can be taken to manage these tensions. The key starting point is to acknowledge and accept HRM paradoxes. Then, through balancing or integration, HRM can cope with complex and often polar opposite demands placed on it. According to Ehnert (2014), successful navigation of organizational paradoxes is particularly important in the light of the demand for HRM creativity and innovativeness.

The notion that sustainable HRM expands our understanding of strategic HRM was also highlighted by Harry (2014) who argued that

Strategic HRM aims to build upon organizational strategy to have the 'right' human resources, at the 'right time' in the 'right place'. With sustainable HRM this will be supplemented by other factors related to sustainability such as the 'right focus' on the 'right contribution' to wider stakeholder needs.

Skill check

Discussing the strategic nature of sustainable HRM. This is a key skill because it helps us to understand the evolution of HRM and how the new approach can support organizational objectives.

Resource-based view (RBV)

Sustainable HRM and its strategic element can be discussed in relation to two main theoretical frameworks that also underpin traditional strategic HRM. These are the RBV and strategic fit. Let's start by explaining what RBV is, how it can be expanded with the NRBV (natural resource-based view) and how both RBV and NRBV represent strategic ideas that are relevant to sustainable HRM. Then, we will move on to the discussion of strategic fit.

Aims of RBV

The main assumption of RBV is that internal resources, as opposed to, for example, industry structure, are pivotal in achieving organizational success. From this perspective organizations are not homogenous, and they differ in terms of their resources. The RBV was advocated by Barney (1991) who is commonly cited as one of the key authors in this field. According to Barney, to attain superior performance organizations need to understand what resources and capabilities they have, or can develop, and how they can strategically use them. Barney argued that in order to gain a *sustainable* competitive advantage our resources need to be valuable, rare, inimitable and non-substitutable. Wright et al (1994) explained what this strategic approach means for the HRM practice.

Valuable resources

In labour markets, where there is a heterogeneous supply of and demand for human resources, value is created by matching job candidates' qualities with the requirements of the organization. Wright et al (1994) pointed out that managing qualified and suitable labour forces is often linked to the financial success of the organization.

Rare resources

There are a variety of different attributes that are attractive to employers (e.g. being self-driven) but Wright et al (1994) believed that cognitive skills stand out. Cognitive skills represent general mental ability and relate to employees' critical thinking, speed of acquiring new knowledge, effectiveness of applying information and capacity to solve problems. Individuals with high levels of cognitive ability are rare. If an organization has employees who are well matched to their roles and pose qualities that are difficult for the competition to acquire, this begins to set foundations for a competitive advantage. Note that once we have employees who are valuable and rare this creates an obligation for long-term investment into the development of their human resources and ensuring a sustained level of staff retention.

Inimitable resources

Physical resources such as equipment can be relatively easily bought. Thus, they produce little long-term advantage for companies because rivals can soon acquire identical or similar assets. However, imitating competitive advantage based on human resources is challenging. Employees' talent and ability to work effectively can be difficult to copy across organizations. Even if the competition convinces some of your qualified employees to work for them, the employees who jumped ship may not be able to recreate what they did for your organization. Complex social factors, such as organizational culture, stimulate and empower employees. This means that without replicating the specific conditions that allowed your best employees to perform well in your organization, the competition may not benefit as much from the poached talent. Social complexity of how employees interact with the organization makes human resources a potential source of long-term competitive advantage (Wright et al, 1994). The tacit and causally ambiguous nature of human resources and its relationship with the employer makes them particularly difficult to imitate (Colbert, 2004).

Non-substitutable resources

In order to achieve sustainable competitive advantage, organizations need to invest in resources that are not easily substituted by other assets. Wright et al (1994) argued that HR is one of the few organizational means with the potential to be non-substitutable. Imagine that your organization already has employee talents that are valuable, rare and inimitable. You have high-ability staff who are deeply committed to the organization. Your competition develops a new valuable technology that increases their productivity and allows them to rival the performance of your organization. If the new technology is not rare or is imitable then your organization should soon be able to purchase, develop or even copy the innovations and regain competitive advantage. In other words, 'the only resources that can substitute for human resources are those resources that are themselves valuable, rare, inimitable and non-substitutable' (Wright et al, 1994).

RBV highlights that investment in employees, and their relationship with the organization, increases their value and can lead to more sustainable success. RBV is concerned with developing a strategic advantage by finding, nurturing and retaining human resources. Thus, RBV reinforces the strategic importance of a long-term horizon for people management.

The RBV stresses the significance of intangible assets and how they can be a source of competitive advantage in the business environment. Not all resources can be recorded in financial statements. Employees' capabilities, their quality and embeddedness in the organization, are vital for achieving outcomes such as innovation or organizational resilience (Muñoz-Pascual and Galende, 2020). RVB already addresses the human and economic sides of sustainability, but it is missing a more explicit discussion of the relationship between organizational resources and the natural environment. This is covered by the NRBV.

Natural resource-based view (NRBV)

The NRBV framework was developed in 1995 by Hart. It builds on the literature of RBV and explains how organizations can generate competitive advantage through strategic capabilities that support eco-friendly sustainable development. Hart (1995) noticed that 'It is likely that strategy and competitive advantage in the coming years will be rooted in capabilities that facilitate environmentally sustainable economic activity'. On the basis of this observation Hart introduced NRBV, which proposes development of three interconnected strategic capabilities: a) pollution prevention, b) product stewardship and c) sustainable development.

- **Pollution prevention.** This is related to minimizing emissions and waste. It can enhance an organization's performance by reducing compliance and liability costs, reducing raw resource material and disposal costs, and simplifying the process.

- **Product stewardship.** This capability includes pro-environmental activities in the whole lifecycle and value chain of products. It addresses concerns such as product design, green logistics or even development of new products with lower environmental costs. Wider stakeholder engagement is vital in building product stewardship.

- **Sustainable development.** This organizational capability refers to practices that go beyond mere reduction of environmental damage. It focuses on production that can be maintained long term or even indefinitely into the future. From this perspective organizations should examine how they can contribute to sustainable local, international and global markets. Commitment to sustainable development combined with the other two capabilities of NRBV can generate long-term competitive advantage (Hart, 1995; Hart and Dowell, 2011).

RBV and NRBV suggest HRM practices must be created and directed toward resources that are valuable, rare, inimitable and non-substitutable, and towards capabilities of pollution prevention, product stewardship and sustainable development (Almada and Borges, 2018). Each organization operates under particular circumstances and the relationships between a) human resources, b) the natural environment and c) the employer will differ. From the perspective of RBV (and NRBV) this creates an opportunity for gaining a competitive advantage. RBV and NRBV highlight the sustainability aspect within HRM practice.

Management teams that create a positive environment for relevant people resources and capabilities can also improve their position in the labour market by increasing their employer attractiveness. The way in which the public evaluates your organization, relative to other employers, will have an impact on the pool and quality of job seekers as well as staff retention.

Strategic fit

The 'fit' perspective, also referred to as the 'contingency approach', underlines the development of HRM strategies, policies and practices in congruence with internal and external environment. Internal fit (or 'horizontal integration') is concerned with attaining consistency in HRM choices and policies and fitting them with the already established organizational practices. When this is achieved, HRM activities make a 'coherent whole' (Torrington et al, 2021). External fit (or 'vertical integration') conveys the importance of linking HRM with business strategy and any situational constraints that an organization may be facing, e.g. laws and regulations or labour market trends. If the alignment between HRM and organizational strategy leads to improved performance it suggests a positive external fit. When internal and/or external fit are in place this can be a source of competitive advantage.

Lopez-Cabrales and Valle-Cabrera (2020) discussed both forms of strategic alignment with reference to sustainable HRM. First, it can be argued that sustainable HRM supports the idea of internal fit. Sustainable HRM does not propose to adopt individual HRM practices but rather to consider a whole HRM system with synergies between different long-term and short-term activities and policies. For example, if underlying policies advocate good work–life balance then corresponding HRM practices (e.g. job design, performance management) should also be implemented to achieve desirable long-term social goals.

Sustainable HRM also attempts to achieve external fit. The approach highlights the strategic alignment and consideration of a wide range of external stakeholders. It places at its centre the idea of listening and responding to different actors in the external environment.

Strategic positioning in relation to sustainable HRM

Drawing on the literature of strategic fit and previous research on organizational arrangements (Tsui et al, 1997), Lopez-Cabrales and Valle-Cabrera (2020) proposed a framework of four types of strategic positions and employment relationships that are reached in sustainable HRM. The strategic positions they proposed are based on two dimensions: 'inducements offered by an organization' and 'expected employee behaviours'. When you plot these two factors against each other and consider the sustainability context it creates a matrix of four solutions: under-investment, quasi-spot contract, mutual investment and over-investment.

Under-sustainability/under-investment in sustainability

This position represents an imbalanced relationship between the organization and its employees. Employers that adopt this model invest little in human resources while having high expectations for their staff's behaviours and performance. There tends to be little to no consideration of social or environmental sustainability. The organizations take a reactive approach to strategic planning, and thus can face issues of high staff turnover and labour conflict (Lopez-Cabrales and Valle-Cabrera, 2020).

The under-investment approach can lead to situations, for example, where employees receive low remuneration, but are simultaneously required to upgrade their educational achievements without any financial support from the employer. The management may even ignore employment laws, such as provision of a safe working environment, assuming that employees are unlikely to report them (see, for example, Richards and Sang, 2021).

Lopez-Cabrales and Valle-Cabrera (2020) labelled this position in employment relationships 'unsustainable' and 'reactive'. Organizations that follow this approach risk their long-term economic condition. When the strategic focus is merely on demanding short-term extra effort from staff the organization has little resilience against changing circumstances in its internal and external environment.

Under-investment in staff can also have a detrimental impact on an organization's reputation and credibility. Advances in social media allow current or former employees to easily post anonymous, damaging information online, spreading negative word of mouth about their company (Lee and Suh, 2020). For example, Glassdoor.com is a platform where employees can write anonymous reviews of their organizations. Information from the website affects job candidates' willingness to apply for a job or to recommend it to other job seekers (Melián-González and Bulchand-Gidumal, 2017). Negative publicity can also affect customers' opinions about the offered products and services.

Quasi-spot sustainability

This form of employment relationship is based on a narrow set of inducements offered by the organization and low expectations for employees' behaviour. Employers following this model comply with the legislation and regulations regarding social, economic and environmental operations but solely to avoid fines and penalties. The dominant focus in HRM remains on maximizing profit with minimization of costs and little consideration of the impact on internal and external stakeholders. Performance and reward management are used primarily for controlling behaviour rather than for long-term commitment.

Lopez-Cabrales and Valle-Cabrera (2020) argued that theoretically the quasi-spot contract can be considered a balanced position because 'firms are looking to achieve the bare minimum in terms of sustainability (solely compliance) by investing minimal resources'. However, it is open to discussion to what extent this represents an equitable exchange when we also consider the negative externalities (see Chapter 3) created by organizations. Minimal compliance with the law often leads to employees' poor financial well-being or even working in poverty (Richards and Sang, 2021). In the business environment, merely conforming to the letter of the law, rather than its spirit, can lead to practices that the public would consider irresponsible or even unethical (McBarnet, 2009).

Similar to under-investment, the 'quasi-spot' represents a position that is not oriented towards long-term sustainability. It tends to occur in arrangements for jobs that are simple in nature with short periods of employment (Lopez-Cabrales and Valle-Cabrera, 2020).

Mutual sustainability

The third type of employment relationship, and a strategic positioning in relation to sustainability, is mutual investment. This approach is characterized by a high level of inducements offered by the employer and high responses from employees; thus Lopez-Cabrales and Valle-Cabrera (2020) label this position as balanced. Organizations taking this strategy will go beyond regulatory compliance, but they will not attempt to become leaders in sustainable practices. Rather their actions will be geared towards matching competitors' attention to social and environmental sustainability. This position is about 'acting through imitation' (Lopez-Cabrales and Valle-Cabrera 2020). As a response to stakeholder pressure, the organizations make investments in different areas of sustainability. If the 'quasi-spot contract' is about compliance, then mutual investment centres around monitoring the competition and the wider market forces (e.g. local community expectations). Efforts towards the long-term viability of employment relationships are partly driven by a concern about what would happen to the reputation of the organization if improvements related to social and economic initiatives were not introduced (Lopez-Cabrales and Valle-Cabrera, 2020).

In the mutual investment approach recruitment and selection can be used to add new employees who value sustainability. Remuneration will be competitive not only in terms of provided incentives but also in how they are connected to environmental and social dimensions. Performance management can be based on practices of empowerment and engagement in different areas of sustainability (Lopez-Cabrales and Valle-Cabrera, 2020). This setting incorporates sustainable HRM practices, but they would not be as extensively introduced as in the next option.

Over-sustainability

The final strategic position identified by Lopez-Cabrales and Valle-Cabrera is termed over-sustainability and is adopted in organizations that take a proactive, radical and innovative stance on sustainability practices. Here, sustainability is seen as the essential element of competitiveness. Organizations that adopt this position attempt to outperform other actors in the market in terms of engagement in social and environmental efforts, while also considering economic risks. In this strategy the investments made in human resources and sustainability exceed the responses expected from employees. This in turn reinforces employees' commitment to the organization.

For example, Bridgeway Capital Management is a small business with fewer than 50 employees. It offers a purpose-driven work environment and uses its culture of philanthropy to attract and retain talented staff. The company donates 50 per cent of its profits to organizations that solve societal or environmental problems. In the past, the company supported non-profit organizations such as SEARCH Homeless Services and Living Water

International (Bridgeway, 2022). Bridgeway also allows staff to serve in the local community during workdays and pays for 50 per cent of the charitable service trip expenses for employees and their family members. Moreover, the company offers its staff additional paid time to travel globally to support charitable goals. Bridgeway is a multi-year winner of *Pensions & Investments'* competition for 'Best Places to Work in Money Management' (Pensions & Investments, 2020).

Meanwhile, the Children's Hospital of Philadelphia (CHOP), a large business with over 15,000 employees, has received multiple employer awards, including number 1 rank in *Forbes'* 'America's Best Large Employer' list in 2022. CHOP is committed to creating an organization where both the patients and employees can thrive.

The hospital's website explains:

> CHOP is a unique work environment, with exceptional team members, supportive managers and state-of-the-art training. Our employees are all empowered to realize their well-defined goals, because we believe everyone makes a difference – it's the very foundation on which our hospital is built (CHOP, 2022).

In addition to extensive learning and career growth opportunities, wellness and health management services for employees, and flexible work arrangements, CHOP also offers a comprehensive benefits programme which includes, for instance, educational assistance, with tuition reimbursement and student loan repayments (CHOP, 2022).

In the 'over-sustainability' position organizations place long-term improvements at the centre of their strategy. In other words, these organizations are truly dedicated to sustainability and often outperform others in their social and environmental efforts. In the original framework, this employment relationship is categorized as 'imbalanced' because the inducements offered by the organization surpass employees' contributions. However, if we extend the analysis by the third dimension and consider externalities, i.e. the impact on third parties such as staff families or the local community, it can be argued that over-sustainability represents a balanced approach (see Table 6.1).

Wider organizational culture, and the values present in the workplace, will influence which strategic positioning is adopted.

Table 6.1   Forms of strategic positioning in relation to sustainable HRM

	Employment relationships	Without a consideration of externalities	With a consideration of externalities
Under-sustainability	– Narrow set of inducements offered by the organization – High expectations for employees' behaviour (Negative externalities)	Imbalanced	Imbalanced
Quasi-spot	– Narrow set of inducements offered by the organization – Low expectations for employees' behaviour (Negative externalities)	Balanced	Imbalanced
Mutual-sustainability	– High level of inducements offered by the employer – High expectations for employees' behaviour (Neutral or positive externalities)	Balanced	Balanced
Over-sustainability	– Inducements offered by the employer exceed expectations for employees' behaviour (Positive externalities)	Imbalanced	Balanced

SOURCE Adapted and expanded from Lopez-Cabrales and Valle-Cabrera (2020)

Organizational culture

In simple terms *organizational culture* (OC) can be defined as 'the way we do things around here' (Deal and Kennedy, 1982). According to Ravasi and Schultz (2006), OC is 'a set of shared mental assumptions that guide interpretation and action in organizations by defining appropriate behaviour for various situations'. Ogbonna and Harris (2014) defined OC as 'the set of values, beliefs, norms and assumptions that are shared by a group and that guide their interpretations of and responses to their environments'. Most academics agree that OC is something that affects all aspects of the organization and shapes employees' behaviours and attitudes. OC is based on formal and informal rules, as well as explicit and implicit assumptions about the work and its environment. OC teaches employees how they should perceive, think and feel in relation to organizational problems (Schein, 1992).

OC is one of the key factors affecting how much effort is driven internally towards sustainability. Because OC provides a guideline for everything that happens in the organization it will also affect what strategy should be taken in relation to sustainable HRM. Organizations that already have an established culture, which considers the long-term vision and stakeholders' needs, may find it easier to create and approve sustainability strategies.

According to Schein (1990), we can identify three main layers of OC: artefacts and creations, values and beliefs, and basic assumptions. The discussion below explains each of these layers and what they mean in the context of sustainable HRM.

Artefacts and creations

This is the most explicit and superficial layer of organizational culture. Anyone encountering these elements of OC can observe, hear or feel them. This layer includes the way members of the organization talk with each other, what they talk about and what myths and stories they share. This also is related to the physical elements of the organization such as the furniture, the building, the offices and what technology is used.

In the context of sustainable HRM, this layer of OC could be manifested, for example, in a form of a basic sustainability course included as a part of the staff induction. Another example would be a written document clarifying the policy on work–life balance and the formal support that the organization provides in helping employees oscillate between their professional and private responsibilities.

Values and beliefs

In Schein's view, what we create and how we behave at work is based on employees' values. This represents the second layer of organizational culture. *Organizational values* are shared convictions about what is or is not good for the organization, which guide employees' behaviour. Values can be held consciously or unconsciously. They can be captured by slogans such as teamwork, excellence, transparency or diversity. These can be actively promoted and encouraged by the organization. The stronger the value the more it will shape employees' attitudes and actions.

Environmental protection, quality employment, diversity and inclusion, employee voice, organizational citizenship – these are some of the organizational values that are related to sustainable HRM. These shared beliefs shape how HRM is practised. It is HRM's responsibility to translate organizational values into policies, practices and strategies.

Basic assumptions

According to Schein, this is the deepest layer of organizational culture. 'Basic assumptions' are so ingrained in organizational memory that employees are not even aware of them. Yet, these unspoken and taken-for-granted ideas influence employees' thoughts, feelings and actions. The underlying assumptions represent deep essence of culture and are well integrated in the reality of the organization. With time, the accepted values, beliefs and attitudes become so established that they no longer need to be stated or discussed by employees. When that happens they become a core element of OC.

If a basic assumption, shared by the staff, is that the organization exists solely for the benefit of the owner, this prevents employees from exploring practices and strategies that would benefit a wider range of stakeholders. How much responsibility should organizations have for their social and environmental impact? Is it an employer's duty to provide certain minimum remuneration that will allow employees to financially support themselves? Does an employer have a responsibility to provide a work environment that will not harm employees? Honest answers to these questions represent some of the underlying assumptions integrated in organizational culture which will affect practices and strategies related to sustainable HRM.

Organizational values and sustainability

Values distinguish one organization from another. Thus, the management needs to make a strategic decision about which ones they plan to emphasize or develop. Values that are successfully embedded in organizational fabric will have an impact not only on current employees and their behaviour but also on prospective members of the organization (Vandenberghe and Perió, 1999). Values that are well-established in the organization influence all elements of its performance. The more the values are aligned with the organization's initiatives and plans, the more they impact how the organization functions (Richards, 2006). Mariappanadar (2019) identified seven sustainable organizational values:

1 **Social consciousness.** High organizational consciousness exposes more connections between the organization and its internal and external environment. This collective social self-awareness can make organizations more compassionate and altruistic. When applied to HRM this value leads to a more democratic approach to people management and a more egalitarian culture. Employees vote or participate in policy initiatives directly. There is more openness to new information and increased awareness of multiple perspectives (Chiva, 2014).

2 **Ethics of care.** This value is about making ethical decisions when navigating the balance between profit making and the well-being of employees and their families. When introduced to organizations and HRM it develops a culture of trust between an employer and its staff, as well as respect for individuals' right to well-being. The value emphasizes the reduction of harmful aspects of HRM such as irresponsible work intensification (Mariappanadar, 2012).

3 **Utilitarian instrumentalism.** This represents quantitative and strategic elements of HRM and using employees' attributes to achieve organizational goals. For sustainable development this needs to be weighed against other values, particularly 'developmental humanism' (Mariappanadar, 2003).

4 **Developmental humanism.** This value emphasizes the importance of developing human resources. When introduced as a part of the organizational culture, this idea fosters practices that are meant to increase employees' commitment. The value highlights individuals' potential for development, participation and involvement (Mariappanadar, 2003; Legge, 1995).

5 **Humanistic organizational values.** Here the organization pays attention to basic human needs (such as stability and safety) and taps into the more sophisticated needs of belonging and accomplishment. This conviction has a direct impact on how to design practices that are meant to motivate, reward, develop and retain staff. It focuses on the search for practices that place a greater emphasis on interpersonal relationships but also allow achievement of productivity and long-term economic goals.

6 **Altruistic employee motivation (empathy).** This value underlines the positive emotion that affects reasoning and decision-making processes.

Empathy is crucial to broaden the thoughts and actions of members of the organization (Wright, 2003). It also reinforces other sustainability values related for example to enhancing employees' growth or reducing harm.

7 Pro-social orientation. Compared to 'individualistic' or 'competitive', the 'pro-social' orientation is linked with greater efforts for improving joint outcomes for the self and others. This value represents cooperation and striving for equality (Van Lange, 1999).

Skill check

Analysing organizational values. This is a key skill because organizational values determine how we behave at work. Understanding formal and informal values will help you identify areas of your organization's culture that already are or could be related to sustainability.

Organizational values and sustainable HRM strategies

Mariappanadar (2019) linked organizational values with three main sustainable HRM strategies: functional, capacity and results-oriented.

Functional sustainable HRM strategy

This strategy concentrates on the development of HRM functions, such as reward management, performance appraisal, etc., through the prism of sustainable values. This would include training specialist sustainable HR professionals who will work with line managers and will help them achieve their goals with a view to wider sustainable organizational values. The strategy would be used to develop HRM practices and policies that allow the organization to achieve its social, environmental and economic objectives. The functional sustainable HRM strategy may set specific requirements for different areas of HRM and how they should evolve. For example, the strategy may provide guidelines for how the performance management process could emphasize values of developmental humanism and pro-social orientation.

Capability-oriented sustainable HRM strategy

This strategy is dedicated to ensuring that the organization has the people that it needs, and that employee and organizational values are aligned. More specifically the strategy covers attracting, training and motivating individuals with the necessary capabilities and values. The strategy can also present a case for competitive advantage gained through fostering of values such as ethics of care or altruistic employee motivation. It is essential for HR leaders to outline what skills are required to develop sustainable culture and help the organization achieve its goals. In other words, the strategy deals with anticipating, developing and enabling sustainable capabilities.

Results-oriented sustainable HRM strategy

The final strategy identified by Mariappanadar (2019) centres around achieving sustainability goals. A key element of this strategy is setting HRM-related targets for the organization which exceed legal requirements. Rather than merely meeting required employment standards, the strategy aims to make a positive impact on the social and natural environment. The results-oriented HRM strategy is vital for any employer with CSR goals but also organizations that focus on sustainable development. The strategy derives from and further reinforces sustainable values, such as social consciousness.

WORKSHOP DISCUSSION 5

HS1 Ltd

HS1 Ltd is a large private company registered in England and Wales. In 2022 it reported £150 million turnover and £3.5 billion assets. The company has the 30-year concession to own, operate and maintain High Speed 1 (HS1), which is a 67-mile (108 km) high-speed railway linking London with the Channel Tunnel. HS1 is the only high-speed railway in the UK. It allows maximum speeds of up to 300 kph for international services and 230 kph for domestic services.

The aim of HS1 Ltd is to 'be the world's leading high-speed rail experience, providing the most sustainable option for transport across the UK and Europe'. To zero in on sustainability practices the company developed its own sustainability strategy. Due to the nature of HS1 Ltd's services, a large portion of the strategy is dedicated to environmental protection. For example, the company sets ambitious targets and then reports on reducing gas emissions, reducing energy wastage, maximizing use of sustainable energy and minimizing water usage. Although sustainable strategy focuses more on the green aspects, HS1 Ltd also recognizes the importance of wider sustainable relationships with a range of stakeholders including employees and local communities.

In their Environmental, Social and Governance Report the company explained: 'HS1 has developed strong values to help mould its culture and guide its actions. Ethics are at the heart of HS1's relationships with our employees, partners and stakeholders and we are adopting a strong framework to fulfil the Group's integrity and transparency responsibilities.'

The company developed a separate roadmap dedicated to social sustainability. It is called 'People Strategy' and is used for 'attracting, developing and retaining our most valuable asset – our people. Our strategy continues to put our people at the very heart of our business as we recognize that the collective talents, input and commitment of our people will keep us on course for the successful delivery of our strategic business objectives.'

Details of how the company acts on their people strategy are included in HS1 Ltd annual sustainability reports. HS1 Ltd has:

- developed a well-being programme for employees;
- added equality, diversity and inclusion (EDI) questions to the employee survey to gather information and track progress;
- developed an EDI policy on menopause;
- benchmarked family-friendly policies to remain competitive;
- embedded sustainability into a performance management system;
- embedded sustainability impacts into staff's personal objectives;
- set a number of hours for staff volunteering in local communities and charity activities (during 2021/22, 736 volunteer hours were registered).

HS1 Ltd's socially sustainable policies and practices seem to be working because their 2022 employee survey showed that:

- 100% of respondents believe HS1 takes sustainability seriously (a 15 per cent increase from 2020);
- 98% of respondents believe HS1 takes health and safety seriously;
- 94% of respondents believe HS1 takes health and well-being seriously;
- 94% of respondents believe HS1 takes EDI seriously.

Sphere

Sphere Digital Recruitment is a recruitment agency with a vision to 'be a specialist digital media, marketing, creative and technology recruitment business that will achieve great results for our people and our customers by having meaningful and engaging experiences with them that enable growth and get results.' The company was started in 2012 in London and since then has grown to 70 employees. Sphere explains that creating an excellent workplace environment played a major role in the success and rapid growth of the company.

Sphere's focus on employees has been acknowledged in employer competitions. For example, in 2022 the agency received an award for the 'Best Small Company in the UK' at the Best Company Awards Q2 2022. The ranking is based on results of an internal anonymous survey. At Sphere the survey showed that:

- 100% of staff agree with the statement 'I believe I can make a valuable contribution to the success of this organization';
- 96% of staff agree with the statement 'This organization has a strong social conscience';
- 89% of staff agree with a statement 'I feel I receive fair pay for the responsibilities I have in my job'.

A strong focus on social sustainability comes from the top. The CEO explained: 'Sphere has and always will be a people first business. (…) We do this with tangible action and support and a culture that is full of authentic encouragement and belief in what we are doing, how we do it and by doing this together.'

On its website the company also lists seven values that influence all its practices and policies:

'**Expertise**: Know our markets and know our customers. Be specialist. Be an expert.

Partnership: Work together, listen, add value. Build long-lasting relationships with customers and peers. Be a partner.

Purpose: Start projects with an end in mind. Have a reason behind our action. Focus on a result. Be solutions driven. Be purposeful.

Responsibility: Work with integrity. Understand our responsibility in everything that we do. Look first at ourselves. Be an example to others. Be responsible.

Simplicity: Do small and basic things brilliantly all the time. Be clear and concise. Keep things simple.

Ambition: Go above and beyond. Never settle for mediocrity. Expect and strive for excellence in everything we do. Be ambitious.

Adaptability: Be prepared. Embrace and drive change. Be opportunistic. Be adaptable.'

The company nurtures and develops staff who in turn nurture and develop customers. In 2021, 23 staff members were promoted. This internal growth of talent is possible thanks to 'personalized training, bespoke career development plans and an enviable list of customers'.

Sphere also takes care of its employees through:

- enhanced paternity pay;
- flexible working hours;
- finishing work at 3 pm on Fridays;
- weekly incentives;
- encouraging sport clubs within the workplace (football team, yoga and running groups);
- quarterly and twice-yearly pay reviews based on targets;
- charity actions such as raising cash for the homeless, and staging events for Roald Dahl's Marvellous Children's Charity;
- well-being activities for staff such as puppy therapy and cocktail making;
- regular strategy mornings, CEO lunches and discussion groups, which give anyone, regardless of their level, a chance to voice their ideas.

Investing in the team allows the company to better retain, motivate and attract talented employees. The company has an 18 per cent staff turnover, which is significantly below its industry average of 40 per cent.

On the company's website an anonymous testimony from an employee reads: 'The culture was the main reason I joined and it felt like a great company to work for – one which was doing great things and one which really cared about their employees.'

Questions

1 Drawing on the examples of HS1 Ltd and Sphere, discuss how sustainability can be embedded in organizational strategy.

2 Drawing on the examples of HS1 Ltd and Sphere, discuss how sustainability can be embedded in organizational culture and values.

3 Compare and contrast strategic approaches to sustainability at HS1 Ltd and Sphere. Do you think that the type of services offered by an organization affects how it approaches social sustainability?

4 What benefits of sustainable HRM can we identify in the cases of HS1 Ltd and Sphere?

Sources

https://find-and-update.company-information.service.gov.uk/company/03539665/filing-history

https://highspeed1.co.uk/about-us

https://highspeed1.co.uk/sustainability

https://highspeed1.co.uk/media/34ll44us/hs1-esg-report-2021-22.pdf

https://highspeed1.co.uk/media/dielj5iu/hs1-sustainability-strategy-2020.pdf

www.spheredigitalrecruitment.com/about-us

www.spheredigitalrecruitment.com/work-for-sphere-digital-recruitment

www.spheredigitalrecruitment.com/about-us/vision-and-values

www.spheredigitalrecruitment.com/work-for-sphere-digital-recruitment/life-at-sphere

www.b.co.uk/companies/sphere-digital-recruitment

Organizational values and the Great Resignation

What happens when organizational values mismatch the values of individual employees? Studies suggest that value discrepancy affects employees' health, performance and job satisfaction (Edwards and Shipp, 2007; Dyląg et al, 2013). For example, Dyląg et al (2013) conducted a study of 480 white-collar workers employed in Polish public and private organizations from various service industry sectors, including education, health care and sales. The researchers found that employees who perceive that there is a dissonance between their own and organizational values are at a higher risk of occupational burnout and lower work engagement.

The issues of organizational value discrepancy and work expectations were highlighted by the Great Resignation. The **Great Resignation**, sometimes also called the Big Quit or the Great Reshuffle, is an economic trend in different parts of the world, which started in 2021, where employees in large numbers voluntarily resigned from their jobs. In 2021, 47.8 million US employees quit their jobs, an all-time record (US Bureau of Labor Statistics, 2022). In the UK, at the end of 2021 the number of resignations hit a 20-year high (ONS, 2022). Similar insights were shared by LinkedIn (2022):

> Our most recent data showed a 54% increase in the number of global members who changed jobs year-over-year – talent is leaving at an unprecedented rate for greener pastures. Companies that don't prioritize their needs face being left behind.

There are many possible reasons for the increased number of people quitting jobs during the Great Recession. First, we need to recognize that in 2020 at the beginning of the Covid-19 pandemic many workers delayed their decision to resign. They decided to stay put in their jobs because of the uncertain circumstances in the market. In 2021, when employees started to see signs of transition towards normalcy, many looked for better opportunities. In other words, some of the resignations were simply pushed in time.

However, the pandemic has also made employees reassess their priorities in their private and professional lives. Many re-evaluated whether their job was meaningful to them, provided an acceptable work–life balance and provided an option to work remotely (see also Tessema et al, 2022).

In a study on the Great Resignation, Sull et al (2022) examined 34 million online profiles of US employees to find out who resigned between April and September 2021. Additionally, the authors utilized a dataset provided to them by reveliolabs.com. In their study, Sull et al focused on 'Culture 500' companies, which is 'a sample of large, mainly for-profit companies that together employ nearly one-quarter of the private-sector workforce in the United States' (Sull et al, 2022). The researchers found that companies with a reputation for healthy work culture experienced lower-than-average turnover during the examined period and lower attrition of workers than their competitors. For example, Enterprise Rent-A-Car had a 2.9 per cent attrition rate compared to Hertz's 13.2 per cent; Southwest Airlines had 3.6 per cent compared to JetBlue's 7.6 per cent.

Moreover, Sull et al analysed the text of more than 1.4 million Glassdoor reviews and examined which topics best predicted loss of staff at a company during the studied six months of the Great Resignation. They identified 'toxic corporate culture' as the best predictor for employees leaving jobs. According to their findings, toxic culture was 10.4 times more likely to contribute to loss of staff than compensation. The authors explained: 'Our analysis found that the leading elements contributing to toxic cultures include failure to promote diversity, equity, and inclusion; workers feeling disrespected; and unethical behavior' (Sull et al, 2022).

The financial price for harmful organizational culture is high. On the one hand, it can lead to increased loss of employees. On the other hand, a toxic employer can struggle to attract job candidates.

The Great Resignation gave employees, and especially skilled workers, an opportunity to choose organizations that better align with their values. For this reason, the event is also sometimes labelled as the Great Reshuffle. Many employees were looking for employment that would provide better conditions and flexibility.

The issue of increased voluntary resignations is exacerbated by a contemporary 'strategic' approach to resourcing staff. When an employee leaves the organization, the management team asks itself a question: 'Do we need to replace this person? Or can we dissolve this role and spread the responsibilities across our employees?' If the answer to this question is based only on a short-term economic rationale it leads to prioritizing cost-cutting over well-being of existing employees. This can lead to a vicious cycle of stress, burnout and more resignations, because the additional burden related to a dissolved role may encourage other workers to also leave. Even when the organization is planning to replace the employee who has left, the additional work related to the temporary cover of duties can tip the scales for another employee to step down. Quitting can be infectious. When one person leaves a job, other staff members may be inspired to do the same and cause *turnover contagion*, or in other words en masse resignation in a relatively short period of time. Once the exodus of employees begins it can be difficult to stop.

The increased number of people who have voluntarily left their jobs during the Covid-19 pandemic also needs to be viewed in the perspective of wider online social movements and communities describing dissatisfaction with employment.

Lying flat and antiwork

Lying flat (or tang ping) is a Chinese social movement, which began in 2021, protesting the pressures of overworking. Many Chinese employees are required to work excessively long hours and risk professional burnout. For example, in internet companies this practice is an established part of the work culture and is represented by the term '996'. It means that companies demand their employees work from 9 am to 9 pm, six days a week. Lying flat is one of the forms of a social protest against such practices. Those who 'lie flat' reject the pressures of professional life because of the physical and mental burden coupled with limited financial rewards. This means giving up on paid work or performing only enough of it to sustain yourself and satisfy your most basic needs. The movement is a sign of resistance against exploitive work practices and emphasizes the value of a well-rounded lifestyle (see e.g. Davidovic, 2022).

The Reddit.com antiwork community (or '*r/antiwork*') represents a similar trend. The antiwork thread on the popular social platform has over 2.2 million subscribers (or 'idlers') and it is 'for those who want to end work, are curious about ending work, want to get the most out of a work-free life, want more information on anti-work ideas and want personal help with their own jobs/ work-related struggles' (Reddit, 2022).

In this online group, members post their negative experiences of work. This is often coupled with pictures of messages from their managers suggesting poor working conditions or inadequate staff treatment. The users of the group share a range of views from abolishing work altogether to more moderate reformist perspectives on work. However, the common theme for all members is the feeling that their workplace takes advantage of them and makes unreasonable demands (e.g. long hours, low wages, poor working conditions).

The above-mentioned examples of social trends illustrate what happens when employee and employer values do not align. The current circumstances in the job market highlight the importance of sustainable HRM, which if introduced earnestly can lead to a strategic competitive advantage.

Summary

A competitive strategy allows organizations to make plans for strengthening a business's long-term position in its market environment. By its nature, sustainable HRM is geared towards the long-term objectives of an enterprise, but it also expands the idea of success by attending to social and environmental goals.

RBV is commonly used in the academic literature as a theoretical framework for strategic HRM. It explains how people management can be used to achieve competitive advantage for an organization. The discussion in this chapter shows that RBV, and its similar form of NRBV, also apply to sustainable HRM. The new approach to people management also corresponds with the 'strategic fit' or contingency perspective. In terms of internal fit, sustainable HRM proposes a system with synergies between different long-term and short-term activities that will mutually reinforce themselves. In terms of external fit, sustainable HRM emphasizes the consideration of the business strategy and a wide range of external stakeholders, including the education system, NGOs and trade unions. The literature connecting strategy, sustainability and HRM is still evolving. However, there are already solid theoretical and empirical foundations that help us make sense of the relationship between these three components.

Like everything that exists in an organization, a business strategy is influenced by the organizational culture. A key element of organizational culture is values shared by its employees. This chapter discussed a list of sustainable organizational values and connected with them three sustainable HRM strategies identified by Mariappanadar (2019). In the next chapter we will examine in more depth different factors that impact implementation of sustainable HRM.

Study questions

1 In what ways does sustainable HRM represent a new, extended approach to the strategic position that HRM takes in organizations?

2 How, according to the resource-based view, can organizations gain a sustainable competitive advantage?

3 What is the natural resource-based view and how does it complement RBV?

4 Which of the strategic positionings presented by Lopez-Cabrales and Valle-Cabrera (2020) symbolize balanced employment relationships?

5 What are three main levels of organizational culture and how are they related to sustainable HRM?

6 What are the three sustainable HRM strategies identified by Mariappanadar (2019)?

7 Explain the phenomenon of the Great Resignation and discuss what unsustainable HRM practices could be related to it.

Key reading

Sull, D, Sull, C and Zweig, B (2022) Toxic culture is driving the Great Resignation, MIT Sloan Management Review, https://sloanreview.mit.edu/article/toxic-culture-is-driving-the-great-resignation

Tessema, M T, Tesfom, G, Faircloth, A, Tesfagiorgis, M and Teckle, P (2022) The 'Great Resignation': causes, consequences, and creative HR management strategies, *Journal of Human Resource and Sustainability Studies*, **10** (1), pp 161–78

Wright, P M, McMahan, G C and McWilliams, A (1994) Human resources and sustained competitive advantage: a resource-based perspective, *The International Journal of Human Resource Management*, **5** (2), pp 301–26

References

Almada, L and Borges, R (2018) Sustainable competitive advantage needs green human resource practices: a framework for environmental management, *Revista de Administração Contemporânea*, **22** (3), pp 424–42

Baird, L and Meshoulam, I (1988) Managing two fits of strategic human resource management, *Academy of Management Review*, **13** (1), pp 116–28

Barney, J (1991) Firm resources and sustained competitive advantage, *Journal of Management*, **17** (1), pp 99–120

Bridgeway (2022) Giving back: what matters most is having a positive impact, https://bridgeway.com/giving-back (archived at https://perma.cc/4KXG-L9SP)

Chandler, A D (1962) *Strategy and Structure*, MIT Press, Boston, MA

Chiva, R (2014) The common welfare human resource management system: a new proposal based on high consciousness, *Personnel Review*, **43** (6), pp 937–56

CHOP (2022) Why Work at CHOP? https://careers.chop.edu/content/Why-Chop/?locale=en_US (archived at https://perma.cc/7ZJP-XHNE)

Colbert, B A (2004) The complex resource-based view: implications for theory and practice in strategic human resource management, *Academy of Management Review*, **29** (3), pp 341–58

Collings, D G, Wood, G T and Szamosi, L T (2019) Human resource management: a critical approach. In D G Collings, G T Wood and L T Szamosi (eds.) *Human Resource Management: A critical approach* (pp 1–23), Routledge, London and New York

Davidovic, I (2022) 'Lying flat': why some Chinese are putting work second, BBC News, www.bbc.com/news/business-60353916 (archived at https://perma.cc/AYE7-RC64)

Deal, T and Kennedy, A E (1982) *Corporate Cultures*, Addison–Wesley, Reading, MA

Dyląg, A, Jaworek, M, Karwowski, W, Kożusznik, M and Marek, T (2013) Discrepancy between individual and organizational values: occupational burnout and work engagement among white-collar workers, *International Journal of Industrial Ergonomics*, **43** (3), pp 225–31

Edwards, J R and Shipp, A J (2007) The relationship between person-environment fit and outcomes: an integrative theoretical framework. In C Ostroff and T A Judge (eds.) *Perspectives on Organizational Fit* (pp 209–58), Jossey-Bass, San Francisco

Ehnert, I (2009) *Sustainable Human Resource Management. A conceptual and exploratory analysis from a paradox perspective*, Physica-Verlag, Berlin/Heidelberg, Germany

Ehnert, I (2014) Paradox as a lens for theorizing sustainable HRM. In I Ehnert, W Harry and K J Zink (eds.) *Sustainability and Human Resource Management: Developing sustainable business organizations* (pp 247–71), Springer, Berlin/Heidelberg, Germany

Ehnert, I, Parsa, S, Roper, I, Wagner, M and Muller-Camen, M (2016) Reporting on sustainability and HRM: a comparative study of sustainability reporting practices by the world's largest companies, *The International Journal of Human Resource Management*, **27** (1), pp 88–108

Harry, W (2014) The relevance of the vision of sustainability to HRM practice. In I Ehnert, W Harry and K J Zink (eds.) *Sustainability and Human Resource Management: Developing sustainable business organizations* (pp 401–19), Springer, Berlin/Heidelberg, Germany

Hart, S L (1995) A natural-resource-based view of the firm, *Academy of Management Review*, **20** (4), pp 986–1014

Hart, S L and Dowell, G (2011) Invited editorial: a natural-resource-based view of the firm: fifteen years after, *Journal of Management*, **37** (5), pp 1464–79

Lado, A A and Wilson, M C (1994) Human resource systems and sustained competitive advantage: a competency–based perspective, *Academy of Management Review*, **19** (4), pp 699–727

Lee, S B and Suh, T (2020) Internal audience strikes back from the outside: emotionally exhausted employees' negative word-of-mouth as the active brand-oriented deviance, *Journal of Product & Brand Management*, **29** (7), pp 863–76

Legge, K (1995) *Human resource management: rhetoric and realities*, Macmillan, London

LinkedIn (2022) New data on employer brand, marketing talent and the Great Reshuffle, www.linkedin.com/business/marketing/blog/research-and-insights/new-data-on-employer-brand-marketing-talent-and-the-great-reshuffle (archived at https://perma.cc/FD3D-FZS5)

Lopez–Cabrales, A and Valle-Cabrera, R (2020) Sustainable HRM strategies and employment relationships as drivers of the triple bottom line, *Human Resource Management Review*, **30** (3), p 100689

Mariappanadar, S (2003) Sustainable human resource strategy: the sustainable and unsustainable dilemmas of retrenchment, *International Journal of Social Economics*, **30** (8), pp 906–23

Mariappanadar, S (2012) Harm of efficiency-oriented HRM practices on stakeholders: an ethical issue for sustainability, *Society and Business Review*, **7** (2), pp 168–84

Mariappanadar, S (2019) Sustainable HRM practices: values and characteristics. In S Mariappanadar (ed.) *Sustainable Human Resource Management: Strategies, practices and challenges* (pp 81–103), Red Globe Press, London

McBarnet, D (2009) Corporate social responsibility beyond law, through law, for law, *University of Edinburgh School of Law Working Paper*, (2009/03)

Melián-González, S and Bulchand-Gidumal, J (2017) Why online reviews matter for employer brand: evidence from Glassdoor, www.glassdoor.com/research/app/uploads/sites/2/2017/01/GD_Report_ReviewsMatterEmployerBrand_FINAL.pdf (archived at https://perma.cc/7EMS-VETZ)

Muñoz–Pascual, L and Galende, J (2020) Sustainable human resource management and organizational performance: an integrating theoretical framework for future research, *Small Business International Review*, **4** (2), pp 1–17

Ogbonna, E and Harris, L C (2014) Organizational cultural perpetuation: a case study of an English Premier League football club, *British Journal of Management*, **25** (4), pp 667–86

ONS (2022) Employment and employee types, X02: Labour Force Survey Flows estimates, www.ons.gov.uk/employmentandlabourmarket/peopleinwork/employmentandemployeetypes/datasets/labourforcesurveyflowsestimatesx02 (archived at https://perma.cc/H84K-Z9ZQ)

Pensions & Investments (2020) Bridgeway Capital Management, www.pionline.com/best-places-work/bridgeway-capital-management (archived at https://perma.cc/UQ53-ZSSG)

Ravasi, D and Schultz, M (2006) Responding to organizational identity threats: exploring the role of organizational culture, *Academy of Management Journal*, **49** (3), pp 433–58

Reddit (2022) Antiwork: unemployment for all, not just the rich! www.reddit.com/r/antiwork (archived at https://perma.cc/F3AR-SG83)

Richards, D A (2006) High-involvement firms: compensation strategies and underlying values, *Compensation & Benefits Review*, **38** (3), pp 36–49

Richards, J (2022) Putting employees at the centre of sustainable HRM: a review, map and research agenda, *Employee Relations*, **44** (3), pp 533–54

Richards, J and Sang, K (2021) Socially *irresponsible* human resource management? Conceptualising HRM practice and philosophy in relation to in-work poverty in the UK, *The International Journal of Human Resource Management*, **32** (10), pp 2185–212

Schein, E H (1990) Organizational culture, *American Psychological Association*, **45** (2), pp 109–19

Schein, E H (1992) *Organizational Culture and Leadership*, Jossey-Bass, San Francisco

Stankevičiūtė, Ž and Savanevičienė, A (2018) Designing sustainable HRM: the core characteristics of emerging field, *Sustainability*, **10** (12), p 4798

Sull, D, Sull, C and Zweig, B (2022) Toxic culture is driving the Great Resignation, *MIT Sloan Management Review*, https://sloanreview.mit.edu/article/toxic-culture-is-driving-the-great-resignation/ (archived at https://perma.cc/7G8J-6JZV)

Tessema, M T, Tesfom, G, Faircloth, M A, Tesfagiorgis, M and Teckle, P (2022) The 'Great Resignation': causes, consequences and creative HR management strategies, *Journal of Human Resource and Sustainability Studies*, **10** (1), pp 161–78

Torrington, D, Hall, L, Atkinson, C and Taylor, S (2021) *Human Resource Management*, 11th edn, Pearson, Harlow, Essex

Tsui, A, Pearce, J, Porter, L and Tripoli, A (1997) Alternative approaches to the employee-organization relationship: does investment in employee pay off? *Academy of Management Journal*, **40** (5), pp 1089–121

US Bureau of Labor Statistics (2022) Job Openings and Labor Turnover Survey (JOLTS), www.bls.gov/jlt/ (archived at https://perma.cc/JX4N-3SMA)

Van Lange, P A (1999) The pursuit of joint outcomes and equality in outcomes: an integrative model of social value orientation, *Journal of Personality and Social Psychology*, **77** (2), pp 337–49

Vandenberghe, C and Peiró, J M (1999) Organizational and individual values: their main and combined effects on work attitudes and perceptions, *European Journal of Work and Organizational Psychology*, **8** (4), pp 569–81

Wright, P M and McMahan, G C (1992) Theoretical perspectives for strategic human resource management, *Journal of Management*, **18** (2), pp 295–320

Wright, P M, McMahan, G C and McWilliams, A (1994) Human resources and sustained competitive advantage: a resource-based perspective, *The International Journal of Human Resource Management*, **5** (2), pp 301–26

Wright, T A (2003) Positive organizational behavior: an idea whose time has truly come, *Journal of Organizational Behavior*, **24** (4), pp 437–42

Implementing sustainable HRM

7

LEARNING OBJECTIVES

After completing this chapter, you should be able to:

- Define sustainability mindset and explain its role in the implementation of sustainable HRM.

- Build a business case for sustainable HRM initiatives.

- Understand what changes sustainable HRM brings to the role and profession of HR.

- Understand what leadership capabilities organizations need to develop as a part of sustainable HRM.

- Understand what skills HR professionals need for a successful implementation of sustainable HRM.

- Explain the introduction of essential sustainable HRM practices.

- Understand the importance of employees' input into the planning and implementation of sustainable HRM.

Introduction

The difficulty level of introducing sustainable HRM may correspond with the size and complexity of the organization. Nevertheless, some of the points remain constant. In order to effectively implement and maintain sustainable HRM in any organization we need to secure the support of its leadership. This is critical to ensure that resources, such as time, are allocated to pursue sustainability. Additionally, employees need to be consulted and included in the decision-making process. It is impossible to achieve social sustainability without listening to the staff. Line managers and the HR team may also need to develop new capabilities including deeper understanding of what sustainability has to offer. In this chapter we will explain each of these points and many more. Let's start our discussion with the sustainability mindset and how it can be developed among organizational leaders.

Sustainability mindset

The support of senior and executive members of the organization is vital to successfully achieve change, such as transforming HRM to a more sustainable approach. However, what is it that inspires organizational leaders to champion sustainability initiatives? Rimanoczy (2010) conducted a qualitative study that examined the experiences of 16 US business leaders who have successfully introduced sustainability initiatives without being asked to do so. The participants represented a variety of businesses such as food retail, floor treatment, household products, technology, coffee, apparel, pharmaceutical, restaurants and agribusiness (Rimanoczy, 2010). The study revealed three interconnected elements that contributed to the leaders' engagement in sustainability initiatives: 'the knowing', 'the being' and 'the doing' (see Table 7.1).

The aspects discussed by Rimanoczy contribute to paradigm shifts in organizations. Rimanoczy (2010, 2019) grouped together the three elements and called them *sustainability mindset*, which is 'a way of thinking and being that results from a broad understanding of the ecosystem's manifestations as well as an introspective focus on one's personal values and higher self, and

Table 7.1   Framework of sustainability mindset

	Elements of the sustainability mindset
The knowing	The information that leaders learn about the state of social challenges is key to developing a wider awareness about the necessity for sustainability.
The being	This refers to how the leaders personally relate to the information that points towards the need for change. Reflective practices allow leaders to connect the data with their own contribution to the sustainability problems encountered. The review of the information and introspective methods lead to a deeper exploration of responsibility, mission and legacy.
The doing	Once the personal connection is made this creates a sense of urgency to act.

SOURCE Based on Rimanoczy (2010, 2019)

finds its expression in actions for the greater good of the whole' (Kassel et al, 2016). Rimanoczy's research originally focused on ideas of respecting and restoring the natural environment. However, the framework was later expanded by the dimension of social sustainability.

The development of a sustainability mindset begins with having access to the key information necessary for organizational sustainability shift. This emphasizes the importance of management education that shows the link between traditional business and social and environmental longevity. It also highlights the need for organizations to internally discuss societal issues, and how they are connected to the operations of the organization.

According to Vere and Butler (2007), for the HR function to facilitate change it must engage managers in the design of the transformation, ideally from the outset of the programme. Furthermore, the initiative should use the language and logic of the organization to receive support from all key parties. In other words, developing a business case can be useful in shifting leaders' mindsets.

Building a business case

Sustainability initiatives – similar to any other organizational undertakings – require allocation of time and resources. In instances where sustainable HRM is not yet a part of the organizational strategy or culture, senior leadership may have to be persuaded that this is the right direction for the organization. Without a clearly structured rationale, senior management may push back against sustainable HRM ideas. The preparation of the rationale is also a chance to carefully consider what future opportunities sustainability will open up for the organization.

The end goal of sustainable HRM is to create effective practices across the whole organization where sustainability is an integral part of people management. Implementing *individual sustainability programmes* or practices is far from what the new approach represents. Having said that, working on separate effective initiatives can be a practical early step. It can be useful for a wider transformation of HRM, as long as it is not seen as the final objective. For example, a gradual introduction of sustainable practices can be necessary in organizations that show initial resistance to the notion of change and introducing sustainability as a central part of organizational values, strategy or overall culture.

The justification for sustainable HRM practices and policies does not have to be a business case. Nor does it have to be a written document. In some cases, it can be an evidence-based presentation in front of the key stakeholders. Depending on the type and size of the organization there may be different conventions for giving a well-organized reasoning for a change. However, in the private sector, and increasingly in public organizations, written business cases are often seen as a standard for justifying initiatives.

A business case examines an existing situation and proposes solutions that will lead to the new desired status. It is a tool that can be used to spell out the value of sustainable HRM practices and connect them with the overall strategy/vision of the organization. Depending on the proposed scale of the change the rationale can focus on a wider scope of sustainable HRM (e.g. multiple elements of social and environmental responsibility) or on a selected few practices (e.g. introducing financial and non-financial incentives for green behaviour). When planning new sustainable initiatives, particular attention should be given to modifying existing harmful and inadequate practices (Macini et al, 2022).

In each organization managers may have a slightly different preference for the exact format or specific metrics that should support the business case. Thus, before preparing the document it may be a good idea to informally discuss with the key stakeholders what they would expect to see in the rationale they will review. You may also have to seek help from colleagues in other departments such as finance to get access to key data that will support your case. This could be an opportunity to signal to a senior finance manager or a managing director that you are preparing such proposal. If they provide you with the information necessary for the document, they may feel partly involved in the initiative, which can increase the chances of them showing sympathy towards the final version of the proposal.

A meaningful business case, or a proposal for change, needs a consultation with employees or their representative. While sustainable initiatives are meant to balance the social, environmental and business objectives they can focus too strongly on the financial side of the equation and dismiss employees' views. A key idea behind sustainable HRM is that it uses a 'two-way' perspective (Paulet et al, 2021). Employees must be given an opportunity to shape sustainability objectives from the bottom up, simultaneously with the support we seek from the organizational top.

Mayberry (2008) identified 10 main elements that the HRM business case can include:

1 **Problem statement.** This is usually a one-paragraph explanation of the current issue that the HRM initiative attempts to solve. It is not enough to point out a problem. It must also pass the 'so what' test. In other words, the current concern needs to be connected to specific organizational goals justifying why management should care about the identified problem. The issue could be linked to the organizational vision or strategic objectives, such as to provide the best service, attract and retain the best people, reduce waste or remain competitive. For instance, this part of the business case can identify inefficiencies related to low job satisfaction and high staff turnover. The document would point out how these issues contribute to unfavourable customer experience. Another example would be the missed opportunity of promoting green behaviour among staff to boost employees' morale and improve the organization's external image. A persuasive problem statement is prepared based on documents such as the organization's mission statement or operating plan.

2 **Background/analysis of the situation.** In this section we provide a more detailed explanation about the problem, opportunity and need for change. The presented arguments can relate to academic research and/or internal data highlighting the issue. Complex HRM matters such as low job satisfaction, and low-quality employment provided by the organization, can be difficult to quantify or measure in terms of costs. Nevertheless, the diagnosis should attempt to estimate expenses related to challenges such as replacing employees. This part can also identify ineffective or missing processes contributing to the problem, for example, poor communication and failure to adequately implement policies that are meant to help employees avoid professional burnout. There should be a clear link between the presented analysis and the next section.

3 **Project objectives.** This is often several bullet points stating what the initiative aims to achieve. Examples may include improving paid leave policies or appointing more staff to reduce the burden on the existing team.

4 **Current process.** This highlights the existing processes that will be affected by the proposed initiative. Such discussion may consider the impact on HR and other departments, partnerships with trade unions, business alliances, customers, NGOs, community groups, government agencies and the business's position with respect to its competition.

5 Requirements. In this section we outline the required budget, time and other resources needed to implement the change.

6 Alternatives. The business case should list three or more possible alternative solutions that were considered but rejected. One of those options would be to take no action. This is because doing nothing is an alternative the leadership may be interested in evaluating. The document is meant to describe the impact of each alternative and break down the risks, initial and ongoing costs and resource requirements involved in each option.

7 Compare alternatives. Here we compare the proposed initiative and each of the alternative solutions. This section highlights the strengths and weaknesses of each option. Here you can contrast alternatives based on different metrics and assess which contributes best to the business objectives. This section can also highlight the consequences of failing to act on the proposed initiative. The logical conclusion of this section would be an explanation as to why the proposed programme is the most effective solution for the identified problems.

8 Additional considerations. This section gives us an opportunity to list any other critical success factors not previously reviewed. Are there any aspects that can affect the start or completion of the initiative? Does the proposed project rely on any partnerships or work which is currently being carried out?

9 Action plan. The leadership may want to see a detailed plan of how the proposed initiative will be implemented. Hence, in this section we recommend several courses of action and a timeline proposed for them. This section explains when each of the points will be implemented and when the overall initiative will be complete. Each component should be specific, outlining what needs to be added, removed or changed. The plan must also clarify what metrics will be used to measure the success of the proposed changes.

10 Executive summary. Depending on the length of the document it may be necessary to prepare a summary of the whole proposal. If used, this usually would be the first section opening the business case. It is meant to provide a succinct overview of the identified problem, considered options and the proposed solution. A good summary follows the same order as the whole document.

When the business case is well written it presents a narrative explaining how the changes towards sustainable HRM will make the leadership's job easier. A good business case paints a picture of why the proposed changes are not only good for the organization, but necessary. The CEO gives HRM policies legitimacy. For a consistent and effective implementation of sustainable practices the support of most senior leaders is vital.

Executives may want to see return on investment (ROI) estimates or a cost-benefit analysis. However, monetizable measures can also be supplemented by an assessment of not readily quantifiable benefits and risks. To present the full picture, elements of a qualitative story may need to be included. A qualitative narrative can convey emotions and make the case more impactful. Similar to the quantitative data, the qualitative perspective needs to be based on evidence (e.g. staff survey, exit interviews, Glassdoor reviews or focus groups).

Skill check

Building a business case. This is a key skill for presenting a structured rationale for sustainable HRM programmes.

Expanded role of HR

In many organizations 'there is no clear owner for sustainability' (SHRM, 2011). This is a chance for HR professionals to step up and lead preparation of new policies and practices. If sustainability initiatives are still underdeveloped in the organization, the HR function can help to define key terms and goals. Doing so would demonstrate that sustainability is more than just legal compliance and environmental protection.

According to Kramar (2022), sustainable HRM expands the role of senior HR managers. By presenting strategic HRM ideas, which are meant to help the organization achieve its long-term goals, HR executives strengthen their position at the senior level. If HR illustrates how sustainable HRM contributes to social, environmental and business goals then it can be involved in shaping future organizational plans. Kramar argued that in extreme cases the input from HR executives could even lead to a change in the products or services offered by an organization. Sustainable HRM has the potential to clarify the meaning of organizational culture. If done correctly it adds pride to the answer for 'who we are' and 'what we stand for'. Creating best employee experience and facilitating positive impact on the environment adds value to the organization and its services.

The HR executives should be involved in the key decision-making processes, working in a team with the CEO. As sustainability has shifted from a marginal to a strategic issue, it is a subject many CEOs are interested in. However, the HR function is not always considered when this matter is discussed at the highest level. The challenge for HR leaders is how to gain visibility in this area and demonstrate that their function can spearhead sustainability. HR leaders, supported by their team, should educate internal stakeholders about what 'sustainability' has to do with HRM. To do so the HR team itself needs to gain a strong understanding of the subject. Many HR leaders and professionals are still gaining a grasp of sustainability or its link to HRM beyond staff wellness programmes (Owen, 2020). This shows an opportunity for development.

The sustainable approach also requires HR to embrace closer collaboration with other functions. Successful introduction of sustainable HRM depends on effective cooperation between leaders across different parts of the organization (Kramar, 2022). Initially, HR, and other employees who engage in sustainability programmes, may not realize that their work is connected. This is because sustainable HRM represents a new approach and is not a norm yet. HR professionals can find it useful to work in collaborative teams with employees from other parts of the organization involved with sustainability. However, if the initiative comes from the HR officers, they may need to first gain approval from their department leaders before they start working more closely with sustainability professionals across the organization (Owen, 2020).

Sustainable HRM also means participating in more external work such as public affairs, collaborations with educational institutions or community engagement. HR professionals need to explore how different HRM practices (recruitment, job design, etc.) can benefit from partnership opportunities with outside stakeholders (Owen, 2020).

Sustainability makes HR professionals' work more meaningful. Guerci et al (2019) conducted a cross-country survey of European HR managers and officers. They found that sustainable HRM practices increased research participants' job satisfaction and decreased their turnover intentions. When sustainability is embedded in the organizational culture, and is a part of the

HRM efforts, it increases the likelihood of HR professionals perceiving their own work as more important. The contribution to the social and environmental success of the organization helps to support the development of HR.

Evolution of the HR profession

According to the survey conducted by SHRM (2011), sustainability already affects the HR profession in a number of ways and it will continue to reshape it moving forward. SHRM listed examples of how sustainability influences the function and its responsibilities. These findings illustrate what needs to be considered when an organization plans to add sustainability to the list of HR objectives:

Changing employee contract. As employees show concern for social and environmental sustainability, they expect their employer to take action in these areas. This can be related to increased pressures for meaningful work and environmental protection. The changing expectations for the employment contract mean that HR professionals have a responsibility for recognizing these trends and communicating them to the organization's leaders. The task is to create a culture that corresponds with stakeholders' interests.

Recruitment and selection. The HR profession needs to incorporate sustainability into recruitment efforts. Sustainability goals and values may need to be discussed during job interviews.

Brand. The communication involved in advertising vacancies is critical for building the brand of an attractive employer. If sustainability is embedded in the organizational fabric this should be reflected in how job applicants perceive the company.

Engagement. As SHRM explained, 'It is important to give employees a way to act on their interests in promoting social and environmental responsibility' (SHRM, 2011). Employees can respond positively to sustainability initiatives if they are educated on the issue, have the ability and permission to engage, there is a strong call for action and a recognition of their achievements (Center for Climate and Energy Solutions, 2015). The HR function plays an essential role in all the above elements of engaging employees in sustainable practices. If employees already have a passion for sustainability, HR can support them in acting on those interests by highlighting options for action and reinforcing desirable behaviours.

How people work. With the aim to achieve social and environmental sustainability, organizations and their HR professionals need to rethink how work is meant to be carried out. Is it possible to perform some of the roles or duties in a more sustainable manner?

Accountability and measurements. HR staff should integrate sustainability targets into performance management and support the organization's attempts at measuring and reporting sustainability progress.

Training/leadership development. The HR function also supports sustainability by developing leadership's capabilities. Professionals in this area can explore how to effectively train managers and motivate them to fill gaps in their sustainability knowledge and skills. Moving forward the HR team needs to incorporate sustainability into the processes of knowledge management.

Developing leadership's sustainability capabilities

When an organization sees social and environmental dimensions as a basis for achieving long-term competitive advantage it becomes logical to invest in leadership that can drive sustainability forward. Managers across the organization influence other members of staff. They evaluate employees' performance and development, make decisions about who joins the organization and who gets promoted. Their actions shape how HRM is put into effect. Therefore, the role of managers and leaders in promoting and introducing sustainable HRM cannot be overstated.

Leadership is crucial for fostering employees' commitment, directing the dialogue and transforming organizations. Years of 'bad habits' can be difficult to change. In order to modify past behaviours and establish new ways of thinking, organizations need to develop leadership's sustainability capabilities (e.g. knowledge, skills and passion for sustainability). Management devoted to the mission of sustainability can inspire and support actions towards more empathic and reflexive day-to-day operations.

According to Gloet (2006), sustainable leadership must be able to set a clear direction and a socially responsibility vision for others to follow. If managers can demonstrate that their leadership is purpose-driven and extends beyond short-term financial profit this can strengthen staff connection with organizational goals. Managers can inspire others by balancing idealism with pragmatism and acting as role models. By being committed to see sustainability results managers show that this issue is important to them, and subsequently that sets sustainability as one of the pressing matters for other employees.

Gloet pointed out that sustainable leadership entails working with different stakeholders, establishing new and maintaining existing relationships within and outside of the organization. It requires understanding of the interconnectedness of the social, environmental and business pressures. To maintain good relationships with diverse actors (e.g. trade unions, investors, workers, local communities), managers need to be good communicators. Championing sustainability also involves open-mindedness and willingness to consider new perspectives. Managing relationships will test leaders' adaptiveness and their ability to anticipate challenges.

The capabilities needed for sustainable leadership emphasize the role of strategic selection and training of managers. Leadership roles will amplify HRM practices as well as their effect on staff and the longevity of the organization. After the organization approves the strategic importance of sustainability, the HR team should present plans for developing the necessary capabilities in the management team. This involves the creation of suitable training programmes based on the identified skill gaps.

Line managers' contribution to sustainable organizations is indispensable. Yet, some supervisors may passively resist the idea of promoting staff well-being and championing environmental protection. When managers' responsibilities become related to sustainability they need to be provided with the necessary resources to succeed (e.g. guidance and time allocation).

HR skills needed for successful implementation

Owen (2020) created a how-to guide for sustainable HRM. The document is based on 43 qualitative interviews with people strategy professionals and sustainability professionals from US Fortune 500 companies and large human resources consulting firms. One of the themes Owen identified is key skills that HR managers need to succeed in sustainable HRM.

Change management and consulting mindset

Sustainable HRM represents adjusting to, and even embracing, ever-shifting expectations that stakeholders have for organizations. This means that HR professionals need to feel comfortable with breaking status quos. Rather than simply enduring change, HR needs to proactively participate in talks about transformation and, where possible, lead the discussion. According to Owen (2020), the role of a change agent involves mastering a 'motivational management style'. To get buy-in from teams and individual employees HR professionals need to understand how to inspire others and encourage managers to also use engaging practices.

Moreover, HR staff may need to prepare to take the role of an 'internal consultant', i.e. explore best practices, identify solutions and work with the stakeholders. Tight budgets mean that employers may seek internal expertise rather than appoint external consultation. The HR team should be ready to fill these shoes.

Analytical business mindset

HR professionals should develop business acumen and understand organizations' competitive environment, main operations and profit model. According to Owen (2020), sustainable HRM emphasizes the need for HR professionals to be 'holistic systems-thinkers'. Social and environmental sustainability have strategic potential. To realize it HR needs to be familiar with the organization's internal business processes. The skill of business analysis can give the HR team confidence in their sustainability proposals and earn them more credibility with executives.

Communication

Excellent communication skills are one of the top requirements for HR professionals and this quality is also needed for successful sustainability initiatives. Managing relationships with internal and external stakeholders requires persuasion, negotiation abilities and being an excellent listener. Developing sustainable plans and then explaining them to management and front-line staff highlights the need for good conversational and written communication skills. HR professionals need to be good storytellers. Once the data pointing to change is analysed it needs to be presented in the form of a narrative that is logical and inspires action (Owen, 2020).

Courage and creativity

Professional courage is one of the key qualities that any HR employee should strive to develop. It is needed to confront resistance and speak up when we notice something wrong (CIPD, 2022). This quality is especially important when we want to introduce a more sustainable approach to managing people. Promoting ideas of good employment standards can be difficult in organizations with economic models focusing on short-term gains. Confident HR professionals will be able to articulate their vision and handle the fear of stepping into uncharted territories. Implementation of a new approach takes courage to break away from the established unsustainable mindset and operations.

Designing new standards and solving problems in people management also requires creative intelligence. Rather than relying on business as usual you need to be able to imagine how practices could be different (Owen, 2020).

Resilience

HR initiatives often promote employees' resilience. However, HR professionals themselves should develop the ability to cope with confusing situations. The progress of change can be frustratingly slow or exhaustively fast. HR professionals need to build their own 'mental toughness' to grapple with the process. As Owen pointed out, HR staff 'must have the inner resilience to hear "no" repeatedly for years, then have a leader magically say, "Let's do it!", and not take this personally' (2020). It takes grit to lead and implement organizational transformation. Budhiraja and Yadav (2020) explained: 'Creating a team cohesive enough to pull together toward achievement of organizational goals and values requires not only time and experience but also persistent perseverance in preserving the core values of HR across managerial hemisphere.'

Essential sustainable HRM practices

There are different perspectives on what fundamental practices need to be implemented as a part of sustainable HRM. Mishra and Sarkar (2020) argued that organizations can focus on the most essential sustainable HRM practices, including the following.

Getting rid of unsustainable rules. HR, in cooperation with other departments, senior leadership and employee representatives, should examine existing policies and practices in terms of their impact on long-term social, environmental and business goals. Policies and rules that limit sustainability may have to be reconsidered and the HR team should be a part of these discussions. Removing unsustainable practices can be challenging if they are entrenched in the basic assumptions about how the organization should achieve its goals.

Integration. As the organization grows it can face a misalignment between its different parts, processes, strategies and practices. For the sustainable approach to succeed it requires integration of all the right partners across the organization. According to Mishra and Sarkar (2020), internal coordination can prove to be more difficult than the development of sustainability vision or tools.

Creating a culture of sustainability. The HR function is instrumental in building a sustainable culture. When the long-term perspective and social responsibility are part of shared values, and are embedded into organizational formal and informal agendas, this gives sustainability initiatives legitimacy. HR professionals can and should support sustainability norms, traditions and symbols. The HR function is in a position to reinforce desirable ethical conduct and help solve problems related to unsustainable management. When the organization goes through cultural transformation, consistent messaging will promote a better understanding of sustainability changes and solidify the new ways of working.

Using frameworks. This involves creating formal organizational structures that will help us achieve sustainable HRM goals. Collective logical frameworks are necessary to reach social, environmental and business objectives. These frameworks can be used to set out milestones.

Reporting practices. The HR team needs to be actively involved in preparing and contributing to sustainability reports. This responsibility may also involve a discussion with a number of stakeholders and collection of data across organizational levels of hierarchy. Measuring and reporting is another area that highlights the role of HR professionals in sustainability plans.

Establishing the sustainability council. A *sustainability council* is an internal body that guides the organization towards social and environmental sustainability. For example, in 2016 the Volkswagen Group established a sustainability council that advises the company on issues related to sustainability. The council reviews the organization's activities and prepares adequate recommendations (Volkswagen AG, 2022). The HR function should be represented on the council and cooperate with it.

Initiating sustainability-focused HR initiatives. This represents shifting from defensive expense cutting to strategic initiation of sustainable initiatives.

Promotion of employees' well-being

One of the central elements of sustainable HRM is the preservation of employees' physical and mental ability to perform well at work. The initial step in this process is diligently following the work safety best practices promoted by national and international organizations (e.g. the Health and Safety Executive in the UK). This is a basic duty of each employer often regulated by the law. However, some employers cut corners by neglecting their responsibilities. They reduce spending on safety measures, turn a blind eye when managers and employees engage in risky behaviours or even deliberately create performance targets that pressure employees to disregard their own physical and mental well-being. One of the infamous examples is Amazon. The company was accused of 'relentless working practices' with some employees allegedly not having enough time to use the toilet at work and having little choice but to urinate in plastic bottles (BBC, 2021).

At the same time, mere compliance with health and safety regulations does lead to sustainable HRM. To develop a more resilient workforce, organizations need to consider proactive measures, as discussed in more detail in Chapter 4. HR should identify gaps between existing work experience and standards for good-quality employment. Then, suitable structures and processes need to be designed and put into operation.

The implementation process can be supported by clearly defining whose responsibility it is to protect employees' mental and physical well-being. First, each manager should have a clear understanding of their role in sustainable HRM. Second, larger organizations can appoint a separate HR officer, or establish a team/committee dedicated to managing employees' well-being. The central oversight can break down the implementation process into four steps: 'diagnostics', 'planning', 'intervention' and 'evaluation'. The wider HR function can support the well-being committee by executing policies and coordinating efforts with internal and external stakeholders (Hoeppe, 2014).

Collecting information directly from employees is imperative. For example, employee surveys have been seen as a standard tool for collecting data on employees' well-being. Hoeppe (2014) analysed how a German bank implemented sustainable HRM. The author found that every two years the financial organization conducted surveys that examined areas such as 'work environment', 'health', 'culture' and how employees cope with the work activities.

WORKSHOP DISCUSSION 6

ActewAGL Retail

ActewAGL Retail is an Australian business that sells electricity and natural gas. It manages the customer service and marketing function for its parent company ActewAGL. ActewAGL Retail has approximately 160 staff members.

In 2017 ActewAGL Retail joined a programme called 'Healthier Work' provided by the government of the Australian Capital Territory (ACT). Healthier Work supports employers by sharing guides, training and tools on promoting health and well-being among staff. Since then, the company has taken a more structured and planned approach to health and well-being. In an interview from 2018, ActewAGL Retail representatives said:

> Previously we risked overloading staff with initiatives. With Healthier Work we're still giving a monthly message on health and well-being, but our 12-month programme is better structured – more focused and fresh: you can tell because our health and well-being committee is more energized, participation has increased, and our feedback on activities has become much more positive.

Small changes and activities started to drive a change in ActewAGL Retail's culture. For example, the company introduced short daily stretches. Initially employees were reserved about this initiative but over time it became a welcome part of their daily routine. The company also organized a seminar from Nutrition Australia. This, combined with colleagues' posters on healthy habits, started a conversation among staff about different ways to improve well-being and how they could commit to various personal goals.

An ActewAGL Retail Healthier Work champion said:

> Our staff are clearly more engaged now. There are subtle changes everywhere. People keep the office cleaner, they are aware of the environment around them, and they are much more willing to take the initiative and raise health and safety issues with managers. Instead of two leaders promoting safe and healthy behaviours, staff across all levels and teams are leading the way.

In 2019–20 ActewAGL Retail decided to further liven up its practices related to health and safety. The company began a programme called Retail Safety Ninjas! Retail Safety Ninjas are a group of employees championing good health, well-being and safety. Ninjas develop and run activities throughout the year for everyone at the company. For instance, they introduced sun safety education and interactive personal security and safety classes. Ninjas also organize events supporting the local community. In 2019–20 they arranged a trivia night to raise funds for Care Financial, a free counselling programme that supports people experiencing financial difficulty.

Retail Safety Ninjas also promote mental health by running activities for the RUOK? Day. In 2019–20 the company gave away 2-for-1 coffee vouchers. The aim was to encourage colleagues to have coffee with someone else and ask them, RUOK?

Barmco Mana McMurray (BMM)

BMM is an Australian company that offers consulting expertise in projects, commercial buildings, specialized engineering services and related activities within the property and construction industry in ACT and surrounds. BMM has 16 members of staff and tries to embed a commitment to a healthy workplace into the company's culture.

Director Trent Gourgaud says that BMM offers something to everyone, from physical and outdoor activities and a 20-minute daily break for foosball, to six-monthly blood donation and multicultural Fridays.

The company also purchased an e-bike for shared use by colleagues. It can be used to quickly get from one site to another for meetings or to take quick ride during a break.

According to BMM, their management practices help the company keep a healthy workplace and a more positive work environment.

Goodwin Aged Care

Goodwin Aged Care is a community-based, not-for-profit organization that provides Canberra and local communities in Australia with aged care services and accommodation. Goodwin has approximately 540 members of staff. The organization recognizes that the productivity of its employees depends on their well-being.

Turin Prasantha, Executive Manager, said: 'Supporting and looking after their [employees'] well-being is key to our continued ability to serve the health needs of our community and deliver exceptional and consistent care into the future.'

Goodwin offers its employees a mix of activities including on-site yoga, meditation and Staff Appreciation Week. The organization has also been using a wellness calendar for several years and since its introduction there has been a noticeable improvement in staff morale. Moreover, as well-being became more and more embedded into the workplace culture employees started to encourage each other to be healthier.

Goodwin offers its employees discounted fruit and vegetables at local markets. It also reimburses staff for products that help them quit smoking (e.g. nicotine patches).

Emma Woods, Well-being and Rehabilitation Advisor at Goodwin Aged Care, explains: 'It's best to start small with your activities, and then as staff become more engaged, gather their ideas and feedback to tailor some of your wellness activities.' Goodwin also suggests that in larger organizations having several champions of well-being helps to encourage colleagues and spread the word about available events and programmes.

Coordination of activities can be challenging. 'A lot of our employees work across a 24/7 roster, so aligning events and activities so that all employees have a chance to participate can be difficult', said Emma. For this reason, when Goodwin organizes workshops, they schedule more than one session and on more than one day to give more employees a chance to attend them.

The Goodwin management team leads by example. They are positive and open to different new wellness initiatives and projects. 'Our well-being at work strategy guides all aspects of wellness at Goodwin, (…) our aim is to have a team of the most talented and committed people', said Turin.

Questions

1   Discuss examples of health and well-being practices from ActewAGL Retail, BMM and Goodwin Aged Care. In your estimation would employees from these organizations be likely to view their employer as caring for health and well-being?

2   What do you think could be the benefits of successful health and well-being practices used by ActewAGL Retail, BMM and Goodwin?

3   Imagine you are an HR manager at a small company with 80 employees. You have been asked by the director to lead a project that is meant to update the company's health and well-being practices. The manager mentioned that one more person will help you with your task. What are the main steps that you would take to successfully deliver the project?

Sources

www.healthierwork.act.gov.au/wp-content/uploads/2020/06/ACT-Government-Healthier-Work-2019-2020-Case-Study-Booklet-web.pdf

www.healthierwork.act.gov.au/wp-content/uploads/2019/06/Healthier-Work-Case-Study-Book-2018-19-for-website.pdf

www.healthierwork.act.gov.au/wp-content/uploads/2015/01/Healthier-Work-2017-18-ACCESSIBLE.pdf

www.accesscanberra.act.gov.au/s/article/healthier-work-tab-overview

HR meets organizational green policy

According to Ramasamy et al (2017), for successful GHRM implementation organizations need to assess their existing green policies and what they try to achieve. This involves collection of information on present environmental guidelines, but also gathering of any relevant data on offered products and services. The process will require approval from senior management, as well as support from other internal stakeholders. The team responsible for collecting the information would most likely include members from different functions. HR should be a part of this process and feed information on how we can use people management to promote green employee behaviours and green culture. The team should also form (or revise) a green strategy.

Alternatively, HR can take a lead and create a comprehensive document elaborating the value of green organizations, benefits of green people management and an action plan for introducing changes. The internal understanding of green HRM policies and their potential contribution to organizational goals is a prerequisite for any meaningful attempts at implementing GHRM. This includes educating stakeholders on the benefits of employees engaging in pro-environmental behaviours, green innovation and green culture.

General barriers to sustainable HRM

The practice of HRM is evolving and many organizations are listening intently to their stakeholders' demands for sustainability. Nevertheless, there still exist barriers that stop some employers from changing their people management practices.

Industry barriers

The industry in which we operate can drive sustainability initiatives forward or hinder the transformation of HRM. In the business environment where organizations are competing fiercely for highly skilled staff, employers may outdo each other in practices to attract, motivate and retain. Many employers will be more persuadable to introduce social and environmental sustainability practices; this in turn will put pressure on other players in the industry to follow the trend.

Conversely, in an industry where unsustainable practices are deeply rooted into organizational logic there can be competitive pressure that creates a barrier for changing HRM. Mariappanadar (2019) used the example of Australian chains of convenience stores and the fuel retailing industry. In this context many organizations were reported to be underpaying and overworking staff. Concern for cost and avoidance of potential competitive disadvantage creates a barrier for sustainable HRM.

However, organizations can disrupt industry practices. Instead of conforming to the established short-term irresponsible methods employers can take a lead and develop new practices or introduce adjustments to their HRM. In this case, breaking away from the industry rules corresponds with the interest of local communities, employees, investors and government regulators. Thus, overcoming negative industry norms can mean getting ahead of the competition (Mariappanadar, 2019).

Empty rhetoric

There is an ongoing public debate about the negative impact of organizations' short-term profit maximization at the expense of basic employee rights and environmental destruction. As a result, consumers put pressure on brands to engage in societal issues. According to the Edelman's 2020 report, which examined brand trust in 11 countries, 80 per cent of respondents wanted brands to 'solve society's problems'. In the 2021 version of the survey 86 per cent of participants felt that CEOs must publicly speak out about societal challenges (Edelman, 2020, 2021). This forces organizational leaders to *say* that they care or that they are *trying* to address pressing issues of sustainability. However, these intentions, which are often publicly announced, do not always match the practice.

According to the Accenture (2021) report on 'Business Futures', 'For 43 per cent of 521 of the world's largest companies, their ability to deliver multi-dimensional value does not match their intent.'

Accenture called this the 'intention-delivery' gap. Many executives show an understanding of how their organizations should engage in sustainable and responsible practices. Nonetheless, they struggle to put the intentions into practice. Accenture predicts that in the future organizations will face even more pressure to demonstrate results behind their sustainability pledges. There is a growing trend for stakeholders to hold employers accountable for their social and environmental impact. Organizations that *purposely fail* to produce sustainable results will struggle to maintain good relationships with their stakeholders.

Complexity

Sustainability expands HRM, but it can also add complexity. Balancing the long- and short-term perspectives requires initial increased effort. Planning, monitoring and evaluating effective interventions, to improve work–life balance, for example, means investing time and resources. Not to mention that the environmental dimension is something new to the practice of people management. Green HRM entails working across departments and gaining better understanding of how the organization affects the environment. To achieve results, isolated activities will not be enough. At the same time, integrated multi-level changes can be demanding to design and approve. A well-incorporated sustainable approach means handling internal intricacies and the trouble of managing external relationships.

However, overcoming the complexity of sustainable HRM can be a source of competitive advantage. Organizations that manage to introduce new proactive HRM may be better positioned to tackle future demands. Breaking the status quo is difficult. But private companies that spend time on examining the trends and complexities involved in sustainability can gain a lead over competitors. At the same time, public and voluntary organizations that tackle the added difficulty of sustainability are better positioned to serve their stakeholders.

Misconceptions

Sustainability is a relatively well-known term. Most employers should be familiar with it, but they may not be fully informed on the subject. When organizations and their members do not have a clear understanding of the topic this can create false impressions and perceptual barriers against sustainable HRM. Therefore, HR should be aware of common misconceptions and be ready to correct them.

First, there is a common misunderstanding that sustainability is just about the natural environment and has little to do with HRM. While the green aspect is crucial, it is only one of the three main elements of sustainability. Social and economic/business goals constitute the remaining two pillars. As discussed in Chapters 4, 5 and 6, HRM is perfectly positioned to help organizations work towards sustainability in all three dimensions.

Second, some organizations may see sustainable HRM as a passing trend. In this scenario executives may hesitate to approve more responsible HRM practices because they may think that these initiatives are based on a new fad that will die out. However, sustainable HRM has long roots in attempts to make people management more focused on employees' needs. It is related to well-established debates of re-humanizing work (De Prins et al, 2014). Business trends also suggest that sustainability will become more relevant in the near future. According to Bloomberg Intelligence, between 2018 and 2022, investment in ESG companies has grown from $30.6 trillion to $41.0 trillion and it is expected that in 2025 it will exceed $50 trillion (Tattersall, 2022). ESG stands for environmental, social and governance. It is an acronym used to represent companies that engage in sustainable operations. With high interest from investors and customers, sustainable management can continue to develop.

Third, some managers may believe that only large businesses can adopt sustainable HRM. Operations that are socially and environmentally responsible could be seen as a luxury that is out of reach for small and medium-sized organizations. For smaller organizations with limited financial and technological resources, 'people are their business' (CIPD, 2012). However, this only highlights the importance of implementing practices that recognize stakeholders' concerns. For example, when an organization relies on a small number of staff, retaining them by provision of decent-quality employment is critical. Similarly, if an SME depends on the support of a local community, or a small number of big clients (e.g. government agencies or other businesses), it may need to demonstrate that its operations are environmentally friendly. Harney and Dundon (2006) pointed out that 'the extent of formalization of HRM should not be seen to be indicative of the substance of HRM'. Smaller organizations do not need an elaborately written strategy to introduce sustainable HRM practices that will improve motivation and retention of staff. Regardless of the size of the company, staff induction and training can include discussions about more efficient use of energy and resources. Smaller businesses can still encourage their team to use more sustainable forms of work commute. This can be done by providing information on local car- and bike-share schemes and incentivizing employees with symbolic rewards for sustainable transport and other eco-friendly behaviours. Smaller companies often depend on being resourceful and creative, which sustainability promotes and enables.

Moreover, sustainable HRM is not limited to businesses. Public- and voluntary-sector organizations are important employers who are responsible for managing their staff in a sustainable manner. Due to their social goals, public and voluntary organizations are often expected to operate on even stricter accountability standards than businesses.

Skill check

Analysing barriers to sustainable HRM. To successfully implement sustainable programmes, policies and initiatives you need to be able to identify potential barriers that could stop or limit the approaches you want to introduce.

Understanding employees' roles and perspectives

The new approach depends on active contributions and involvement in the decision-making process from non-managerial staff. At the same time, we need to recognize that employees are not a homogenous group. HR professionals work with pluralist workforces in complex social relationships that extend beyond simple transactional exchanges (Nuis et al, 2021).

Even though collectively staff represent 'a key stakeholder', they hold various interests. Podgorodnichenko et al (2022) identified three main roles that employees play in relation to sustainable HRM: a) employees as a driving force for sustainability, b) employees as consumers of HR practices, and c) employees as members of a community. The researchers argued that sustainability is strongly integrated in HRM only in organizations where policies and practices attempted to simultaneously address all three employee roles. The study was based on 35 interviews with HR managers from New Zealand and Australia.

Employees as a driving force for sustainability. From the perspective of HR, it is perhaps easiest to recognize employees as a group whose engagement we need to mobilize to effectively introduce different policies and practices. This also applies to sustainable HRM. Professionals in people management will use, for example, internal communication, reward management and volunteering activities to get employees on board with sustainability initiatives. Employees are a group who turn ideas into practice and HR has many tools to facilitate that.

Employees as consumers of HR practices. Unlike typical strategic HRM, the sustainable approach pays equal attention to the staff's second role – namely, employees are targets of concern for sustainable HRM. The new approach places employees' needs at the heart of its policies. It means thinking about the implications of practices on staff and their interests. When developing and introducing HRM programmes it is possible to overemphasize the business goals and neglect our responsibilities towards employees as individuals. HRM initiatives need to take into account employees' well-being and development, rather than simply seeing staff as a means to an end.

Employees as members of a community. Employees as stakeholders also represent the interests of a local community. Podgorodnichenko et al (2022) explained: 'Some participants argued that as employees are embedded in their communities, HRM could develop policies and practices that create value beyond organizational boundaries and may address social issues (e.g. family violence, lack of literacy and numeracy skills, ageing generations).' HR practices such as diversity and inclusion or supporting employee well-being have a positive impact on local communities where the organization is based. Employers can make a conscious effort to recruit staff locally or work in partnership with charities and educational institutions to develop competencies of members who belong to underrepresented groups. Employees who personally benefit from these and similar initiatives are more likely to feel engaged with their work. Even employees who do not directly benefit from these actions can be more enthusiastic about their organization. Seeing how the employer gives back to the community adds additional meaning to their work (Rupp et al, 2018).

Implementation of sustainable HRM requires a consideration of at least three roles that employees play. The interests of employees as individuals and members of a community do not always align with the immediate goals of the organization. Thus, sustainable HMR needs to recognize the plurality of interests and cope with potential dilemmas and tensions (Ehnert, 2009). In real-world scenarios this often means 'educating employees about organizational needs and objectives as well as educating their organizations about the needs of employees as individuals and community members' (Podgorodnichenko et al, 2022).

According to Van Buren III (2022), for organizations to move towards more sustainable HRM we need to consider the following questions.

- Who defines 'sustainability'? In relationships between the employer and employees, who determines what sustainable practices and policies are and how?
- What input do employees have in discussions and decisions about sustainable HRM?
- To what extent is data and information provided by employees taken into account?
- How does the new HRM approach discuss and balance social, environmental and business sustainability?

Van Buren III (2022) highlights that if management's definition and under-standing of sustainability is different to that of employees then organizations can find it difficult to implement sustainable HRM initiatives. What is more, fundamental disagreement between managers and employees on the subject of sustainability can worsen employment relations. If employees' perspectives are not taken into account, HRM will be sustainable only on paper. For ex-ample, imagine a situation where staff are already frustrated and disenchanted with their work because of long working hours, being understaffed, continual cost savings and high levels of stress. Having heard the previous rhetoric of 'empowering staff', which turned out to be excessive work intensification, the team is already cynical and does not trust management initiatives (see, for example, Cartwright and Holmes, 2006). In these circumstances sustainable practices that do not take into account the employees' perspective might not only fail; seen as an additional burden, play-acting false sustainable initiatives can negatively impact already fragile employee-employer relationships.

One of the ways through which employees voice their interests is trade unions. Trade unions have a long history of defending employees' rights and fighting for better working conditions. As such, they are an important stake-holder for sustainable HRM (Richards, 2022). Working with trade unions is one of the obvious ways to include employee representation in the discussion about sustainability. Partnerships with trade unions can strengthen HRM policies. At the same time, rejection of employee voice and representation resembles traditional strategic HRM 'where the mechanisms of employee voice are primarily instituted to improve organizational performance rather than to achieve other social or human outcomes' (Gutiérrez Crocco and Martin, 2022). Trade unions help to identify and confront unsustainable HRM practices that individual employees may not be able to voice during their employment contract (Macini et al, 2022).

Summary

In this chapter we looked in more depth at the implementation of sustainable HRM. We discussed the importance of developing a sustainability mindset among organizational leaders. This is related to educating management about the state of environmental and social issues and how these are connected to the organizations the leaders run. The framework of a sustainability mindset un-derscores the value of integrating more ethical discussions in wider management education. But it also forces us to think about the language and logic that organizations use to present the case for sustainability. One of the tools we can use to change leaders' mindset is a clearly structured rationale, for example, in the form of a written business case. This is an opportunity for HR professionals to show initiative and take charge of planning more sustainable practices and policies. Whether there already is a clear owner of a sustainability agenda, or there is an opening for someone to step up and take charge, HR needs to gain visibility in this area and prove that it is a critical partner in making the organization more sustainable.

The chapter explained that the new approach involves a considerable number of skills. Not only does it require the HR staff to develop new competencies, but it also necessitates new capabilities among the managers. Many of the HRM responsibilities are carried out by line managers (e.g. employee selection or performance management). While HR can introduce new sustainability policies they will not be effective unless supervisors who run day-to-day operations support them.

In addition to navigating the social, environmental and business objectives, sustainable HRM means balancing management and employee perspectives. Engaging multiple stakeholders is hard and at times it can test our patience. Championing sustainable practices requires perseverance and professional courage.

One of the elements of implementing the new approach is measuring and reporting sustainable HRM efforts. This is a topic that deserves its own separate discussion in the next chapter.

Study questions

1 What is a sustainability mindset and why is it important in the practice of sustainable HRM?

2 Does implementation of sustainable HRM require a business case? Discuss.

3 In what ways does sustainable HRM expand and evolve the role of HR?

4 What leadership capabilities does an organization need to develop in order to effectively introduce sustainable HRM?

5 Discuss the key skills HR professionals need for implementation of sustainable HRM.

6 What are some of the common misconceptions about sustainable HRM?

7 Discuss whether it is possible to introduce sustainable HRM without consulting employees.

Key reading

Accenture (2021) Business futures 2021, signals of change, the essential radar that leaders need to see and seize the future, www.accenture.com/us-en/insights/consulting/business-change

Podgorodnichenko, N, Akmal, A, Edgar, F and Everett, A M (2022) Sustainable HRM: toward addressing diverse employee roles, *Employee Relations*, **44** (3), pp 576–608

Ramasamy, A (2017) A study on implications of implementing green HRM in the corporate bodies with special reference to developing nations, *International Journal of Business and Management*, **12** (9), pp 117–29

References

Accenture (2021) Business futures 2021, signals of change, the essential radar that leaders need to see and seize the future, www.accenture.com/us-en/insights/consulting/business-change (archived at https://perma.cc/9DCV-VAND)

BBC (2021) Amazon apologises for wrongly denying drivers need to urinate in bottles, www.bbc.com/news/world-us-canada-56628745 (archived at https://perma.cc/5PZ2-TXA7)

Budhiraja, S and Yadav, S (2020) Employer branding and employee-emotional bonding—the CSR way to sustainable HRM. In S Vanka, M B Rao, S Singh, M and Rao Pulaparthi (eds.) *Sustainable human resource management, transforming organizations, societies and environment* (pp 133–49), Springer, Singapore

Cartwright, S and Holmes, N (2006) The meaning of work: the challenge of regaining employee engagement and reducing cynicism, *Human Resource Management Review*, **16** (2), pp 199–208

Center for Climate and Energy Solutions (2015) Best practices in sustainability engagement, www.c2es.org/wp-content/uploads/2017/10/C2ES-Best-Practices-Sustainability-Engagement.pdf (archived at https://perma.cc/23PN-L6C3)

CIPD (2012) Achieving sustainable organization performance through HR in SMEs, www.cipd.asia/Images/achieving-sustainable-organisation-performance-through-hr-in-smes_2012-research-insight_tcm23-9103.pdf (archived at https://perma.cc/9BL8-2CW)

CIPD (2022) Core behaviours. Professional courage and influence, showing courage to speak up and skilfully influencing others to gain buy-in, https://peopleprofession.cipd.org/profession-map/core-behaviours/professional-courage-influence (archived at https://perma.cc/4PRP-Y6J6)

De Prins, P, Van Beirendonck, L, De Vos, A and Segers, J (2014) Sustainable HRM: bridging theory and practice through the 'Respect Openness Continuity (ROC)'-model, *Management Revue*, **25** (4), pp 263–84

Edelman (2020) Edelman Trust barometer special report: brand trust in 2020, www.edelman.com/research/brand-trust-2020 (archived at https://perma.cc/LDK8-2NH5)

Edelman (2021) 2021 Edelman Trust barometer, www.edelman.com/trust/2021-trust-barometer (archived at https://perma.cc/7VDQ-PEUS)

Ehnert, I (2009) *Sustainable Human Resource Management: A conceptual and exploratory analysis from a paradox perspective*, Physica-Verlag, Berlin/Heidelberg, Germany

Gloet, M (2006) Knowledge management and the links to HRM: developing leadership and management capabilities to support sustainability, *Management Research News*, **29** (7), pp 402–13

Guerci, M, Decramer, A, Van Waeyenberg, T and Aust, I (2019) Moving beyond the link between HRM and economic performance: a study on the individual reactions of HR managers and professionals to sustainable HRM, *Journal of Business Ethics*, **160** (3), pp 783–800

Gutiérrez Crocco, F and Martin, A (2022) Towards a sustainable HRM in Latin America? Union-management relationship in Chile, *Employee Relations*, **44** (3), pp 650–62

Harney, B and Dundon, T (2006) Capturing complexity: developing an integrated approach to analysing HRM in SMEs, *Human Resource Management Journal*, **16** (1), pp 48–73

Hoeppe, J C (2014) Practitioner's view on Sustainability and HRM. In I Ehnert, W Harry and K J Zink (eds.) *Sustainability and Human Resource Management: Developing sustainable business organizations* (pp 273–94), Springer, Berlin/Heidelberg, Germany

Kassel, K, Rimanoczy, I and Mitchell, S F (2016) The sustainable mindset: connecting being, thinking and doing in management education. In *Academy of Management Proceedings*, 2016 (1), pp 16659, Academy of Management, Briarcliff Manor, NY

Kramar, R (2022) Sustainable human resource management: six defining characteristics, *Asia Pacific Journal of Human Resources*, **60** (1), pp 146–70

Macini, N, Fernandes Rodrigues Alves, M, Oranges Cezarino, L, Bartocci Liboni, L and Cristina Ferreira Caldana, A (2022) Beyond money and reputation: sustainable HRM in Brazilian banks, *Employee Relations*, **44** (3), pp 702–28

Mariappanadar, S (2019) Implementing sustainable HRM practices. In S Mariappanadar (ed.) *Sustainable Human Resource Management: Strategies, practices and challenges* (pp 157–87), Red Globe Press, London

Mayberry, E (2008) How to build an HR business case, society for human resource management, www.shrm.org/resourcesandtools/hr-topics/behavioral-competencies/leadership-and-navigation/pages/businesscase.aspx (archived at https://perma.cc/4KTM-MYSF)

Mishra, R K and Sarkar, S (2020) Sustainable HRM practices – a drive towards sustainability (The case of NLCIL). In S Vanka, M B Rao, S Singh and M Rao Pulaparthi (eds.) *Sustainable Human Resource Management: Transforming organizations, societies and environment* (pp 183–96), Springer, Singapore

Nuis, J W, Peters, P, Blomme, R and Kievit, H (2021) Dialogues in sustainable HRM: examining and positioning intended and continuous dialogue in sustainable HRM using a complexity thinking approach, *Sustainability*, **13** (19), p 10853

Owen, C L (2020) *Sustainable HRM: A how-to-guide*, University of Michigan School for Environment and Sustainability

Paulet, R, Holland, P and Bratton, A (2021) Employee voice: the missing factor in sustainable HRM? *Sustainability*, **13** (17), p 9732

Podgorodnichenko, N, Akmal, A, Edgar, F and Everett, A M (2022) Sustainable HRM: toward addressing diverse employee roles, *Employee Relations*, **44** (3), pp 576–608

Ramasamy, A, Inore, I and Sauna, R (2017) A study on implications of implementing green HRM in the corporate bodies with special reference to developing nations, *International Journal of Business and Management*, **12** (9), pp 117–29

Richards, J (2022) Putting employees at the centre of sustainable HRM: a review, map and research agenda, *Employee Relations*, **44** (3), pp 533–54

Rimanoczy, I B (2010) *Business Leaders Committing to and Fostering Sustainability Initiatives* [PhD thesis], Teachers College, Columbia University, New York

Rimanoczy, I B (2019) Personal development toward a sustainability mindset. In R R Sharma (ed.) *Human Resource Management for Organizational Sustainability* (pp 19–32), Business Expert Press, New York

Rupp, D E, Shao, R, Skarlicki, D P, Paddock, E L, Kim, T Y and Nadisic, T (2018) Corporate social responsibility and employee engagement: the moderating role of CSR-specific relative autonomy and individualism, *Journal of Organizational Behavior*, **39** (5), pp 559–79

SHRM (2011) *Advancing Sustainability: HR's role. A research report by the society for human resource management, BSR and Aurosoorya*, SHRM, Alexandria, VA

Tattersall, M (2022) The rise of ESG investing, how investment managers can seize a $50 trillion AUM opportunity, www.emarketer.com/content/rise-of-esg-investing (archived at https://perma.cc/P2SZ-55PF)

Van Buren III, H J (2022) The value of including employees: a pluralist perspective on sustainable HRM, *Employee Relations*, **44** (3), pp 686–701

Vere, D and Butler, L (2007) *Fit For Business: Transforming HR in the public service*, CIPD, London

Volkswagen AG (2022) Sustainability council, https://cw.volkswagenag.com/en/sustainability/strategy-policy-engagement/engagement/sustainability-council.html (archived at https://perma.cc/QN7Y-4YU7)

Measuring and reporting sustainable HRM

8

LEARNING OBJECTIVES

After completing this chapter, you should be able to:

- Identify key measures for the social sustainability of HRM.
- Identify key measures for the environmental sustainability of HRM.
- Identify key measures for the business sustainability of HRM.
- Explain the difference between international sustainability reporting standards, frameworks and indices.
- Explain international sustainability reporting standards provided by the Global Reporting Initiative and the International Organization for Standardization.
- Explain the international sustainability framework promoted by the Sustainable Development Goals.
- Identify organizations that combine international sustainability standards and frameworks.
- Critically discuss the system of international sustainability standards and frameworks.
- Understand what international sustainability indices are and critically evaluate them.
- Discuss examples of leading international sustainability indices.

Introduction

Improving sustainability requires transparency. Without relevant and accurate knowledge on what the organization does, stakeholders may not be able to support it. Openness about financial and non-financial performance is crucial for building trust. This in turn is needed for maintaining positive relationships with the stakeholders. With increased pressure from different interest groups (customers, employees, government, investors) organizational transparency is often seen as a necessity (Crane et al, 2019).

One of the ways in which organizations can improve their openness is by monitoring and then internally and externally reporting key information. Different models, indicators and guides have been developed to measure sustainability efforts. Although sustainable HRM is a relatively new field it draws from domains of CSR, psychology, economics, environmental and medical research. Thus, there are many tools we can use to measure sustainability of people management. In fact, the amount of choice can be disorienting. What further complicates the matter is a broad landscape of international sustainability standards. The aim of this chapter is to help you organize your knowledge on common measuring and reporting methods useful for sustainable HRM.

Assessment of sustainability performance is needed for transparency, but it is also about achieving organizational effectiveness and solving problems. Which of our current practices are unsustainable and require our increased attention? What risks is our organization currently facing in relation to HRM? Are we meeting targets for our sustainable strategy? How impactful are the changes we introduce to people management? These are all valid questions that the management will be able to address if it decides to evaluate sustainable HRM performance.

This chapter first looks at measures proposed by the academic and practitioner community. We will discuss measures for monitoring employee health, work engagement and green behaviours. We will also explain how metrics commonly adopted by HR professionals can be used to assess sustainability. Then we will examine international sustainability standards, frameworks and indices. They provide even wider guidelines, covering issues from monitoring child labour to supplier environmental assessment. They also set global best practices for sustainable HRM.

Multi-dimensionality and multi-purposiveness of measures

Sustainable HRM is a complex practice. Each of its three pillars opens opportunities for different objectives and thus a variety of measurement options. Mariappanadar (2019) even goes as far as to say that using a single measure in such a multifaceted domain would be 'inappropriate and inadequate'.

To help navigate different types of available measures, the discussion below is divided into three main groups of instruments:

1 Measures focusing on the social dimension

2 Measures focusing on the environmental dimension

3 Measures focusing on the business dimension

Note that this separation of assessment methods is introduced for didactical purposes. Some of the measures collect information on practices that represent a combination of social, environmental and business sustainability.

The discussion below covers tools that were developed with the intended use for academia, practice or a combination of the two.

Measures focusing on the social dimension

Employment quality

One of the ways to measure social sustainability of HRM practices is to evaluate the overall quality of employment experience. The work environment and everyday duties that employees perform have a direct impact on staff well-being and their social relationships. Methods representing this approach explore employees' perceptions regarding the standard of work-related aspects.

Work-Related Quality of Life Scale (WRQoL)

This is a broad measure examining individuals' work experience. Van Laar et al (2007) developed a 23-item WRQoL questionnaire that focuses on six psychosocial subfactors:

1 general well-being

2 home–work interface

3 job and career satisfaction

4 control at work

5 working conditions

6 stress at work

The measure demonstrates excellent reliability. This means it consistently measures what it is supposed to measure. It was successfully tested in studies of the UK higher education industry (Edwards et al, 2009), Malaysian public health sector (Chen et al, 2014) and Iranian occupational therapists (Rostami et al, 2021). It was adopted in research in more than 45 countries (QoWL, 2022a). The tool was designed to be applicable in a wide range of national and industrial contexts.

The questionnaire used for this measure is concise. It fits on a single page. Easton and Van Laar (2018) have also prepared a comprehensive user manual for the tool. The WRQoL scale is free to use for non-commercial, educational or research purposes, but profit-making organizations have to request permission to use it (QoWL, 2022b).

The measure developed by Van Laar et al (2007) is only one of several versions of work quality assessment. Other examples include:

- Quality of Work Life Scale (QWLS) (Sirgy et al, 2001)
- Quality of Work Life Questionnaire (Elizur and Shye, 1990)
- Quality of Working Life Systemic Inventory (Martel and Dupuis, 2006)

There is an extensive amount of research showing a link between quality of working life and benefits for employees and employers. High scores are linked with more motivated staff, reduced absenteeism and lower personnel turnover (see e.g. Jabeen et al, 2018). At the same time, low quality of work life is associated with higher risks of anxiety and burnout, which are known to lower employees' performance and increase organizational costs (Leitão et al, 2021).

WORKSHOP DISCUSSION 7

Somerset County Council

Somerset County Council (from here on the Council) is the county council of Somerset in the south west of England. The Council is a large public-sector employer responsible for functions and services ranging from education (e.g. schools), social services, managing roads and transport to waste disposal.

In 2001 the Council hired a team of experts to conduct a Quality of Working Life (QWL) audit. The aim of the QWL assessment was to focus on the psychological risks of employees' work, specifically stress.

The Council wanted to identify how it could lower high levels of absence from work and the associated costs. In 2001/02 the Council estimated that it lost approximately 10.75 full-time-equivalent (FTE) working days per one FTE employee, due to sickness absence. This cost the Council around £677 per FTE employee and resulted in an estimated total annual loss of £7.4 million due to health-related absence. Each day of reduced average annual sick leave would allow the Council to save north of £750,000. What's more, the Council's average annual sick leave was significantly above the government's targets for local authorities (9.1 days). The Council was eager to act and meet the target within the five-year time frame provided by the government.

In addition, during this time county councils were targets of stress-related litigation. Public-sector workers, such as social services employees and teachers, were taking their employers to court for excessive workplace stress. The Council had a history of such legal actions and wanted to take more proactive steps in addressing the psychosocial risks at work.

The initiative of the QWL audit was also supported by trades unions and elected members within the Council. The stakeholders agreed that the council should aim for excellent work performance but not at the expense of its people's well-being.

The audit gave employees a chance to provide information about their well-being at work and report on elements of their work environment which they believe had a negative impact on their overall quality of working life. The data collection then allowed planning of necessary recommendations and solutions. The audit also informed the employer on how it was performing in terms of QWL compared to other organizations.

As a part of the QWL audit, 14,000 questionnaires were distributed, and 6,500 employees returned completed forms. The quantitative data was supplemented with focus groups and one-to-one interviews which were carried out between November 2001 and January 2002. The data was analysed, then reported in the form of a written summary and a presentation for key stakeholders.

The audit identified these main causes of stress at work:

- unmanageable workloads
- organizational change
- threat of and actual violence/verbal abuse at work
- challenges related to information technology

After receiving the audit results the Council formed a QWL Project Team. The team was chaired by a senior HR manager and included HR managers from different directorates of the council (Economy, Transport & Environment, Social Services, Education), a health and safety manager, a training and development manager, and trade union representatives. The objective of the team was to develop an action plan based on the audit's results. The team took a participative approach in designing the proposed interventions to ensure that the actions were as realistic and as relevant to the organization as possible. Management groups and staff across departments were consulted. The goal was to collect appropriate information and also give staff a chance to be a part of the decision-making process. The assumption was that the consultative approach to planning would also help to promote the QWL project and minimize any potential resistance against proposed changes.

The main interventions taken by the Council included the introduction of:

- Guidelines for managers on proactive approaches to stress management, including instructions on what can be done to avoid stress and how to alleviate increased levels of stress.
- Practical training sessions for managers on limiting staff's and their own stress.
- A training course developed for the executive board of the council.
- Updated guidelines for managers on performance review.
- Training for managers on the updated performance review system.
- Training for staff explaining the updated performance review system.
- Training for managers on sickness absence management, explaining the compassionate approach to managing employees' sickness and their return to work. The training highlights the importance of finding out if the organization contributed in any way to the employees' poor health.
- A presentation for senior managers on linking stress and sickness absence.
- Training for managers related to equality and diversity.
- A pamphlet for all staff about the QWL audit, its results and planned actions.
- A pamphlet for all staff about stress management.
- Training for staff who interface with the public on how to deal with and prevent harmful episodes.
- An independent and confidential counselling service available 24 hours a day by telephone or face to face.

- 'Listeners service' – an internal confidential support service where trained listeners help employees cope with experiences of mistreatment at work.

Most of the action points were funded from existing resources but in 2003/04 and 2004/05 additional funds of £100,000 and £160,000 were allocated to further support specific interventions.

The QWL audit was undertaken between the end of 2001 and the beginning of 2002. The action plan and funding were approved by Spring 2003. In 2003/04 the annual average FTE days lost to sickness absence was 8.29 and in 2004/05 it was 7.2 days. The saving related to reduced sickness absence levels was approximately £1.57 million. The cost/benefit analysis showed a net saving of over £1 million.

Questions

1 What were the main drivers for conducting a QWL audit at Somerset County Council?

2 Consider your own or your friends' experiences of stress at work. What is it that you or your friends find stressful about work? How similar or different are your experiences to the identified main causes of stress at Somerset County Council?

3 Critically examine the list of main interventions taken as a result of the audit. Can you identify any actions useful in stress management that could be missing from the list?

Sources

Adapted from Tasho, W, Jordan, J and Robertson, I (2005) Case study: Establishing the business case for investing in stress prevention activities and evaluating their impact on sickness absence levels, HSE Books, www.hse.gov.uk/research/rrpdf/rr295.pdf

Easton, S and Van Laar, D (2018) User manual for the Work-Related Quality of Life (WRQoL) Scale: a measure of quality of working life, University of Portsmouth

CIPD Good Work Index

Every year CIPD conducts a survey that is a 'snapshot of job quality in the UK' (CIPD, 2022). The CIPD Good Work Index measures seven main factors of job quality:

- pay and benefits
- employment contracts
- work–life balance

- job design and the nature of work
- relationships at work
- employee voice
- health and well-being

These seven dimensions are based on 18 sub-indices (e.g. subjective pay, pensions, benefits) which are examined with a series of questions. Overall, the CIPD Good Work Index consists of 95 survey items.

CIPD uses this index to present the overall picture of work quality in the UK. However, with CIPD's permission (and/or permission of any other required parties) individual employers might be able to adapt the structure and questions from the survey. An additional benefit of this measure is that after an organization collects its data internally it can compare its results against the national scores published on the CIPD website.

Based on the internal survey results organizations can plan and introduce initiatives aiming to improve employees' work experience. For example, imagine that the survey findings indicate that a majority of your employees poorly assess their working relationships with line managers. As an employer, you may want to focus on this issue, collect more data and prepare an adequate training programme for line managers.

Health management

Some measures focus specifically on collecting data related to employees' health. Staff well-being is an important indicator of how socially sustainable people management is. According to the World Health Organization (WHO), we can identify three main domains of health and well-being: physical, mental and social. Measures used to monitor employees' health cover one or more of those areas.

Affective well-being at work

This is an example of a measure that focuses specifically on employees' psychological health. The frequency and intensity with which people experience positive or negative feelings is one of the key indicators of mental well-being. Daniels (2000) developed a version of this measure which consists of 30 items and examines five factors:

- anxiety–comfort
- depression–pleasure

- bored–enthusiastic
- tiredness–vigour
- angry–placid

In this tool respondents are asked a question: 'Thinking of the past week, how much of the time has your job made you feel each of the following?' (Daniels, 2000). Then on a scale of 1 to 6 they need to rate how often they felt anxious, cheerful, active, aggressive, patient, etc. Daniels and Harris (2005) also created a shorter version of the measure which consists of only 10 items.

The measure can be used, for example, to assess the effects of a job redesign or other major changes in the work environment. Employees' affection can be evaluated before and after modifications were introduced.

PROWELL workplace health and well-being

This is a workplace analytic platform for practitioners that uses a combination of measures to assess health and well-being performance in a workplace. The tool was developed by the Innovative Workplace Institute (IWI) in collaboration with industry leaders from workplace design, management and strategy, as well as researchers in health and well-being (Lee and Aletta, 2019). It examines all three aspects of health and well-being, i.e. physical, mental and social. More specifically it assesses these seven dimensions:

- physical fitness
- physical comfort
- physical nourishment
- cognitive well-being
- emotional well-being
- social well-being
- environmental well-being

The tool exists in a free form that analyses workplace health and well-being performance 'in an instantaneous manner, informing practitioners of already enhanced features as well as features to be improved in the workplace being assessed' (Lee and Aletta, 2019). IWI also offers PROWELL PLUS, which includes additional features such as analysis of workplace health and well-being scores in relation to organizational performance and customized recommendations for individual employers (IWI, 2022).

Positive psychological states

Some measures focus on selected positive psychological states, such as employees' capacity and willingness to invest energy into their work. For example, Xu et al (2020) argued that employee work engagement can be used as a 'leading indicator of turnover intention and an early diagnostic tool for sustainable human resource management.'

Gallup's employee engagement survey Q^{12}

One of the most popular measures in the domain of employee engagement was established by Gallup, Inc. in 1998 (Schaufeli and Bakker, 2010). Based on decades of research the company developed a tool called 'Q^{12}' which, as the name suggests, includes 12 survey items. Q^{12} was administered to more than 7 million employees from more than 100 countries (Harter et al, 2006) and over 50 different industries (Gallup, 2022). The Q^{12} was designed to be practical and provide insights that are actionable. It provides information related to four main levels of engagement:

- basic needs
- individual contribution
- teamwork
- growth

Utrecht Work Engagement Scale (UWES)

This is another popular measure assessing employee engagement. UWES was developed by Schaufeli and colleagues (2002) and in its original form it consisted of 17 items that were psychometrically validated. UWES looks at three dimensions:

- vigour
- dedication
- absorption

The initial measure was translated into 31 languages and has been altered into multiple shorter versions (e.g. UWES-15, UWES-9) including the ultra-short UWES-3 which consists of only three survey items (Merino-Soto et al, 2022).

Employee engagement has been linked to positive strategic organizational outcomes. For example, by increasing engagement Caterpillar managed to generate $8.8 million annual savings in one plant from reduced attrition, absenteeism and overtime. Another company, Molson Coors, found that their highly engaged employees were five times less likely to have a safety incident than disengaged employees. Moreover, safety incidents of disengaged employees were on average six times more costly than safety incidents of highly engaged staff (Vance, 2006).

Thriving at work

This is another positive psychological state that has been linked to sustained performance of employees. ***Thriving at work*** means experiencing a sense of vitality and learning (Spreitzer et al, 2005). Porath et al (2012) developed a 10-item measure for this construct. It consists of two factors:

- vitality
- learning

Employees flourish at work when they feel both elements. On the one hand they acquire knowledge and skills. On the other hand they feel energized and have a zest for work. Imagine your employees experience professional development, but are depleted of energy. According to Porath et al (2012), this limits the extent to which they thrive. The opposite is also true. If a person has plenty of energy at work yet few opportunities for growth and learning, then this also limits their sense of prospering. Porath et al argued that when we examine 'thriving' as a continuum, rather than a simple yes/no dichotomy, this allows a more detailed understanding of people's experiences (Porath et al, 2012).

Knowing the extent to which employees thrive at work is the first step to improving this psychological state. But why should managers care about this topic? Thriving helps us to resolve issues such as lost productivity due to absenteeism. Prospering employees are less likely to miss work because they are in good health and have high morale. This positively affects organizational performance and reduces staff healthcare costs. When employees score highly on this measure, they also tend to be more committed to their organizations (Walumbwa et al, 2018).

Negative states

Measures that fall into this category prioritize assessment of negative constructs, for example the extent to which work intrudes into our private lives. By assessing negative effects that an organization has on employees, their families and local communities the management team can get closer to planning and developing more sustainable HRM practices.

Social harm of work

This measure examines employees' perceptions of the extent to which work restricts their family life and work–life balance (Mariappanadar and Aust, 2017; Mariappanadar, 2019). The tool includes 14 items and focuses on three main dimensions:

- work–family restrictions
- negative impacts of work–family restrictions
- reduced work–family role facilitation

Organizations that help employees manage their professional and personal responsibilities show their staff that they are valued in their workplace. Better work–life balance and family life help to reduce employees' levels of stress and risk of burnout.

An organizational stress screening tool (ASSET)

This is a comprehensive work-related stress measure. The tool is based on the stress model of Cooper and Marshall (1976). Faragher et al (2004) evaluated the instrument and found that it is psychometrically valid for examining stress. ASSET quantifies the extent to which employees are exposed to common stressors such as:

- work–life balance
- overload
- resources and communication
- work relationships
- job security
- pay and benefits
- control
- aspects of job (working conditions)

The measure includes 37 items but there is also a shorter version of the tool (ASSET Pulse) which has the potential to reliably examine the same number of job stressors but with only 10 items (Johnson et al, 2018). According to the authors of the updated version, ASSET Pulse is as effective in predicting negative outcomes of stress as the original tool. However, the concise format means that the survey is easier and quicker to administer and may result in better response rates. The size of the survey and how long it takes to complete it are important factors to consider, particularly when we collect data from a workforce that could be experiencing excessive amounts of pressure at work (Johnson et al, 2018).

Skill check

Analysis of negative states. The ability to systematically examine employees' negative states is key to maintaining good employee well-being and for developing relevant solutions in cases when staff experience difficulties at work.

Measures focusing on the environmental dimension

Green innovation and creativity

With limited natural and energy sources some organizations may value generation and implementation of new ideas for sustainable products and processes. HRM is key for bringing in, developing and retaining staff with creative talents. In relevant cases employers may wish to measure how successful people management practices are in cultivating green innovation and creativity.

Arici and Uysal (2022) conducted a review of academic literature on this topic and identified 23 main measures. From their comprehensive list of instruments, the two most commonly used were the green creativity scale developed by Chen and Chang (2013) and the green innovation scale developed by Chen et al (2006). *Creativity* is concerned with generation of ideas, and *innovation* captures implementation of ideas.

Green creativity

Chen and Chang (2013) investigated the impact of green dynamic capabilities and green transformational leadership on green product development performance. They found that the first two variables, in a direct and indirect manner, positively impact green product development. The indirect influence is through employees' creativity. As part of their investigation, they developed a popular scale for green creativity which consists of six questionnaire items.

Creativity is the starting point for innovation. Organizations that value environmental performance and development of new green products or practices may want to first measure their employees' green ingenuity. This assessment can be particularly useful when a new sustainability practice is introduced (e.g. green training or a green reward system) and we want to gauge what impact it has on the individuals' or teams' ability to put forward new green solutions.

Green innovation

Chen et al (2006) set out to examine the impact of green innovation on competitive advantage. They collected 232 survey responses from managers working in Taiwanese information and electronics companies. The data suggested that pioneering in green innovation can help companies achieve competitive advantage. Additionally, the authors have prepared two measures of green innovation looking at:

- green product innovation
- green process innovation

Each of the factors is examined with the use of four items. Chen et al (2006) explained that organizations that invest in green innovation can have the 'first mover advantage' in the market. Companies that choose to build their business model around innovation and championing environmental sustainability may find it useful to keep track of green innovation levels.

Green behaviours

Employees can show a range of pro-environmental actions that are valuable to the employer, e.g. recycling, reusing or choosing eco-friendly alternatives. GHRM practices are essential for motivating these and similar pro-environmental actions.

Francoeur et al (2021) reviewed academic literature about green behaviours. They examined 53 papers and identified 22 measurement scales published between 1994 and 2016. The authors compiled all of the data from these tools and created a list of 170 items. The catalogue of survey questions was then divided into the following five categories and 16 subcategories of behaviours (Francoeur et al, 2021):

- **Reducing waste and preserving resources**
  - recycling (21 items)
  - reusing (12 items)
  - reducing (48 items)
- **Avoiding environmental harm**
  - pollution (3 items)
  - monitoring environmental impact (4 items)
- **Working sustainably**
  - choosing responsible alternatives (2 items)
  - creating products and processes (1 item)
  - embracing innovation for sustainability (4 items)
  - performing sustainable daily work (7 items)
- **Influencing others**
  - educating and training (7 items)
  - encouraging and supporting (11 items)
- **Taking initiatives**
  - initiating programmes and policies (17 items)
  - lobbying and activism (4 items)
  - putting environmental interest first (7 items)
  - environmental voice behaviour (9 items)
  - environmental-civism (13 items)

The items summarized by Francoeur et al (2021) represent a combination of measures which target:

- **Individual employees,** e.g. 'at work, I offer ideas for reducing our impact on the environment'.
- **Leaders,** e.g. 'prior to making decisions with environmental implications, I prefer to obtain the opinions of environmental or community groups'.

- **Leaders' assessment of group member behaviour,** rating the extent to which group members are, e.g., 'recycling reusable things in the workplace'.
- **Collective behaviour,** e.g. 'employees do everything they can to protect the environment at work'.

Main GHRM practices

Researchers have also prepared survey scales that examine specific GHRM practices, such as green recruitment. From the existing instruments assessing HRM practices two stand out: one developed by Tang et al (2018) and one created by Shah (2019). Both tools are comprehensive and examine a whole spectrum of GHRM components. However, depending on need, researchers or practitioners can use parts of these measures focusing for example only on assessment of green recruitment or green training (see e.g. Khan and Noorizwan Muktar, 2020).

Survey scale developed by Tang et al (2018)

This measure consists of 18 items covering five main components of GHRM:

- green recruitment and selection
- green training
- green performance management
- green pay and reward
- green involvement

Survey scale developed by Shah (2019)

This measure examines GHRM through 28 items. They cover seven key areas:

- green compensation management
- green health and safety
- green job design
- green labour relations
- green performance management
- green recruitment and selection
- green training and development

Measures focusing on the business dimension

Human capital

The financial and business sustainability of HRM practices can be measured, for example, through the lens of *human capital* (HC). HC can be conceptualized as a theory, concept or a measure. It represents employees' knowledge, skills and abilities (Armstrong and Taylor, 2020). HC was originally developed by economists (Schultz, 1963) but it found its way into organizational studies and HRM.

HC is sometimes used interchangeably with the phrase 'human resources'. However, it helps to think of 'capital' as a term that is narrower than 'resource' (Barney, 2011; Osranek and Zink, 2014a). As mentioned in Chapter 1, *human resources* are all assets and characteristics that people possess and contribute to the organization. This includes human capital and other forms of capital such as *aesthetic capital*, which are employee assets and attributes related to physical attractiveness and presentation.

Osranek and Zink (2014a) proposed to use the perspective of human capital to evaluate the sustainability of HRM practices. According to the authors, two measures of HC stand out: the Saarbruecken formula and the German human potential index.

Saarbruecken formula

This is a formula for calculating HC developed by Scholz, Stein and Bechtel in 2004 at the Saarland University in Saarbruecken, Germany (Scholz et al, 2011). The tool estimates the monetary value of HC. The formula first requires division of employees into categories according to their field of activity and collecting data for each group. Then, the formula factors in the following figures per each employee group:

- number of full-time equivalents
- average market-based salary
- average knowledge 'life-span' (how many years before employees require new training in each job position)
- average length of tenure with the organization
- personnel development costs for the last 12 months
- results of the motivation index

The last factor is a result from a staff survey that examines employees' engagement, loyalty to the organization and the work environment in which they operate. Similar to the other figures, the motivation index result needs to be provided per each previously identified employee group.

The formula considers a combination of the 'hard' data (number of employees, average salary and development costs) and 'soft' data (motivation, loyalty). Rather than simply calculating the cost of the workforce, it attempts to measure the potential to perform and translates it into a monetary value (Osranek and Zink, 2014a).

The formula has been implemented by large corporations such as SAP, TNT Express Germany and Austrian Telecom (Weiskopf and Munro, 2012). When applied in practice it can be turned into a software component and linked with the HR department IT systems (Scholz, 2007).

Human Potential Index (HPI)

This instrument was developed and tested by the Federal Ministry of Labour and Social Affairs in Germany in 2009 (Osranek and Zink, 2014b). It aims to assess an organization's structures and instruments that are suitable for promotion and generation of HC. It considers the work conditions that make HC development possible and reviews their effectiveness in relation to the financial success of the organization. According to Osranek and Zink (2014a), the measure looks at:

- general conditions of work (sector, organization size, legal form);
- value-adding processes (e.g. HR strategy, HR planning and selection, compensation and benefits);
- value-adding instruments of sustainability (e.g. corporate values, work–life balance, equal opportunities and diversity);
- indicators of commitment (motivation, employee retention and innovations);
- variables for economic success (earnings before interest and taxes, overall turnover).

Osranek and Zink (2014a) explained that if 'the Saarbruecken Formula calculates a monetary value for human capital' then 'HPI quantifies activities which can influence the amount of a monetary result'. Moreover, compared to most HC measures the HPI more extensively incorporates employees' interests.

HR metrics examining business performance

Commonly known HR metrics can also be used to measure sustainability of HRM practices. Many of these tools represent a combination of the business and social dimensions, with the environmental aspect usually underrepresented.

Whichever HR metric we use it is important to remember that these basic tools should not be applied in isolation. In order to develop a more sustainable approach the essential HR measures would need to be supplemented with more detailed input from employees. The discussion below shows examples of common HR measurements.

Cost per hire

The average cost of hiring a new employee. The cost per hire can be calculated by adding up all the internal and external costs in money, time and resources invested in hiring during a given period. Then, we divide that figure by the number of new hires. This measure shows how effective the recruitment process is. When making calculations it is important to include all relevant expenses, e.g. role advertisement, recruiter/agency fees, resume screening, background checks, interviews and time invested in selection, onboarding, IT and administrative costs as well as training.

If the cost per hire is high this should not automatically be interpreted as a signal for indiscriminate cost cutting and saving on selection methods or onboarding. Bringing in suitable staff requires initial investment. Having said that, high value in this measure could spark a discussion about areas for improvement. For example, Macmillan Cancer Support moved away from outsourcing recruitment and brought it back in-house. This shift allowed the organization to improve control over each step in the process, better leverage the brand, significantly improve job candidates' experience and reduce cost per hire from more than £1,000 to £411 (Gyton, 2017).

Time to productivity

The time it takes for a new employee to become operational and productive. This can be measured through a combination of quantitative and qualitative data. The quantitative approach starts with setting consistent key performance indicators (KPIs) for each role. Then we measure how many days or weeks it takes a new employee to achieve the required productivity. A qualitative approach would include follow-up emails and conversations at set periods of time (e.g. two weeks, three months and six months). For example, Bank of America collects 360-degree feedback on new executives six months after they start the job. This helps to check how the new leader is performing (Conger and Fishel, 2007).

The value of this measure can significantly differ between roles. Employees joining more senior positions may require more time to reach full productivity compared to staff joining early-career roles. Moreover, new joiners who are still gaining experience in their role or have transferred from a different industry may need more time to become fully operational. However, relatively high time to productivity can be an indication that the onboarding process and initial training require improvement.

Demographics

These are the characteristics of the workforce, e.g. age, gender, ethnicity, disability, highest education level, length of service in the organization, full-time/part-time. Basic information about the demographic profile of employees will help organizations examine the extent of workforce diversity. This, combined with the data on employees' positions, will also help to determine diversity across different organizational levels. Many organizations have a heterogenous composition of workforce among the entry-level roles and support staff. However, there may be less diversity in more senior positions. One of the reasons for this could be initial consideration of inclusion at the level of recruitment and selection, but not supporting diverse needs in terms of training, development and mentoring. For example, ineffective work–life balance practices can be a barrier for employees with care responsibilities to progress in their careers.

Overtime percentage

The number of hours an employee works that are outside their regularly scheduled hours. Tracking and measuring overtime is important to monitor employee workload. A temporary spike in the measure could be caused by an unexpected increase in the production schedule. However, high persistent value requires further investigation. Elevated numbers may indicate that workers struggle to keep up with their deadlines and daily responsibilities. This is a symptom of a department or the organization being understaffed. Not having enough employees increases risks of injuries and illnesses, decrease in work standards and customer service, brand damage and higher staff turnover. A high score would indicate a need for hiring more staff to improve performance quality and reduce the burden on the existing team.

Early turnover

The number of new joiners who leave the organization in a given period of time (e.g. in the first year).

Total turnover rate

The number of leavers divided by the total population in the organization and multiplied by 100.

Employee satisfaction

The number of employees who would recommend the organization to their family and friends as a good workplace

Average time stay

The average number of weeks, months or years an employee stays with an organization.

The above measures represent basic tools in examining staff turnover. Retaining employees tends to be less expensive than recruiting and training new ones. In addition, high turnover and low employee satisfaction measures can be alarming symptoms of people management ineffectiveness. For example, it could be a sign of poor working conditions and compensation, job design, interpersonal relationships or leadership.

Absenteeism rate

The number of workdays missed divided by the number of workdays scheduled and multiplied by 100.

Absenteeism refers to unplanned absences from work. There can be many reasons for an employee's habitual poor attendance at their job. Similar to turnover, absenteeism can be an indicator of work dissatisfaction. It may also be a result of chronic health problems. For example, overworked staff are more prone to illnesses and injuries. Furthermore, limited flexibility in terms of when and where work can be carried out increases absence among staff who have care responsibilities or other duties outside of work. A higher rate requires an internal discussion about the root cause of absence.

Time since last promotion

The average number of months between internal promotions. We can track how many employees were promoted in the past year, or in the last several years. Then, we estimate the frequency with which employees advance their career. When there are few promotion opportunities within the organization this increases the risk of talented staff leaving their jobs to seek development elsewhere.

Training expenses per employee

The total training cost divided by number of employees. This measure helps to calculate approximately how much is invested in employees' development. The estimate can include expenses such as course fees, travel expenses, training equipment and compensation for outside help (e.g. instructors). Sustainable development and responsible financial management means keeping track of how much budget is dedicated to employee growth.

Health care costs per employee

The total health care costs divided by the number of employees. This is a simple calculation of how much the organization spends on health care. The measure is particularly important in countries such as the United States where approximately half of the country's total population receive employer-sponsored health care coverage (Kaiser Family Foundation, 2019). Health insurance constitutes the largest employee-related expense for US employers (Bureau of Labor Statistics, 2020).

Health care costs can be lowered through proactive investment in employees' health. For example, Johnson & Johnson's Health & Wellness Program lowered the company's medical care expenditures by approximately $224.66 per employee per year. The initiative decreased expenditures on doctors' office visits, mental health visits and inpatient hospital days (Ozminkowski et al, 2002).

Capital Metropolitan Transportation Authority in Austin, Texas introduced a workplace wellness programme in 2003. Between 2003 and 2006 the organization's health care costs increased. This was partly due to low initial participation in the new programme coupled with increasing health care costs in the United States during this period. However, when employee participation dramatically increased in 2007 the employer saw a 4 per cent decrease in health care costs while the national average in the country increased by 6 per cent in the same period. Overall, during the four years that the programme was examined it generated a 2.43 return on investment (ROI). Meaning, for every $1 that was spent on the programme $2.43 was saved. This ROI consisted of 1.86 saved due to lower health care costs, and 0.57 in savings due to significantly reduced absenteeism (Davis et al, 2009).

International reporting standards for sustainability

As mentioned at the beginning of the chapter, organizations are not interested in measuring their sustainability efforts just for the benefit of improving performance. Employers may also want to communicate to their stakeholders how well they engage in responsible management. For this purpose, various international organizations establish norms that help to unify measurement and reporting practices across countries and industries.

When navigating the literature on international reporting we come across sustainability 'standards' and 'frameworks/guiding principles'. These terms are often used interchangeably. However, according to the Global Reporting Initiative (GRI), it is helpful to recognize a difference between them. GRI (2022) defines *standards* as 'the agreed level of quality requirements, that people think is acceptable for reporting entities to meet'. A standard sets a more specific requirement for what information must be included when the organization reports its practices, processes and policies.

On the other hand, a sustainability *framework* is 'a set of principles providing guidance and shaping people's thoughts on how to think about a certain topic, but miss a defined reporting obligation' (GRI, 2022). In this section we will first focus on reporting standards and then move on to sustainability frameworks.

Global Reporting Initiative

GRI provides the 'the dominant global standard for sustainability reporting' (KPMG, 2020). GRI is a non-governmental body with its headquarters in Amsterdam, the Netherlands. Its standards for sustainability reporting are free and widely respected. According to a survey conducted by KPMG (2020), 96 per cent of the world's largest 250 companies report on their sustainability performance. Of these 250 largest companies, 73 per cent use GRI standards to do so. While GRI is popular among corporations the standards are applicable to organizations of any type and size. For example, public entities all over the world, such as DevelopmentWA in Australia, have successfully produced GRI sustainability reports (GRI, 2021; DevelopmentWA, 2022).

GRI (2021) provides reporting standards in four main categories, as shown in Table 8.1.

Table 8.1   GRI sustainability reporting standards

Standard series	Topic	Description
100 series	Universal standards	These standards set key principles and requirements for GRI reporting.
200 series	Economic standards	This category covers standards for reporting an organization's impact on the economic conditions of its stakeholders. It addresses subjects such as taxes, corruption and anti-competitive behaviour.
300 series	Environmental standards	When an organization addresses these standards it discloses information about its impacts on living and non-living natural systems. The GRI focuses here on topics such as, energy, waste, emissions and biodiversity.
400 series	Social standards	These standards are related to the social dimension of sustainability including child labour, forced or compulsory labour and issues of working conditions.

SOURCE Based on GRI (2021)

The 100 series is essential for any organization that wants to engage in GRI. Moreover, HRM can shape behaviours that will help to meet environmental sustainability targets. These would be then reported according to the criteria set in the 300 series. However, probably the most important for HR professionals would be the 400 series, particularly the reporting standards dedicated to:

- GRI 401: Employment
- GRI 402: Labour/Management Relations
- GRI 403: Occupational Health and Safety
- GRI 404: Training and Education
- GRI 405: Diversity and Equal Opportunity
- GRI 406: Non-discrimination

International Organization for Standardization (ISO)

ISO is one of the largest organizations dedicated to the development of international standards. It is an independent, non-governmental body with a Central Secretariat based in Geneva, Switzerland. ISO standards cover various technical and non-technical fields. Plenty of ISO standards and related documents set norms for sustainable HRM. Notable examples include ISO 14001, 30414 and 26000.

ISO 14001

This is a standard that sets out requirements for an effective environmental management system (EMS). It can be applied for organizations of any type and size. It became one of the world's most recognized measures for whether an employer meets set norms for environmental sustainability. One of the requirements for ISO 14001 certification is provision of environmental training and management of environment objectives. To achieve a certification in ISO 14001 at least basic GHRM practices need to be developed and maintained.

ISO 30414

This standard sets norms for human capital data capture, measurement and analysis (ISO, 2018). It provides guidelines for reporting information on diversity management, organizational culture, available skills and capabilities, recruitment and turnover, and employees' health and safety. Organizations can achieve a certificate confirming that their human capital reporting is in accordance with ISO 30414. Similar to ISO 14001, this standard is applicable to organizations of any type and size.

ISO 26000

This is a standard that provides guidance for managing social responsibility. ISO highlight that this standard is not meant to be seen as a set of certifiable organizational requirements. Still, ISO 26000 is 'increasingly viewed as a way of assessing an organization's commitment to sustainability and its overall performance' (ISO, 2022b). It addresses subjects such as responsible labour practices, human rights at work and fair compensation.

International guiding frameworks for sustainability

Sustainability frameworks provide broader guidance than reporting standards. In this context, frameworks are understood as general guiding principles recommended by international bodies, which influence organizational members' thoughts and shape employers' and governments' actions in relation to sustainability (GRI, 2022).

Sustainable Development Goals (SDGs)

This is arguably the world's most famous sustainability framework, developed in 2015 by the United Nations General Assembly (UN-GA). SDGs represent 17 interconnected and global goals which aim to:

1 End poverty.

2 End hunger.

3 Ensure and promote health and well-being.

4 Ensure equitable quality education.

5 Achieve gender equality.

6 Ensure availability of clean water and sanitation.

7 Ensure access to affordable and clean energy.

8 Promote decent work and economic growth.

9 Build industry, innovation and infrastructure.

10 Reduce inequality.

11 Make cities and communities sustainable.

12 Ensure responsible consumption and production.

13 Take action against climate change.

14 Responsibly use marine resources.

15 Protect and restore life on land.

16 Promote peace, justice, and strong institutions.

17 Strengthen global partnerships for sustainable goals.

The aim of the initiative is to achieve set objectives in each area by 2030 (UN, 2015). The main goals listed above are related to 169 targets and 232 global performance indicators. For example, 'Target 8.5: By 2030, achieve full and productive employment and decent work for all women and men, including for young people and persons with disabilities, and equal pay for work of equal value' (UN, 2022).

The framework suggests two measures for this specific target: the average hourly earnings of employees and the unemployment rates for different demographic groups.

The SDGs list represents a range of societal issues, and several of them are related to how organizations manage their employees. According to Chams and García-Blandón (2019), the key contribution of sustainable HRM is related to goals 3, 5, 8, 10, 12 and 17. SDGs promote a decent work environment with healthy and equitably treated employees. The framework also puts pressure on organizations to sustainably utilize natural resources. This sets obligations for using GHRM.

Employees are the beneficiaries, success initiators and a driving force for achieving SDGs (Chams and García-Blandón, 2019). Due to the wide scope of the SDGs, they represent broader guidelines rather than specific reporting standards set for example by GRI.

Combination of standards and frameworks

Some organizations provide a combination of reporting standards and general frameworks for sustainable management. Notable examples of such mixes come from the Organization for Economic Co-operation and Development (OECD) and the United Nations Global Compact (UNGC).

OECD guidelines for multinational enterprises

In 1976 the OECD established a set of recommendations, made by governments, for multinational enterprises. Since then, the guidelines have been revised several times with the most recent version from 2011. The guidelines represent a general framework of what policies and practices multinational enterprises should implement. At the same time, they set basic norms for what information needs to be disclosed or reported. The guidelines focus on the socially responsible practices in management related to:

- disclosure
- human rights
- employment and industrial relations
- environment
- combating bribery

- consumer interests
- science and technology
- competition
- taxation

The guidelines aim to improve multinational organizations' sustainable development and 'ensure coherence between economic, environmental and social objectives' (OECD, 2011). The document provides ethical requirements for people management. For example, it urges multinational enterprises to promote greater equality of employment opportunity, ensure occupational health and safety, and consult with employee representatives before carrying out substantial changes such as workforce downsizing.

UNGC

UNGC is an initiative led by the United Nations to encourage businesses to implement sustainable and socially responsible practices. The mission was formed in 2000, and according to the UN it is 'the world's largest corporate sustainability initiative' with over 15,000 companies and 3,800 non-business participants from over 160 countries (UNGC, 2022). UNGC evolved from focusing on the promotion of guiding principles to also introducing its own new platform for reporting sustainable practices (UNGC, 2021a, 2021b).

Organizations can join UNGC and by doing so commit to operating according to the 10 principles:

1 Support protection of human rights.
2 Ensure business operations do not breach human rights.
3 Respect freedom of association and the right to collective bargaining.
4 Eliminate forced labour.
5 Abolish child labour.
6 Eliminate work discrimination.
7 Prevent environmental challenges.
8 Ensure environmentally responsible practices.
9 Promote development of environmentally friendly technologies.
10 Fight corruption.

Organizational members of UNGC pledge to follow these principles and integrate them into their strategies and activities. Each associate is expected to submit a Communication on Progress (COP). It is a public report that informs stakeholders on how the business is moving towards sustainability practices. Previously business participants were expected to include in the COP a statement expressing continued support, and a relatively brief narrative on how the business is implementing sustainable practices and how it is measuring the outcomes of sustainable operations (see e.g. UNGC, 2011).

However, starting from 2023 a new revised COP requires a submission of answers to a questionnaire, in addition to a statement of support issued by a CEO. The new questionnaire is developed on the basis of several established reporting standards, including GRI (UNGC, 2021a, 2021b).

Critique of standards and frameworks

Setting sustainability standards and frameworks is meant to encourage individual organizations to operate in a more socially responsible manner. However, due to weaknesses in each scheme, critics raise concerns as to what extent these initiatives really make a difference in how employers operate.

In most parts of the world organizations have the flexibility to choose if they want to participate in this exercise, or which standards and frameworks they should follow. The space for sustainability reporting is 'crowded', with a wide range of different options available (UNGC, 2021a). Thus, organizations can select a standard or framework that best suits their needs and requires little additional investment.

Moreover, when organizations prepare sustainability reports they are in control over what data is included and what information is overlooked. Unlike financial statements, which are audited, sustainability reports are rarely reviewed by third parties. This potentially allows organizations to overemphasize areas where basic standards are met and leave out critical truths about unsustainable practices (Pucker, 2021). A lot of the social and environmental damage can be done by things that organizations choose not to do. For example, we would struggle to find in sustainability reports information about failing to provide comprehensive family-friendly policies. What is more, the success of sustainable management depends on how existing policies are implemented in practice. Even when a company provides generous parental leave, taking it may mean negative consequences for the employees' career prospects. This level of detail, which makes a difference between the sustainable and unsustainable, is not currently reported by organizations. According to Pucker (2021), in the current system the 'measurement is often nonstandard, incomplete, imprecise and misleading'.

While imperfect, however, sustainability standards and frameworks continue to evolve and improve. For example, in response to a common criticism of too many reporting norms, several international bodies have consolidated. The Climate Disclosure Standards Board (CDSB), the International Integrated Reporting Committee (IIRC) and the Sustainability Accounting Standards Board (SASB) were integrated into one organization in 2022 – the International Sustainability Standards Board (ISSB).

With regards to voluntary participation many regulators show interest in introducing mandatory measures. Allison Herren Lee, the acting chairman of the Securities and Exchange Commission (SEC, 2021) said, 'ESGs are front and centre for the SEC'. Lee discussed the merits of a mandatory standards framework.

In 2014 the European Union introduced the Non-Financial Reporting Directive (NFRD). It requires by law large public-interest companies with more than 500 employees to report information on social and environmental challenges. In 2021 the European Commission adopted a legislative proposal called the Corporate Sustainability Reporting Directive (CSRD). The proposal builds on the NFRD and further strengthens and expands sustainability reporting. For example, CSRD establishes a rule of mandatory assurance (auditing) of sustainability information and introduces more detailed reporting requirements (European Commission, 2022). Once introduced they will become unified mandatory EU sustainability reporting standards. These steps represent a continuing evolution of sustainability measuring and reporting.

Skill check

Working with different sustainability standards and frameworks.
With many standards and frameworks available, being able to navigate these materials is a skill in itself. Managers and HR professionals who are interested in sustainable HRM should have a good knowledge of the most common international guidelines.

International sustainability indices

Organizations can enter public sustainability indices, which are tools for quantifying and benchmarking the sustainability performance. Entering an index is another opportunity for the organization to communicate sustainability successes to its stakeholders. The most famous indices target publicly traded companies.

The indices usually do not list companies involved in business areas such as tobacco products, military weapons and firearms, although there are exceptions. In the light of news about companies' unsustainable or unethical practices, indices can also suspend or remove constituents. For example, Dow Jones Sustainability Indices reserve the right to exclude from their lists companies that engage in controversial activities related to issues such as labour disputes, workplace safety violations and breaches of human rights (S&P Global, 2022a).

The sustainability indices can serve several purposes. On their website, FTSE Russell (2022a) point out four main uses.

- Financial products – indices can be used to create investment products such as index-tracking funds.
- Research – to assess companies' performance and identify leaders in sustainability.
- Reference – to create a standard for measuring sustainability.
- Benchmarking – to compare companies' performance against each other.

Individual and institutional investors can check sustainability indices to make informed decisions about companies that may or may not carry additional risks related to their social, environmental and governance performance.

Dow Jones Sustainability Indices (DJSI)

DJSI represent a group of indices that evaluate the sustainability performance of companies publicly traded on S&P Dow Jones Indices. The main sustainability index is the Dow Jones Sustainability World Index, which lists 10 per cent of sustainability leaders from the largest 2,500 stocks in the S&P Global Broad Market Index. Other DJSIs cover specific regions such as North America, Europe, Asia Pacific, Korea, Australia and Chile. Between 10 and

30 per cent of the best-performing companies per industry are listed on each index.

Leaders in sustainability are identified by a Corporate Sustainability Assessment (CSA) conducted by S&P Global. The assessment criteria are related to three dimensions of sustainability: governance and economic, environmental, and social. Depending on the industry the weight of the criteria in each dimension can vary. For example, in the banking industry there is more weight on the governance and economic dimension (49 per cent) than on the environmental (18 per cent) or social (33 per cent) elements. On the other hand, in the multi-utility and water industry 41 per cent of the total sustainability score comes from environmental criteria, and the social and economic dimensions weigh in at 31 and 28 per cent respectively. The methodology for assessment is regularly reviewed (S&P Global, 2022b).

The specific criteria for each sustainability dimension can also vary between industries. For example, for airline companies there are measures of 'passenger safety' and 'fleet management'. Nevertheless, basic criteria related to sustainable HRM are a part of measurement for all 61 industries examined by CSA (S&P Global, 2022b). These include:

- social reporting
- labour practice indicators
- human rights
- human capital development
- talent attraction and retention
- operational eco-efficiency
- climate strategy
- business ethics

DJSIs illustrate that HRM is a sustainability matter relevant across industries.

FTSE4GOOD Indices

This is a family of sustainability indices developed by the FTSE Group. Similar to DJSI, FTSE4GOOD includes indices that cover all world and regional markets (e.g. UK, US, Europe or Japan). Companies considered for a listing must be first included in one of the general FTSE indices such as the FTSE All-World Index.

Each company is given an overall rating ranging from 0 to 5 based on their ESG performance. Businesses from a 'developed' market need a score of 3.3 or above to be added to the FTSE4Good Index Series, whereas companies from an 'emerging' market require an ESG Rating of 2.9 or above (FTSE Russell, 2022b).

The overall rating is based on scores and exposure related to the three pillars: environmental, social and governance records. On average each company is assessed based on 125 indicators, some of which are industry- or geography-specific. The rating system is based on information provided by organizations such as the Health & Safety Executive, International Labour Organization, Institute of Business Ethics and UN Global Compact (FTSE Russell, 2021).

MSCI KLD 400 Social Index (Domini Social Index 400)

This is an index that focuses specifically on 400 US publicly traded companies that show exemplary practice in sustainability. The research universe of this index consists of over 2,400 large-, mid- and small-capitalization companies listed on the MSCI USA Investable Market Index. From this pool 400 best performers in ESG are selected. The social index reserves at least 200 positions for large- and medium-capitalization companies.

The index provides each company with an overall ESG rating on a seven-point scale from 'AAA' to 'CCC' (MSCI, 2021):

- Leader (AAA, AA)
- Average (A, BBB, BB)
- Laggard (B, CCC)

To join the index a company needs to score at least 'BB'. Businesses that are already listed need to achieve at least a 'B' rating to maintain their position. The ratings are based on the information collected from over 1,000 data points on ESG policies, programmes and performance. The key areas of assessment are related to four environmental, four social and two governance themes:

- (E) climate change (e.g. Carbon emissions)
- (E) natural capital (e.g. Water stress)
- (E) pollution and waste (e.g. Electronic waste)
- (E) environmental opportunities (e.g. Opportunities in renewable energy)

- (S) human capital (e.g. Labour management, health and safety)
- (S) product liability (e.g. Consumer financial protection)
- (S) stakeholder opposition (e.g. Community relations)
- (S) social opportunities (e.g. Opportunities in nutrition and health, access to health care)
- (G) corporate governance (e.g. Board, pay)
- (G) corporate behaviour (e.g. Business ethics) (MSCI, 2022)

Critique of sustainability indices

Critics such as Taparia (2021) highlighted that indices measuring long-term social, environmental and governance performance can have surprisingly low standards for inclusion. Phillip Morris International, one of the largest tobacco companies in the world, was included in the DJSI in 2020 and 2021 (Philip Morris International, 2021). Another example is Amazon, which is often included in ESG indices, such as FTSE4Good US Select Index (FTSE Russell, 2022c). Funds investing in companies that are screened for environmental, social and corporate governance criteria (e.g. Vanguard ESG U.S. Stock ETF) also include the tech giant (see e.g. Vanguard, 2022). While Amazon took steps towards achieving environmental goals (Amazon, 2022), it is also one of the fiercest anti-union employers and provides questionable working conditions (Greenhouse, 2022). These extreme examples undermine the public's faith in the accuracy with which indices measure sustainability risks and damages.

Over the years sustainability indices have become more rigorous in their methodologies and company selections (MacMahon, 2020). But, as pointed out by Taparia (2021), there is still significant scope for improving how we benchmark ESG. One of the corrections that may need to be introduced in the future is a measure of the social, environmental and governance damages caused by corporations (Taparia, 2021).

Summary

How can we measure sustainability of people management? In this chapter we explored a variety of approaches to evaluate the effectiveness of sustainable HRM. We started the discussion by looking at different evaluation perspectives proposed by the academic and practitioner community. To help navigate the wealth of methods we divided measures into three broad categories, those focusing primarily on the social, environmental or business dimensions.

In terms of social sustainability, HRM practices can be evaluated through the lens of employment quality and employees' health. In pursuit of better HRM practices, organizations can also assess employees' positive psychological states, such as work engagement or the extent to which people feel they thrive at work. Equally, we may choose to examine the harm that people management causes and the negative states (e.g. stress) that workers experience.

HRM is crucial for success in protecting the natural environment. Thus, some employers may be interested in measuring how people management initiatives affect environmental sustainability. This led us to a discussion of measuring employees' green innovation and creativity before and after introducing changes to HRM practices. Other employers may want to examine progress in developing employees' green behaviours such as reducing waste and preserving resources. We also looked at measures that assess employees' and managers' perceived effectiveness of GRHM practices (e.g. green recruitment, training, performance management, etc.).

Sustainable development is also about achieving long-term business objectives. This chapter has shown, through the perspective of human capital, how employers can measure the monetary value of investing in human resources. Moreover, we discussed common HR metrics that are used to evaluate organizational performance and sustainability of HRM.

Due to the high public interest in socially responsible management, global institutions have begun to develop and popularize standards, frameworks and indices for sustainability. International reporting norms created, for example, by GRI and ISO, help organizations communicate to stakeholders that they are making progress in sustainable management. Critics have pointed out that the current system for international standards is weakened by the voluntary and flexible nature of measuring and reporting sustainability. In response to these concerns regulatory bodies such as the European Commission are taking steps towards setting mandatory measuring and reporting standards.

Study questions

1 Discuss whether measuring and reporting sustainability of HRM is important or not.

2 What are the four main perspectives we can take to measure the social sustainability of HRM? Support your answer with reference to key authors.

3 What is the difference between green creativity and green innovation? How can these concepts be used to evaluate the effectiveness of sustainable HRM?

4 Discuss, with examples, how commonly known HR metrics can be used to measure the sustainability of HRM.

5 What is the difference between sustainability reporting standards and frameworks? Support your answer with one example of each.

6 Explain the contribution of the United Nations Global Compact in the international system of sustainability standards and frameworks.

7 What are international sustainability indices? What are their main uses and limitations?

Key reading

Davis, L, Loyo, K, Schwertfeger, R, Glowka, A, Danielson, L, Brea, C and Griffin-Blake, S (2009) A comprehensive worksite wellness program in Austin, Texas: partnership between Steps to a Healthier Austin and Capital Metropolitan Transportation Authority, *Preventing Chronic Disease*, 6 (2), pp 1–5

Francoeur, V, Paillé, P, Yuriev, A and Boiral, O (2021) The measurement of green workplace behaviors: a systematic review, *Organization & Environment*, 34 (1), pp 18–42

GRI (2022) The GRI perspective: ESG standards, frameworks and everything in between, Issue 4, 10 March 2022, www.globalreporting.org/media/jxkgrggd/gri-perspective-esg-standards-frameworks.pdf

Taparia, H (2021) The world may be better off without ESG investing, *Stanford Social Innovation Review*, https://ssir.org/articles/entry/the_world_may_be_better_off_without_esg_investing

References

Amazon (2022) Amazon sustainability further and faster, together, https://sustainability.aboutamazon.com (archived at https://perma.cc/E6V4-YQV5)

Arici, H E and Uysal, M (2022) Leadership, green innovation and green creativity: a systematic review, *The Service Industries Journal*, **42** (5–6), pp 280–320

Armstrong, M and Taylor, S (2020) *Armstrong's Handbook of Human Resource Management Practice*, 15th edn, Kogan Page, London

Barney, J (2011) *Gaining and Sustaining Competitive Advantage*, 4th edn, Pearson, Boston

Bureau of Labor Statistics (2020) Employer costs for employee compensation, economic news release, www.bls.gov/news.release/pdf/ecec.pdf (archived at https://perma.cc/4W2Q-TYHC)

Chams, N and García-Blandón, J (2019) On the importance of sustainable human resource management for the adoption of sustainable development goals, *Resources, Conservation and Recycling*, **141**, pp 109–22

Chen, W S, Haniff, J, Siau, C S, Seet, W, Loh, S F, Abd, M H et al (2014) Psychometric properties of the Malay work-related quality of life (WRQoL) scale in Malaysia, *World*, **1** (1), pp 57–67

Chen, Y S and Chang, C H (2013) The determinants of green product development performance: green dynamic capabilities, green transformational leadership and green creativity, *Journal of business ethics*, **116** (1), pp 107–19

Chen, Y S, Lai, S B and Wen, C T (2006) The influence of green innovation performance on corporate advantage in Taiwan, *Journal of Business Ethics*, **67** (4), pp 331–39

CIPD (2022) CIPD Good Work Index, www.cipd.co.uk/knowledge/work/trends/goodwork (archived at https://perma.cc/73JY-GYQB)

Conger, J A and Fishel, B (2007) Accelerating leadership performance at the top: lessons from the Bank of America's executive on-boarding process, *Human Resource Management Review*, **17** (4), pp 442–54

Cooper, C L and Marshall, J (1976) Occupational sources of stress: a review of the literature relating to coronary heart disease and mental ill health, *Journal of Occupational Psychology*, **49**, pp 11–28

Crane, A, Matten, D, Glozer, S and Spence, L (2019) *Business Ethics: Managing corporate citizenship and sustainability in the age of globalization*, 5th edn, Oxford University Press, Oxford

Daniels, K (2000) Measures of five aspects of affective well-being at work, *Human Relations*, **53** (2), pp 275–94

Daniels, K and Harris, C (2005) A daily diary study of coping in the context of the job demands–control–support model, *Journal of Vocational Behavior*, **66** (2), pp 219–37

Davis, L, Loyo, K, Schwertfeger, R, Glowka, A, Danielson, L, Brea, C and Griffin-Blake, S (2009) A comprehensive worksite wellness program in Austin, Texas: partnership between Steps to a Healthier Austin and Capital Metropolitan Transportation Authority, *Preventing Chronic Disease*, **6** (2), pp 1–5

DevelopmentWA (2022) Sustainability and innovation, our view, https://developmentwa.com.au/about/sustainability-and-innovation (archived at https://perma.cc/4T98-53BW)

Easton, S and Van Laar, D (2018) *User Manual for the Work-Related Quality of Life (WRQoL) Scale: a measure of quality of working life*, University of Portsmouth

Edwards, J A, Van Laar, D, Easton, S and Kinman, G (2009) The work-related quality of life scale for higher education employees, *Quality in Higher Education*, **15** (3), pp 207–19

Elizur, D and Shye, S (1990) Quality of work life and its relation to quality of life, *Applied Psychology*, **39** (3), pp 275–91

European Commission (2022) Corporate sustainability reporting, https://ec.europa.eu/info/business-economy-euro/company-reporting-and-auditing/company-reporting/corporate-sustainability-reporting_en (archived at https://perma.cc/6ERU-4WZK)

Faragher, E B, Cooper, C L and Cartwright, S (2004) A shortened stress evaluation tool (ASSET), *Stress and Health: Journal of the International Society for the Investigation of Stress*, **20** (4), pp 189–201

Francoeur, V, Paillé, P, Yuriev, A and Boiral, O (2021) The measurement of green workplace behaviors: a systematic review, *Organization & Environment*, **34** (1), pp 18–42

FTSE Russell (2021) Methodology. Guide to FTSE sustainable investment data used in FTSE indexes v1.1, https://research.ftserussell.com/products/downloads/Guide_to_FTSE_Sustainable_Investment_Data_used_in_FTSE_Russell_Indexes.pdf (archived at https://perma.cc/ECJ6-TCWW)

FTSE Russell (2022a) FTSE4Good Index Series, www.ftserussell.com/products/indices/ftse4good (archived at https://perma.cc/463C-4P9Q)

FTSE Russell (2022b) FTSE4Good index series v.4.6, ground rules, https://research.ftserussell.com/products/downloads/FTSE4Good_Index_Series_Ground_Rules.pdf (archived at https://perma.cc/5YAN-ATQM)

FTSE Russell (2022c) FTSE4Good US Select Index, FTSE Russell factsheet, https://research.ftserussell.com/Analytics/Factsheets/Home/DownloadSingleIssue?issueName=F4GUSAP1&IsManual=false (archived at https://perma.cc/L4JW-7RJP)

Gallup (2022) Gallup's employee engagement survey: ask the right questions with the Q^{12} survey, www.gallup.com/workplace/356063/gallup-q12-employee-engagement-survey.aspx (archived at https://perma.cc/VN2R-55RQ)

Greenhouse, S (2022) Amazon chews through the average worker in eight months. They need a union, *The Guardian*, www.theguardian.com/commentisfree/2022/feb/04/amazon-chews-through-the-average-worker-in-eight-months-they-need-a-union (archived at https://perma.cc/FWG9-YJ9U)

GRI (2021) The GRI standards. A guide for policy makers, www.globalreporting. org/media/nmmnwfsm/gri-policymakers-guide.pdf (archived at https://perma. cc/9D9K-G4HW)

GRI (2022) The GRI perspective. ESG standards, frameworks and everything in between, Issue 4–10 March 2022, www.globalreporting.org/media/jxkgrggd/ gri-perspective-esg-standards-frameworks.pdf (archived at https://perma.cc/ Z8PX-GGTC)

Gyton, G (2017) I used to spend half my time on candidates' complaints, *People Management*, September, pp 22–23

Harter, J K, Schmidt, F L Killham, E A and Asplund, J W (2006) *Q12 Meta-analysis*, The Gallup Organization, Princeton, NJ

ISO (2017) ISO/TR 30406:2017 Human resource management – sustainable employability management for organizations, www.iso.org/standard/72327.html (archived at https://perma.cc/KNS6-RLLY)

ISO (2018) ISO 30414:2018, Human resource management – guidelines for internal and external human capital reporting, www.iso.org/standard/69338. html (archived at https://perma.cc/78X6-77GT)

ISO (2022b) ISO 26000 Social Responsibility, www.iso.org/iso-26000-social-responsibility.html (archived at https://perma.cc/Y7MX-63RV)

IWI (2022) Workplace well-being Assessment, www.innovativeworkplaceinstitute. org/workplace-well-being-assessment.php

Jabeen, F, Friesen, H L and Ghoudi, K (2018) Quality of work life of Emirati women and its influence on job satisfaction and turnover intention: evidence from the UAE, *Journal of Organizational Change Management*, **31** (2), pp 352–70

Johnson, S J, Willis, S M and Robertson, I T (2018) Cross-validation of a short stress measure: ASSET Pulse, *International Journal of Stress Management*, **25** (4), pp 391–400

Kaiser Family Foundation (2019) Health insurance coverage of the total population, www.kff.org/other/state-indicator/total-population (archived at https://perma.cc/MX94-TKYH).

Khan, M H and Noorizwan Muktar, S (2020) Mediating role of organizational attractiveness on the relationship between green recruitment and job pursuit intention among students of Universiti Teknologi Malaysia, *Cogent Business & Management*, **7** (1), 1832811

KPMG (2020) The time has come, the KPMG Survey of Sustainability Reporting 2020, https://home.kpmg/xx/en/home/insights/2020/11/the-time-has-come-survey-of-sustainability-reporting.html (archived at https://perma.cc/TB4J-GBRU)

Lee, Y and Aletta, F (2019) Acoustical planning for workplace health and well-being: a case study in four open-plan offices, *Building Acoustics*, **26** (3), pp 207–20

Leitão, J, Pereira, D and Gonçalves, Â (2021) Quality of work life and contribution to productivity: assessing the moderator effects of burnout syndrome, *International Journal of Environmental Research and Public Health*, **18** (5), 2425

MacMahon, S (2020) The challenge of rating ESG performance, *Harvard Business Review*, hbr.org/2020/09/the-challenge-of-rating-esg-performance (archived at https://perma.cc/F2Y2-4TB7)

Mariappanadar, S (2019) Measurements for sustainable HRM practices. In S Mariappanadar (ed.) *Sustainable Human Resource Management: Strategies, practices and challenges* (pp 216–44), Red Globe Press, London

Mariappanadar, S and Aust, I (2017) The dark side of overwork: an empirical evidence of social harm of work from a sustainable HRM perspective, *International Studies of Management & Organization*, **47** (4), pp 372–87

Martel, J P and Dupuis, G (2006) Quality of work life: theoretical and methodological problems and presentation of a new model and measuring instrument, *Social Indicators Research*, **77** (2), pp 333–68

Merino-Soto, C, Lozano-Huamán, M, Lima-Mendoza, S, Calderón de la Cruz, G, Juárez-García, A and Toledano-Toledano, F (2022) Ultrashort version of the Utrecht Work Engagement Scale (UWES-3): a psychometric assessment, *International Journal of Environmental Research and Public Health*, **19** (2), p 890

MSCI (2021) MSCI KLD 400 Social Index Methodology, www.msci.com/eqb/ methodology/meth_docs/MSCI_KLD_400_Social_Index_Methodology_ Nov2021.pdf (archived at https://perma.cc/5859-B9EW)

MSCI (2022) MSCI ESG ratings methodology, executive summary, MSCI ESG Research LLC, www.msci.com/documents/1296102/21901542/ESG-Ratings- Methodology-Exec-Summary.pdf (archived at https://perma.cc/JE7J-6UP8)

OECD (2011) Guidelines for multinational enterprises, www.oecd.org/daf/inv/ mne/48004323.pdf (archived at https://perma.cc/AG9M-JRYY)

Osranek, R and Zink, K J (2014a) Corporate human capital and social sustainability of human resources. In I Ehnert, W Harry and K J Zink (eds.) *Sustainability and Human Resource Management: Developing sustainable business organizations* (pp 105–26), Springer, Berlin/Heidelberg, Germany

Osranek, R and Zink, K J (2014b) A measurement approach to human potential in the context of a sustainable corporate management. In M Russ (ed.) *Value Creation, Reporting and Signaling for Human Capital and Human Assets* (pp 19–47), Palgrave Macmillan, New York

Ozminkowski, R J, Ling, D, Goetzel, R Z, Bruno, J A, Rutter, K R, Isaac, F and Wang, S (2002) Long-term impact of Johnson & Johnson's Health & Wellness Program on health care utilization and expenditures, *Journal of Occupational and Environmental Medicine*, **44** (1), pp 21–29

Philip Morris International (2021) Philip Morris International's ESG performance recognized by S&P Dow Jones Indices, company included in Dow Jones Sustainability Index North America for second consecutive year, www.pmi.com/media-center/press-releases/press-release-details?newsId=24571 (archived at https://perma.cc/KSZ8-AG7F)

Porath, C, Spreitzer, G, Gibson, C and Garnett, F G (2012) Thriving at work: toward its measurement, construct validation and theoretical refinement, *Journal of Organizational Behavior*, 33 (2), pp 250–75

Pucker, K P (2021) Overselling sustainability reporting, *Harvard Business Review*, 99 (3), pp 134–43

QoWL (2022a) International use of the WRQoL scale, where is the WRQoL scale being used? www.qowl.co.uk/researchers/qowl_wrqol_international.html (archived at https://perma.cc/DNP6-DMM9)

QoWL (2022b) Download our scales and manuals, notice to potential users of the WRQoL scale, www.qowl.co.uk/researchers/qowl_download_intro.html (archived at https://perma.cc/5QWY-S8TU)

Rostami, H R, Akbarfahimi, M, Ghaffari, A, Kamali, M and Rassafiani, M (2021) Relationship between work-related quality of life and job satisfaction in Iranian occupational therapists, *Occupational Therapy International*, 2021, pp 1–6

S&P Global (2022a) Dow Jones Sustainability Indices methodology, www.spglobal.com/spdji/en/documents/methodologies/methodology-dj-sustainability-indices.pdf (archived at https://perma.cc/G6D7-2M7F)

S&P Global (2022b) Weights overview. Corporate sustainability assessment 2022, https://portal.csa.spglobal.com/survey/documents/CSA_Weights.pdf (archived at https://perma.cc/NX79-FLRM)

Schaufeli, W B and Bakker, A B (2010) Defining and measuring work engagement: bringing clarity to the concept. In A B Bakker and M P Leiter (eds.) *Work Engagement: A handbook of essential theory and research* (pp 10–24), Psychology Press, London

Schaufeli, W B, Martinez, I M, Pinto, A M, Salanova, M and Bakker, A B (2002) Burnout and engagement in university students: a cross-national study, *Journal of Cross-cultural Psychology*, 33 (5), pp 464–81

Scholz, C (2007) Ökonomische Humankapitalbewertung. Eine betriebswirtschaftliche Annäherung an das Konstrukt Humankapital, *Betriebswirtschaftliche Forschung und Praxis* (BFuP), 59 (1), pp 20–37

Scholz, C, Stein, V and Bechtel, R (2011) *Human Capital Management. Raus aus der Unverbindlichkeit!*, Luchterhand, Munich

Schultz, T W (1963) *The Economic Value of Education*, Columbia University Press, New York

SEC (2021) A climate for change: meeting investor demand for climate and ESG information at the SEC, www.sec.gov/news/speech/lee-climate-change (archived at https://perma.cc/D4RP-WHUT)

Shah, M (2019) Green human resource management: development of a valid measurement scale, *Business Strategy and the Environment*, **28** (5), pp 771–85

Sirgy, M J, Efraty, D, Siegel, P and Lee, D J (2001) A new measure of quality of work life (QWL) based on need satisfaction and spillover theories, *Social Indicators Research*, **55** (3), pp 241–302

Spreitzer, G M, Sutcliffe, K, Dutton, J, Sonenshein, S and Grant, A M (2005) A socially embedded model of thriving at work, *Organization Science*, **16** (5), pp 537–49

Tang, G, Chen, Y, Jiang, Y, Paille, P and Jia, J (2018) Green human resource management practices: scale development and validity, *Asia Pacific Journal of Human Resources*, **56** (1), pp 31–55

Taparia, H (2021) The world may be better off without ESG investing, *Stanford Social Innovation Review*, https://ssir.org/articles/entry/the_world_may_be_better_off_without_esg_investing (archived at https://perma.cc/5GM4-Y7R9)

UN (2015) Resolution adopted by the General Assembly on 25 September 2015, transforming our world: the 2030 agenda for sustainable development, https://sdgs.un.org/2030agenda (archived at https://perma.cc/5KTJ-3DG7)

UN (2022) SDG Indicators, metadata repository, https://unstats.un.org/sdgs/metadata/ (archived at https://perma.cc/9YJZ-YC2L)

UNGC (2011) Communication on progress, www.unglobalcompact.org/participation/report/cop/create-and-submit/detail/13514 (archived at https://perma.cc/AG5V-9F89)

UNGC (2021a) Questionnaire guidebook. Communication on progress, https://info.unglobalcompact.org/l/591891/2022-01-13/49q7nw/591891/1642091777YUCS9o1k/UNGC_CoP_GuideBook.pdf (archived at https://perma.cc/3DB9-XJ7D)

UNGC (2021b) Frequently asked questions. Communication on progress, https://info.unglobalcompact.org/l/591891/2022-02-01/4byhlh/591891/1643749643zyYHKrqu/UNGC_CoP_FAQ_01_28_2022.pdf (archived at https://perma.cc/WKL4-VWKK)

UNGC (2022) One Global Compact. Accelerating and scaling global collective impact, https://info.unglobalcompact.org/l/591891/2022-01-04/493jyf/591891/1641310342EQoLgnAd/UNGC_New_Value_Prop_Brochure_Design.pdf (archived at https://perma.cc/FD7J-KVL9)

Van Laar, D, Edwards, J A and Easton, S (2007) The work-related quality of life scale for healthcare workers, *Journal of Advanced Nursing*, **60** (3), pp 325–33

Vance, R J (2006) Employee engagement and commitment: a guide to understanding, measuring and increasing engagement in your organization, SHRM foundation, www.shrm.org/foundation/ourwork/initiatives/resources-from-past-initiatives/Documents/Employee%20Engagement%20and%20Commitment.pdf (archived at https://perma.cc/R89L-GLP2)

Vanguard (2022) Vanguard ESG U.S. Stock ETF, https://investor.vanguard.com/etf/profile/esgv (archived at https://perma.cc/4Q2N-E8XE)

Walumbwa, F O, Muchiri, M K, Misati, E, Wu, C and Meiliani, M (2018) Inspired to perform: a multilevel investigation of antecedents and consequences of thriving at work, *Journal of Organizational Behavior*, **39** (3), pp 249–61

Weiskopf, R and Munro, I (2012) Management of human capital: discipline, security and controlled circulation in HRM, *Organization*, **19** (6), pp 685–702

Xu, F Z, Zhang, Y, Yang, H and Wu, B T (2020) Sustainable HRM through improving the measurement of employee work engagement: third-person rating method, *Sustainability*, **12** (17), p 7100

Sustainable HRM in different areas of the world

9

LEARNING OBJECTIVES

After completing this chapter, you should be able to:

- Discuss contextual factors affecting sustainable HRM in the United States and Canada.
- Discuss contextual factors affecting sustainable HRM in Latin America.
- Discuss contextual factors affecting sustainable HRM in Europe.
- Discuss contextual factors affecting sustainable HRM in the Middle East.
- Discuss contextual factors affecting sustainable HRM in Africa.
- Discuss contextual factors affecting sustainable HRM in South Asia.
- Discuss contextual factors affecting sustainable HRM in East and Southeast Asia.
- Discuss contextual factors affecting sustainable HRM in Australia and New Zealand
- Recognize the complexities of sustainable HRM in multinational corporations.

Introduction

People management is influenced by internal and external environments. Internal forces shaping HRM practices include work culture, management philosophy, organizational policies and the technology used by the employer. External forces include national and international economic conditions, changing levels of unemployment, government policies, demographic trends, employment regulations and trade unions (Tayeb, 2005). One example that illustrates the powerful impact of the external environment is the Whirlpool Corporation and its attempt to lay off employees in the United States and Europe. It took the company less than a year to dismiss 1,000 people in Arkansas in the US, where the barriers for dismissal are low. At the same time, it took Whirlpool Corporation more than three years to cut 500 jobs in Italy (Ball and Hagerty, 2013).

Chapter 9 focuses on a discussion of the external forces shaping sustainable HRM in different national and regional contexts. Comparative analyses are well established in the field of HRM. As one assessment put it, 'There is… a comparative tradition that shows a preference for exploring the context, systems, content and national patterns of HRM as a result of the distinctive developmental paths of different countries and territories' (Farndale et al, 2017). In a similar vein, authors started to introduce comparative and global analysis specifically in the area of sustainable HRM (e.g. Aust et al, 2018; Kramar and Mariappanadar, 2019).

This chapter outlines contextual forces crucial for sustainable HRM in the following regions:

- United States and Canada
- Latin America
- Europe
- Middle East
- Africa
- South Asia
- East and Southeast Asia
- Australia and New Zealand

Each of the discussed areas presents its own set of opportunities and challenges affecting the sustainability of people management. The last main section of the chapter takes a closer look at sustainable HRM practices in multinational corporations (MNCs).

United States and Canada

The US and Canada share many economic and systemic similarities. Both countries have liberal market economies and a high proportion of immigrants

(Pison, 2019). Many organizations in both countries show commitment to diversity management. The reward systems are performance oriented rather than seniority based, such as in traditional Japanese (Allen et al, 2004) or Arab-Islamic organizations (Bachkirov and Shamsudin, 2017).

The employment relations are also similar. After World War II, Canada adopted characteristics of the industrial relations system present in the US (Block, 2006). In international comparative studies of employment relations, the US and Canada are often paired together (Colvin and Darbishire, 2013).

Work–life balance and employee-friendly policies

Despite many parallels, there also exist contextual differences between the US and Canada, which have significance for sustainable HRM. Compared to their southern neighbours, Canadian employees report better work–life balance (OECD, 2022a). One of the reasons for this could be that Canadian legislators show more initiative in protecting employees' intersection of professional and personal life. For example, to regulate excessive work communication, the province of Ontario passed a bill that protects employees' right to disconnect from work. The new Bill 27, Working for Workers Act, defines *disconnecting from work* as 'not engaging in work-related communications, including emails, telephone calls, video calls or the sending or reviewing of other messages, so as to be free from the performance of work' (Legislative Assembly of Ontario, 2021). According to the regulation, employers with 25 or more staff must clarify their position on disconnecting from work in a written policy which must be shared with all employees. In comparison, in the US there are no regulations protecting the 'right to disconnect'. It remains US organizations' own decision whether to introduce policies clarifying their position on this issue.

Bill 27 introduced in Ontario does not specify what practices must be included in organizational policies. Thus, even if a company is covered by this regulation, HR professionals and senior managers will still need to decide what sustainable practices should be incorporated into their guidelines on disconnecting from work. This could include setting a maximum response time frame for emails (for example, within 24 hours, Monday to Friday), or clarifying rules on scheduling meetings across time zones.

In general, compared to the US, in Canada there are more employee-friendly policies, which set minimum standards for more sustainable people management. Parental leave policy in Canada is more generous in terms of duration, paid benefits and how flexible it is. The Canadian Labour Code grants pregnant employees up to 17 weeks of leave. This statutory period can be longer depending on province and territory. Moreover, natural or adoptive parents are eligible for up to 63 weeks of parental leave. Maternity and parental leaves can be combined although this cannot exceed 78 weeks (Government of Canada, 2022b). Employers do not have to pay staff on maternity and parental leave, but the government provides benefits for employees on maternity and paternity leave (Government of Canada, 2022c). In the US, under federal law parents are protected for up to 12 weeks of unpaid leave (US Department of Labor, 2022). In parts of the country such as California, New York and Washington, regulators introduced state legislation that supplements the national law and provides additional rules about paid leave and/or extending unpaid leave. However, there are also several states (e.g. Alabama, South Dakota) that have no or limited extension of the federal law on maternity and paternity leave. In regions with less regulation there is more onus on employers to show initiative in protecting employees' work–family balance. For example, Alabama Power, an electric utility company, introduced its own policy of 12 weeks of paid maternity and adoptive leave, as well as an additional 80 hours of paid leave available to parents (Vollers, 2019).

In the US the '*at-will employment*' rule allows employers to fire an employee for any reason and without warning, providing that it is not an illegal dismissal (e.g. terminating an employee because of their race, religion, national origin or sex). Some parts of the US put limitations on the at-will employment rule, but all states recognize it (Muhl, 2001). In contrast, in Canada there is a high legal threshold for a justification to terminate an employee without notice or pay in lieu (Government of Canada, 2022a). This gives Canadian employees a higher level of job security. Lack of 'at-will employment' also puts more responsibility on managers to discipline staff to correct their behaviour, rather than resort to immediate dismissal.

Focus on social, environmental and economic sustainability

Historically, Canadian businesses were more active than US firms in promoting social and environmental responsibility (Thorne et al, 2010). Thorne et al (2017) found that 'Canadian firms have a greater tendency to issue standalone CSR reports and have higher CSR scores than US firms'.

According to Taylor and Lewis (2014), US HRM research strongly focuses on a *unitarist managerial perspective,* which is an assumption that managers and employees share the same interests. This neglects the employees' voice in the decision making related to HRM and can influence how sustainable HRM is practised in the US. Taylor and Lewis argued that because of the assumptions common in US organizations about the relationship between employees and employers, US sustainable HRM may prioritize the financial goals and potentially environmental goals, but neglect people matters. Many innovations in the field of management that are key to sustainable HRM originated in the US. For example, the idea of diversity management comes from the US and is championed all over the world by US corporations (Aust et al, 2018). However, Taylor and Lewis (2014) call for 'more emphasis on collective good rather than individualist action and rewards' in US HRM and sustainable HRM.

Skill check

Analysing external forces shaping sustainable HRM in US and Canada. This is a key skill, especially for employers who wish to expand their operations in North America or already have employees in both countries.

Latin America

Latin America is a diverse group of countries at various stages of economic and political growth. Nevertheless, we will attempt to identify the main themes in organizational practices in this part of the world and use these for our discussion of sustainable HRM.

Paternalistic management

One of the challenges that Latin America is facing is high societal inequalities, with many people living in poverty, and weak institutional frameworks (Hernandez-Pozas et al, 2021). The region is also characterized by a *paternalistic style of management*. In this system employers offer a form of protection for employees in exchange for strict autonomy in the decision-making process, loyalty and obedience. The employer promises to tend to employees' needs, but it is also the employer who decides what those needs are. Paternalism uses the analogy of a family to influence employees. However, we should also note that there is a growing trend in Latin America of employees raising their voices and asking to be included in the discussions about HRM and employment conditions (Pipoli et al, 2014; Andonova et al, 2009).

In the context of Chile, Gutiérrez Crocco and Martin (2022) identified three main possibilities for how sustainable HRM can challenge or fit into the established management frameworks. In the first scenario, sustainable HRM is introduced only in name, but does not change the internalized practices of paternalism and a controlling culture. The second option is that the sustainability approach opens opportunities for a recognition of employee voice and collaborations with unions. Third, the adoption of the sustainability approach is mixed, and the traditional paternalism evolves, but does not recognize the plurality of interests in organizations (Gutiérrez Crocco and Martin, 2022). What separates paternalist and sustainable HRM are 'A level of autonomy and participatory egalitarian relationships, horizontal communication, delegation and trust' (Pipoli et al, 2014). Osland et al (2009) argued that 'charity and paternalism do not result in long-term development'.

Davila and Elvira (2018) examined HRM practices in Latin America through the lens of stakeholder management. This study analysed annual sustainability reports of 10 Latin American MNCs. The researchers focused specifically on employment and community initiatives. The dataset relies on self-reported information, and hence may not represent the full picture of HRM practices. Nevertheless, across different organizations Davila and Elvira (2018) identified examples of:

- training programmes open to the entire community
- scholarships for employees' children
- health insurance for employees' families
- support for communities affected by natural disasters
- programmes developing local entrepreneurship
- support for native communities by building infrastructure, provision of health services and charity
- development of employee leadership skills
- coaching programmes
- knowledge dissemination across the organization
- measurement of employee engagement

- work–life balance programmes, including flexible working hours
- collaborations with universities and colleges

Many of these initiatives rely on employees participating as volunteers and providing important environmental and communal support. If combined with a recognition of employee voice (e.g. ensuring that employees' interests are represented at board level, good level of direct employee participation in decision making) then MNCs' efforts would embody a step towards sustainable HRM. However, without the last vital ingredient the projects run the risk of concentrating on 'reputation issues' rather than socially sustainable people management (Gutiérrez Crocco and Martin, 2022).

For example, Macini et al (2022) explained that the Brazilian banking industry is 'internationally recognized for its sustainable practices, its engagement with stakeholders and its publications of complete integrated reports (…) at the same time, this industry has a high incidence of lawsuits and questionable HRM practices.' The authors examined sustainable HRM in the Brazilian banking industry by collecting and analysing data from three main sources: GRI annual sustainability reports, employment tribunal decisions and in-depth interviews with top managers in the Banking Trade Union and the Brazilian Federation of Banks (Macini et al, 2022). According to the research findings, the organizations showed some engagement with sustainable HRM, but there was also a lot of scope for improvement. For instance, the study found that

> Brazilian banks today have a total of twelve thousand people with special needs integrated into their staff. This number might not be as positive as it looks, because banks exploit legal loopholes to pay just half the legal minimum wage to most disabled employees (Macini et al, 2022).

Broadening views on sustainability

One of the key issues is to broaden employers' understanding of responsible management. Alberton et al (2022) explored sustainability in 20 Brazilian hotels by doing interviews with managers and conducting a staff survey. In the examined context researchers found that 'for the hotels, sustainability is linked only to the environment' (Alberton et al, 2022). The survey analysed sustainable practices and individual competencies and found a lack of knowledge about even essential social sustainability factors such as accident prevention. In a different study, Murcia and Tomaselli (2020) surveyed 186

MBA students from six Latin American countries (Argentina, Chile, Ecuador, Mexico, Peru and Uruguay) and concluded that 'A huge challenge lying ahead for us management educators pertains to thoroughly bridging students' knowledge gaps about the relationship among economic growth, society, and the environment'.

Many organizations and managers in Latin America have high aspirations for sustainable development. A study found that the majority of SMEs in Chile, Argentina, Mexico, Peru and Venezuela show a high or at least a medium commitment to CSR practices (Vives, 2006). High commitment meant that sustainable practices were a part of the business's strategy and were routinely performed. Medium commitment meant that specific CSR practices were carried out regularly but were not a part of the business's strategy. SMEs' engagement in sustainable development is crucial because they constitute 95 per cent of the whole business community in Latin America (Vives, 2006). Vives argued that while CSR practices are already common in many SMEs it is worth deepening their involvement. Moreover, we should further promote socially responsible practices among those firms that show ad hoc or no commitment to sustainability.

Europe

The political and economic context in this region varies widely from country to country. However, the formation of the European Union (EU) has facilitated a level of convergence in management and employment practices. The EU made it easier for organizations to trade and operate across borders. Finding work in neighbouring countries, whether seasonally or permanently, is also easier for citizens of EU Member States. The EU also provides an extensive and progressive net of legislation. EU labour law is a vital element of the *European social model*. The model is based on principles of social protection and dialogue, with the emphasis on employee rights, workplace preventative measures and democracy, as well as promotion of equality, diversity and inclusion (Vaughan-Whitehead, 2015). As explained by Claus (2003), 'Through its directives and recommendations, the EU is streamlining HR practices related to health and safety, gender equality, employee involvement in work council participation, parental leave, etc.' The EU law sets the framework for employment relations by protecting workers' freedom of association and the right to collective bargaining and collective action. However, details related to collective labour negotiations are set by each country (Bercusson, 2002). The EU also does not impose one minimum wage on Member States. Denmark, Italy, Cyprus, Austria, Finland and Sweden do not have an official national minimum wage and across the other Member States the lowest legal remuneration ranges from €2,257 per month in Luxembourg to €332 per month in Bulgaria (Eurostat, 2022).

Theoretically European HRM is similar to the US model, for example in terms of the role of HRM and its key assumptions. However, the environmental factors change how HRM is implemented. For instance, in Europe, trade unions are more influential. There is also more emphasis on a wider range of stakeholders, rather than just shareholders (Brewster, 2007).

HRM trends across Europe

Researchers have recognized different HRM paradigms within the European context. Ferreira (2016) examined a set of high-performance HRM practices across 31 European countries. The project analysed data from the 2005 European Working Conditions Survey (EWCS) with more than 24,000 participants. The study did not find a single European approach to HRM. Instead, the results indicated three clusters with different degrees of implementing HPWS. The identified groups also correspond with an approximate geographical pattern (see Table 9.1).

Notably, Ferreira (2016) found that Nordic countries scored higher than other regions in employees' individual autonomy. The South-West countries demonstrated a solid amount of development in job enrichment, whereas countries in South-Eastern Europe presented the highest degree of implementing communication practices (Ferreira, 2016).

Diaz-Carrion et al (2019) focused on socially responsible HRM and examined CSR reports from 153 European companies headquartered in Germany, Spain, Sweden and the United Kingdom. The authors found evidence suggesting that there is no single model of sustainable HRM in Europe. Rather there are significant differences between HRM practices in the examined countries. Swedish companies were more likely to implement socially responsible HRM than businesses from the other examined regions. The Nordic country scored the highest in the implementation of sustainable practices in all six areas of:

- staffing
- training

- performance evaluation and career management
- compensation
- work–family balance and diversity promotion
- occupational health and safety

On the other side of the spectrum companies with headquarters in Germany were the least likely to implement sustainable HRM policies. Diaz-Carrion et al (2019) explained that this could be partly because Germany has high levels of legal employee protection and CSR accounts focus on actions taken above the legal compliance. Thus, reports filled out by German businesses may present less information about sustainable policies, such as generous

Table 9.1   Implementation of HWPS across Europe

Cluster/Region	Countries	Characteristics
'Northern Europe'	Belgium, Denmark, Estonia, Finland, Ireland, Latvia, Malta, Netherlands, Norway, Slovakia, Slovenia, Sweden, Switzerland and United Kingdom	– Widespread implementation of high-performance practices across all, or almost all, bundles of practices.
'South-West Europe'	Austria, Croatia, France, Germany, Italy, Luxembourg, Poland, Portugal, Spain and Turkey	– Lower implementation of HPWS than in the Northern Europe cluster. – Particularly low scores on practices related to communication. – Decent level of job enrichment close to the Northern cluster.
'South-Eastern Europe'	Bulgaria, Cyprus, Czech Republic, Greece, Hungary, Lithuania and Romania	– Overall, lower implementation of HPWS than in the other two clusters. – Particularly low scores on practices related to job enrichment and training. – Communication practices more common than in the other two clusters.

Examined bundles of practices in areas of communication, individual autonomy, training, reward and incentive, job enrichment, self-managed teams and job rotation.

SOURCE Ferreira (2016)

maternity/paternity leave, because many rules are already ensured by the national employment law (Diaz-Carrion et al, 2019). This could potentially explain German companies' lower scores compared with the other examined regions. At the same time, we need to recognize that while Sweden has very progressive employment legislation, it also has significantly higher *union density*, which is the proportion of paid employees who are union members. Sweden has a union density of approximately 65 per cent, against 16 per cent in Germany (ILOSTAT, 2019).

WORKSHOP DISCUSSION 8

Bitė Lietuva, Lithuania

Companies notice that helping staff with their childcare responsibilities may improve employee recruitment and retention. One business that came to such a conclusion is the Lithuanian telecommunications company Bitė Lietuva. Bitė opened its first kindergarten for employees' children in Vilnius in 2009. Each day the childcare room is open to 10 children aged 3 to 12. Parents can head to work with the peace of mind that they are leaving their kids in the hands of a professional nanny. Due to the success of the initiative, in 2015 the company decided to open its second kindergarten, this time for colleagues working at the Ukmergė call centre. More than 30 employees work at this branch.

Company kindergartens are free and available to all employees. They are open from 8 am until 5 pm and are used by 70 per cent of workers with children in the applicable age group. Parents have the flexibility to use the kindergarten for a full day or just a couple of hours. Nannies, trained in pre-school education, keep children entertained by organizing different activities and tasks suitable to the children's age.

In 2019 the company also opened a children's room in the Šiauliai office. This space is designed for older kids who do not need supervision. Children can use the room to do their homework or play while they are waiting for their parents to finish work.

According to Eglė Staniulionė, the People Embassy Manager (Head of HR) at Bitė, company kindergartens benefit all parties involved: children are happy and well cared for; parents are able to concentrate on their work as the company makes it easier for them to balance family and professional life; and onsite kindergartens can save them time and money. Moreover, they may feel better knowing that their children are near them. Finally, the company is able to use the programme to attract talented employees balancing career development and childcare.

Bitė is an award-winning employer with titles for best employer among Baltic countries in 2021 (according to international personnel management company

Kincentric) and is one of the top employers in Lithuania (according to international internet recruitment company CV-Online).

eMAGNETIX Online Marketing, Austria

eMAGNETIX is a small Austrian online marketing agency. In 2015 the company advertised a project management role. Not a single person applied for the vacancy. This forced eMAGNETIX to reconsider its management practices and make the company a more attractive workplace. One of the changes introduced was reduced working time. The company first trailed a policy where employees work a 34-hour week. After a successful test in October 2018, they introduced a 30-hour week with a full salary. In 2019 the same project management role became open but this time the company received 75 job applications. eMAGNETIX managed to gain a reputation as a great employer with innovative solutions to HRM. Since the company revitalized its HRM practices it has won several awards including first place for Austria's Best Employers 2019 in category X-SMALL (20–49 employees).

City of Kankaanpää, Finland

In 2010 the City of Kankaanpää in Finland introduced a more holistic approach to age management. The municipality employs more than 500 people and wanted to ensure that its workplace was suitable for all members of staff including older colleagues.

The municipality introduced policies that benefit all employees, such as flexible work arrangements, a new system for tracking working hours and accumulated overtime, free access to municipal sports facilities and programmes endorsing exercise. However, the City also introduced a few initiatives that specifically targeted older employees. Staff over the age of 55 were encouraged to get health check-ups every three years. These were more frequent doctor visits than the standard once-in-five-years medical check-ups suggested to younger employees. Moreover, staff over the age of 60 could use two additional days of paid leave. The municipality also introduced practices that assist knowledge exchange between younger and older workers. The aim of the more active age management was to increase the average retirement age and provide a more sustainable workplace.

In 2015 the City of Kankaanpää won a prize of €40,000 from the Working Life Award Fund established by the Finnish Ministry of Social Affairs and Health. The employer received recognition for its promotion of elder workers' continuous employment.

Questions

1 Consider the above examples of management practices from Bitė Lietuva, eMAGNETIX and the City of Kankaanpää. What challenges related to employees' lives are these three organizations trying to address?

2 Who do you think are the stakeholders of Bitė Lietuva, eMAGNETIX and the City of Kankaanpää that benefit from the management practices described in the workshop article? What do you think are the benefits for the stakeholders?

3 Do you think that the management actions of Bitė Lietuva, eMAGNETIX and the City of Kankaanpää are unique to the context of Lithuania, Austria and Finland where these organizations operate? Discuss this topic with a consideration of different environmental forces that impact HRM practices in national contexts.

Sources

www.eurofound.europa.eu/sites/default/files/ef20021en2_0.pdf

https://kaunozinios.lt/lietuva/i-lietuvos-bendroviu-biurus-atkeliauja-vaiku-darzeliai-trys-ju-naudos-darbuotojams_97449.html

https://sc.bns.lt/view/item/358027

www.tv3.lt/naujiena/verslas/bite-lietuva-trecius-metus-is-eiles-pripazinta-geriausiu-darbdaviu-baltijos-salyse-n1125933

www.apiedarba.lt/cv-online-top-darbdaviai-2020/

www.kleinezeitung.at/karriere/neuearbeitswelt/5735786/Firmenchef-zieht-Bilanz_30Stunden-volles-Gehalt_Wir-bekommen-die?from=rss

www.emagnetix.at/

www.greatplacetowork.at/workplace/item/1753/eMAGNETIX+Online+Marketing+GmbH

www.kt.fi/uutiset-ja-tiedotteet/2015/vuoden-2015-ty%C3%B6elamapalkinto-kankaanpaalle

Unsustainable practices in regions focusing on sustainability

According to Ehnert et al (2014), on a macro level HRM in Europe is 'more prone to long-term thinking' and leads in the development of sustainable people management. However, research shows that even in regions famous for socially responsible employment practices, such as Sweden and Finland, employees can be subject to unsustainable or even exploitative working conditions (e.g. Axelsson and Hedberg 2018; Ollus, 2016). For example, Ollus (2016) conducted interviews with employers and employees in the Finnish cleaning industry. Staff who had few employment options were vulnerable to arrangements with poor working terms and conditions. Ollus provided examples of 'forced flexibility' where migrants, due to their circumstances, had little choice but to accept zero-hours contracts (see also Chapter 3). Asked about sustainability of management practices, employer representatives shifted the responsibility onto employees (Ollus, 2016):

> Isn't it already a bit stupid of the worker to start to work under such a zero-hour contract? I wouldn't dare [to do it] myself if I had a contract like that.

Middle East

The Middle East has rich diversity in terms of political and economic systems, languages and ethnicities. This region is also a melting pot of religious beliefs such as Islam, Judaism, Christianity, Zoroastrianism and a range of different denominations and minor religious groups. Having said that, the majority of the population in the Middle East is Muslim. In most of the region Islam strongly influences the political system and everyday life. For example, in countries such as Saudi Arabia, the UAE and Oman, 'there is no clear separation between Islam, state affairs and private life' (Koleva, 2021).

Islamic principles and HRM

Literature suggests that Islamic principles affect the practice of HRM in the Middle East (Metcalfe, 2007; Budhwar and Mellahi, 2007). Islam promotes collaboration and mutual respect in private and work environments. Islam also emphasizes work ethic and self-improvement. This suggests that staff need to engage in training and development to achieve better performance. Employees are expected to show long-term commitment to their organizations, and employers should demonstrate care towards their personnel. Nepotism in recruitment goes against Islamic values of equity and fairness, although Ali and Al-Kazemi (2006) argued that not all employees and organizations adhere to these religious principles. Budhwar et al (2019) pointed out that 'wasta' is a major challenge in the region. *Wasta* is an Arabic word for favouritism and providing someone we know with benefits such as getting hired or promoted. As the author explained, 'Despite being a punishable crime in certain countries (e.g. Jordan), the prevalence of wasta in organizations in the region is on the increase because it is proving to be impossible to overcome bureaucratic obstacles in any other way' (Budhwar et al, 2019).

Gender inequality

Another challenge is related to gender equality in work and career opportunities. Traditionally, patriarchal structures with imposed gender roles have strongly impacted employment practices in the Middle East. This is still true in many parts of the region. According to the Global Gender Gap Report, out of the 24 lowest-scoring countries in the gender economic participation index, 18 are from the Middle East and North Africa (WEF, 2021).

Over the last few decades there has been a high integration of the Middle Eastern states with world trade markets. This puts pressure on modernization and recognition of gender equality and diversity (Metcalfe, 2007). For example, in the UAE, Emirati women are in charge of over 23,000 businesses. Collectively these organizations are worth between US $45 billion and $50 billion. The UAE also requires every government organization and every company to have female board members (Patterson et al, 2020). According to the macro data from the Gender Gap Report, the Middle East is making progress in providing equal opportunities. However, the improvements are still slow and at the current pace it will take the region 142 years to close the gender gap (WEF, 2021). For HR professionals and managers this highlights the importance of introducing policies and practices that assist women's employment and career development. This includes:

- challenging gender stereotypes
- providing equal opportunities in recruitment and selection
- supporting female role models and mentoring
- providing professional training for women
- providing maternity and family policies

Perception of socially responsible management

The idea of businesses engaging in socially responsible management is gaining popularity in the Middle East, although the rate of change varies among countries and industries (Al-Abdin et al, 2018). For example, 80 per cent of surveyed Moroccan SMEs perceive CSR as an 'economic constraint' (El Baz et al, 2016). El Baz and colleagues examined organizations in the food processing industry and found that in Morocco SMEs focus on maximizing profit and engaging in sustainable practices only where they align with financial returns (see Table 9.2). With little attention to social or environmental sustainability this limits the amount of socially responsible practices used by Moroccan SMEs. This contrasts with how French SMEs perceive CSR, namely as an 'economic opportunity' or 'global opportunity' (El Baz et al, 2016). When SMEs view CSR as an 'economic opportunity' they are more likely to recognize the importance of employee well-being and safety or creating a good work climate, as these factors can have a strategic and positive impact on the organization (El Baz et al, 2016).

The contrast between French and Moroccan SMEs is related to the wider cultural, institutional and economic differences between the two countries (El Baz et al, 2016). However, for managers and HR practitioners who wish to introduce sustainable HRM in the context of Moroccan SMEs it may be

Table 9.2   Perception of socially responsible business practices – food-processing SMEs in Morocco and France

Perception profile	SMEs in Morocco	SMEs in France	Key characteristics
CSR as an ethical constraint	–	10%	– Significant dissonance between management vision and action. – Economic conditions of the organization limit managers' and employees' ability to behave in a desired way which is sustainable and socially responsible.
CSR as a global opportunity	–	30%	– Focus on innovating sustainable practices. – Search for new sustainable solutions that balance social, environmental and economic development.
CSR an economic constraint	80%	20%	– Focus on maximizing profitability. – Limited attention to the social and environmental dimensions of sustainability. – Limited recognition of responsibility towards a wider group of stakeholders.
CSR an economic opportunity	20%	40%	– Focus on profits combined with active engagement in CSR. – Sustainability and social responsibility seen as a part of business strategy.

SOURCE El Baz et al (2016)

useful to understand and be aware of the dominant perception patterns related to sustainability. The study conducted by El Baz et al (2016) highlights international differences in how SMEs view social responsibility.

Research on sustainable HRM

There is a gradually growing amount of research examining sustainable HRM in the Middle East. Mohiuddin et al (2022) analysed what factors affect the achievement of HRM sustainability in Iranian state universities. The researchers surveyed 334 employees. The study found that 'social factors, psychological factors, employer branding, and economic factors have positive and significant effects on HRM sustainability at universities' (Mohiuddin et al, 2022). Iran is facing difficult economic conditions and there is an increasing interest in sustainable development of cities. According to Mohiuddin et al (2022), managers of the examined universities show commitment to sustainable HRM as a measure to cope with local social and environmental challenges.

Fayyazi et al (2015) set out to explore the barriers to GHRM implementation in the Iranian oil industry. The researchers conducted interviews with 12 industry experts and surveyed 31 HR managers. According to their findings the biggest barriers to introducing GHRM were poor implementation planning and ambiguity of green values (Fayyazi et al, 2015).

Ababneh (2021) examined the impact of GHRM practices on employees' green behaviours in four- and five-star hotels operating in Jordan. The author conducted a survey of staff working in hotels with publicly announced commitments to environmental protection. The study found a positive impact of green HRM practices on the 'firm's successful and efficient implementation of environmentally related policies and strategies' (Ababneh, 2021). Particularly, the study highlighted the importance of green job redesign and carefully planned environmental training programmes.

Many countries in the Middle East rely on oil production and export. Political actors and organizations operating in these economies show determination for sustainable development, particularly in the environmental dimension. This can stimulate the development of GHRM practice and studies. However, we also need to recognize that in the Middle East, political sensitivity and concerns about political repression can limit the scope of research (Clark, 2006), this includes examining in more depth issues such as socially unsustainable practices in people management.

Africa

Africa is the second most populous continent. It also has the youngest population in the world (UN, n.d.) and above-average *labour force participation rate* (ILO, 2020), which is an estimate of a region's active workforce, calculated by summing employed and unemployed people, then dividing it by the total number of working-age population. In other words, in Africa there is a large number of people available to engage in paid work. However, the region is still developing skills that are needed for 21st-century jobs. Estimates suggest that sub-Saharan Africa has a lower level of digital proficiencies compared to other parts of the world (Choi et al, 2020). For organizations this highlights the importance of training, mentoring and creating partnerships with educational institutions (Dieke, 2020). The need for developing skills is also related to management and leadership positions. For more sustainable development, training at the higher levels of organizational hierarchy needs to be more planned and structured rather than informal and conducted in an ad hoc manner (Okupe, 2020). Due to the gap in the supply of many skills, developing the human resource pool in Africa has significant value for supporting local communities. As argued by Mamman et al (2018), 'The HR profession is well equipped to make a significant contribution in developing the human and organizational capacities that can lead to the realization of Africa's potential within the context of SDGs.' According to Mamman et al (2018), this requires HR to extend its boundaries of responsibilities and provide support in areas where institutions and state agencies have created a void. The authors identified seven main challenges that HR professionals are likely to face in Africa:

- limited understanding of the role that HR can play in the sustainable development of communities in Africa;
- low institutionalization and limited formal structures available for the HR profession (e.g. lack of professional bodies or their low profile);
- limited formal training and education available for HR professionals;
- weak regulation and enforcement of rules structuring employment relations;
- the profession has not yet reached the point of critical mass needed to gain visibility and recognition;
- there are cases of underqualified staff working in HR roles, which lowers the profile of the profession and lowers organizations' expectations from the role;

- other wider issues related to the organizational environment in Africa, e.g. corruption, limited technical and managerial competencies, scarcity of financial resources.

Equality, diversity and inclusion

A substantial challenge for sustainable HRM in this region is related to managing equality, diversity and inclusion. For example, inter-tribal conflicts are a particularly sensitive topic in Africa. Tribal diversity is similar to ethnic diversity; however, as explained by Zoogah (2016) the former concept is narrower. In Africa, especially the sub-Saharan region, tribal identification is stronger than ethnic or racial identification, although the literature often uses these terms interchangeably (Zoogah, 2016). Political actors in Africa create divides between tribal groups by exacerbating identity-based differences, spreading stereotypes and presenting the other groups as a 'threat'. At the same time, they elevate the status of their own groups and call for loyalty in conflicts between 'us' and 'them' (Parboteeah et al, 2014). Tribal conflicts pose difficulties for managing diversity and protecting employees' rights to freedom from discrimination. Biased managers may introduce policies and practices that will encourage a lack of tribal diversity. Performance of employees who belong to the same tribe as the manager may be seen more favourably. In-group members may receive higher pay and more career development opportunities (Zoogah, 2016). According to Zoogah (2016), diversity management can be used to 'neutralize high tribal identification in the workplace'. Sustainable HRM in a region with high tribal diversity needs to consider promotion of tribal harmony, de-escalation of conflicts and provision of open channels of communication where employees can discuss issues of mistreatment.

Another challenge related to diversity and inclusion is under-representation of local employees in managerial roles at international companies. One of the studies that came to such a conclusion was conducted by Nwosu and Ogunyemi (2020). The authors set out to examine sustainable HRM in the Nigerian hospitality sector. They found that 'out of 40 international brand hotels in Nigeria, there is currently only one local general manager, the first in the history of branded hotels in Nigeria' (Nwosu and Ogunyemi, 2020). The study also found examples of gender imbalance in managerial roles. Indeed, according to the International Labour Organization (ILO) (2020), Africa shows a high gender gap in the labour force participation rate. This is particularly concerning in Northern Africa where the gap is 47 per cent and almost twice the global average (27.1 per cent).

Green HRM

Edeh and Okwurume (2019) examined GHRM in Nigerian banks. The study found that practices of green recruitment were strongly and positively correlated with organizations' environmental sustainability. At the same time, green training was strongly linked with economic sustainability and green employee relations were positively associated with social sustainability. The authors concluded that the inclusion of GRHM practices can have strategic importance for Nigerian banks. In a similar study, Akpa et al (2022) examined the Nigerian hospitality industry and found that GHRM has a positive impact on employee retention.

Ikhide et al (2021) found that Nigerian millennials are concerned with organizations' socially responsible operations. Similar to other parts of the world, the young generation in Nigeria is more likely to join organizations that engage in CSR. The perception of the potential employer is particularly positive if a job seeker sees that the organization engages in CSR because of altruistic or public-serving motives (Ikhide et al, 2021).

South Asia

South Asia includes Afghanistan, Bangladesh, Bhutan, India, Maldives, Nepal, Pakistan and Sri Lanka. Economically, South Asia is one of the fastest-growing regions in the world. Foreign direct investment to this region has increased from US $3.2 billion in 1999 to $71 billion in 2020, with the majority of this financial capital ($64 billion) flowing into India (UNCTAD, 2000, 2022). The countries in South Asia were heavily affected by Covid-19, then started to gradually recover from the pandemic recession and the economic headwinds in a form of inflation (World Bank, 2022a).

Talent management

South Asia has a large supply of labour force with a population of 1.8 billion. Almost half the people living here are below the age of 24. However, similar to Africa, a large portion of the population does not have the skills needed for decent-quality jobs (UNICEF, 2019). A limited skill base is one of the factors that hinder developing countries such as Pakistan from fully integrating with global businesses and world markets (Asrar-ul-Haq, 2015).

Ali and Guha (2018) argued that talent management can be more challenging in developing parts of South Asia, compared to Western countries. In South Asia the pool of people with professional skills is limited and educated employees often choose to migrate to other countries. For example, many doctors leave Pakistan and move to countries with more developed economies (Sohail and Habib, 2016). Poor financial gains and political instability are quoted as main reasons for the 'brain drain' in the Pakistani medical profession (Tahir et al, 2011). A *brain drain* refers to a substantial departure of highly educated or skilled people from one country (area or economic sector) to another. Covid-19 has temporarily slowed down the emigration of Pakistani workers, and due to layoffs many people migrated back to their home country (Bureau of Emigration & Overseas Employment, 2020). However, without systemic and management changes, skilled employees will feel that they are pushed out of their home country. According to Ali and Guha (2018), HRM inefficiencies impede recruitment, motivation and retention of talent in South Asia. This often includes:

- ineffective, narrow or traditional recruitment practices
- limited use of employer branding
- limited partnerships between industry and educational institutions
- ineffective applicant processing
- inappropriate or outdated selection criteria
- ineffective selection processes
- ineffective organizational systems for learning and developing careers
- uncompetitive remuneration
- lack of strategic planning by HR professionals
- rigid hierarchies
- poor processes related to talent identification and appreciation
- poor attention to leadership development and succession planning

Gender inequality

Tackling gender inequality is another big challenge for the South Asian region. This is related to many areas of private, social and public life including work opportunities and work experiences. As explained in the report from the World Bank (2022a), 'Despite decades of rapid economic growth, rising education, and declining fertility, women in South Asia continue to face greater disadvantages in accessing economic opportunities than in most of the developing world.'

The report also explains that on a global scale the number of people with traditional views about gender roles is decreasing. However, in Bangladesh, India and Pakistan, traditional views about gender inequality have increased over time. The majority of the population in these three countries hold conservative views about gender roles and support 'preferential access to jobs for men' (World Bank, 2022a).

The legal framework in this region also does not provide a strong base for sustainable HRM. The law in Afghanistan, Bangladesh, Nepal and Pakistan does not prohibit dismissal of employees because they are pregnant (World Bank, 2020). Apart from Bhutan and Nepal, other countries in the region do not have a law to protect the right to equal remuneration for equal work (World Bank, 2022a). At the same time, there are legal provisions that restrict women's access to different industries or for how long they can work. In most countries in the region, women cannot work the same night hours as men, they cannot work in mining and in some manufacturing jobs. The Maldives is the only country in the region where there are no legal restrictions on women's employment (World Bank, 2018).

There are wider macro-societal factors (e.g. legal, socio-cultural) which affect women's work in South Asia and are beyond the influence of the employer (Ali, 2013). However, there are also organizational policies related to diversity and work fairness which sustainable HRM can champion in the South Asia region. First, in instances where the legal framework does not protect basic employee rights (e.g. equal pay for equal work), sustainable HRM should introduce policies that cover such issues. Second, where the legal framework exists it can be poorly implemented in practice (Strachan et al, 2015). Even if sexual harassment is illegal, employees may not know how to identify instances of harassment, or they may be afraid and ashamed to report those cases. The HR function plays a vital role in increasing awareness and setting zero-tolerance policies for harassment and discrimination. HR should create channels through which employees can safely bring to light information about experiences of mistreatment. Induction and training of employees should cover the subjects of equality, diversity and inclusion. Managers and supervisors should be directly responsible for implementing EDI policies and for promoting a work environment free from harassment and discrimination (Suram, 2015).

Research on sustainable HRM

Mariappanadar (2020) examined the impact of HPWS on Indian employees' well-being. The researcher surveyed employees from three organizations with 250–500 employees, one in each industry of finance, health and higher education. Mariappanadar (2020) found that 'High-quality bundles of motivation-enhancing HRM practices used to improve organizational performance also impose increased health harm of work on employees'. Similar findings related to HPWS and health harm were also found in Indian IT companies (Chillakuri and Vanka, 2022).

Mishra (2017) examined GHRM in India by conducting interviews with HR professionals from six manufacturing businesses. The researcher found that while some elements of GHRM were implemented, these practices were often introduced in an ad hoc manner without a formal structure. For example, employers used workplace posters to increase employees' awareness about green behaviours but only half of the organizations provided formal environmental training. Mishra (2017) argued that active participation and visible support from senior management is vital for promoting employees' green behaviours.

East and Southeast Asia

One of the significant factors affecting sustainability of HRM in East and Southeast Asia is the 'demographic window of opportunity' (DWO) and its different stages across the region (Debroux, 2010). DWO is 'a period of several decades that countries go through when moving from a situation of high fertility and mortality to low fertility and mortality' (Crombach and Smits, 2022). During the DWO, economies can experience rapid economic growth due to a large working-age population coupled with a relatively small group of people who are too young or too old to engage in paid work.

In Japan and South Korea the DWO is already closed (> 15 per cent over age 64). In China, most economically developed parts of the country are also in the post-window phase, while other regions are in the 'late' stage of DWO (< 20 per cent under 15 and < 15 per cent over 64). However, the DWO is still open in Southeast Asian countries such as Indonesia, the Philippines and Malaysia, where there is a large number of young people (20–30 per cent under 15) coupled with a small population over 64 (less than 10 per cent) (Crombach and Smits, 2022; World Bank, 2022b).

These demographic profiles emphasize the strategic importance of different practices in sustainable people management. For example, in regions with ageing populations it may be more urgent to promote elder workers' continuous employment. With higher average age there may also be more need to consider what motivates employees at different stages of their careers and to implement training programmes that transmit knowledge and skills between employees (Pinto et al, 2014). These are standard practices in diversity management, but they become even more pressing in regions such as East Asia where the population is ageing and declining.

At the same time, in Southeast Asian countries that have a large young population (e.g. Indonesia, the Philippines, Malaysia) it may be more urgent to gain a deeper understanding of what motivates new generations of employees. Do the HRM practices need to be updated to keep up with the wave of young employees? For example, faster provision of performance feedback may be needed to keep younger employees engaged (Vraňaková et al, 2021).

Japan

Japan is transitioning out of a system of lifetime employment. According to the traditional HRM practice, large Japanese companies would recruit fresh school and university graduates and provide them with employment for the rest of their careers. In exchange, employees were expected to show loyalty to their employer and fully devote their time and energy to the success of the organization. The number of employees who enjoy this lifetime employment has been decreasing since the 1990s (Shimoda, 2015). Traditional job security is currently offered mostly to core employees at the expense of peripheral staff who are on temporary or part-time contracts. It is possible that in the near future core workers will also not be provided with lifetime employment. In 2019 the chairman of the Japan Business Federation (Keidanren) made a statement, ahead of annual spring negotiations with labour unions, that Japanese-style employment, which includes a lifetime employment system, needs to be reconsidered (Kawate, 2019). This is one of several public statements made by business leaders signalling the continuing transformation of Japanese HRM.

On the surface, Japanese lifetime employment could be seen as a sustainable approach to HRM. However, it is key to note that in Japan the by-product of this system has been a significant extension of employees' working hours, poor-quality employment contracts for non-regular employees and strong gender segregation of employment (OECD, 2021). Many authors have pointed out that in the traditional Japanese HRM system women have limited promotion opportunities. According to a survey conducted by Reuters, women constitute less than 10 per cent of managers at most Japanese companies and changing this number requires a dramatic shift in 'Japan's male-oriented corporate culture' (Kajimoto, 2021). The price that Japanese employees and their families pay for the maintenance of the old HRM system is high (Lewis, 2016; Uzama, 2008). Perhaps a transformation of Japanese HRM will create an opportunity for more sustainable forms of people management.

China

After joining the World Trade Organization (WTO) in 2001 China soon became known as the 'world's factory'. Due to a large workforce, limited labour laws and poor regulatory compliance Chinese companies were able to achieve low production costs and became extremely competitive in global markets, particularly manufacturing. With rapid economic growth, real wages (wages adjusted for inflation) of Chinese employees also started to increase (ILO, 2016) and Chinese authorities began to shift their focus towards gradually improving the quality of work and offering more advanced forms of production. In 2016 the ILO and Chinese constituents started a programme focusing on promoting a decent work agenda. In 2019 the ILO and China signed a Memorandum of Understanding to 'promote decent work, social justice and a human-centred future of work with the Ministry of Human Resources and Social Security' (MoHRSS) (ILO, 2022). In 2021 the Supreme People's Court and MoHRSS released guidelines that impose limitations on overtime (Huang, 2021).

There is a growing interest in China in social, environmental and economic sustainability. Since 2006 a number of laws, regulations and guidelines have been released in this region to promote and set standards in CSR (Wu and Hąbek, 2021). For example, in 2008 the Shenzhen and Shanghai Stock Exchanges mandated that a subset of listed companies has to issue stand-alone CSR reports and offered incentives for companies that promote CSR. Irrespective of the regulatory push, employers may want to voluntarily engage in sustainable practices and this includes manufacturing companies. Lin-Hi et al (2019) examined what determines job choice for blue-collar employees working for a Chinese garment factory. The study found that socially responsible HRM practices had a positive and strong impact on the perception of employer attractiveness, employer prestige and how likely a person is to recommend the factory as an employer. According to the authors, more sustainable human resource management is 'a powerful instrument for factories in emerging countries to cope with the new reality whereby labour is becoming a scarce resource' (Lin-Hi et al, 2019).

Indonesia

Indonesia has the largest economy in Southeast Asia. The country has seen remarkable growth, with GDP increasing from the 26th largest in the world in 2000 to the 16th largest in 2021 (World Bank, 2022c). In 2021 Indonesia was ranked the second-best country in the world in which to invest (US News, 2021). These economic opportunities are taking place in parallel with HRM practices being strongly influenced by a complex culture and pluralistic society (Novianti, 2018). Indonesia is composed of approximately 17,000 islands, and due to its geographic area, is one of the most ethnically diverse countries in the world. This, coupled with a mosaic of non-indigenous ethnic minorities, creates challenges and opportunities for managing cross-cultural differences.

Moreover, MNCs that open subsidiaries in Indonesia can face friction when transferring HR practices from their home country. For example, Soehardjojo et al (2022) found that Indonesian managers resisted the adoption and adaptation of Japanese HRM and employment relations practices.

Ideas of social justice and prosperity are deeply embedded in the Indonesian state philosophy (Pancasila). They influence institutional frameworks and organizational practices including HRM (Supangco and Los Baños, 2018). Thus, the concept of sustainable businesses corresponds with the local culture (Sitorus, 2016). However, the field of corporate social responsibility is still in its early stages of development. Ridho (2017) found that the majority of CSR managers in Indonesian-listed companies perceive CSR as limited to donations and community development programmes. This means that there is an opportunity for local HR practitioners to demonstrate how people management practices can help organizations improve and broaden their CSR performance.

Australia and New Zealand

Australia and New Zealand share many similarities that affect their HRM practice. Since the early 1990s employment relations in both countries have been converging towards a comparable neoliberal approach. Colvin and Darbishire (2013) argued that in terms of labour market regulation, Australia and New Zealand have moved towards the model of Anglo-American countries that is also shaping standards in Canada, the UK and the US. In this shift employers are gradually increasing their discretion over the labour market and the role of labour unions is challenged. At the same time union membership has been declining. In Australia, union density fell from 51 per cent in 1976 to 14.3 per cent in 2020 (Australian Bureau of Statistics, 2020), and in New Zealand it decreased from 56 per cent in 1975 to 17.7 per cent in 2018 (Ellem and Franks, 2008; Centre for Labour, Employment and Work, 2020).

Small businesses dominate the private sector in New Zealand, and this influences the style of HRM practised in the country. According to OECD (2022b), 99 per cent of businesses in New Zealand have between 0 and 49 employees and they employ 41.5 per cent of the national workforce. Boxall et al (2018) explained that with a large number of smaller businesses, HRM in New Zealand can be less formal and more oriented towards agile operations. Smaller organizations do not engage in extensive labour planning or formal job analysis. Employers may also have more limited budgets dedicated to staff training, with a lot of the personnel development taking place through informal mentoring and coaching.

The business landscape in New Zealand is changing, however. Between 2000 and 2020 the number of big employers with more than 100 staff increased by 58 per cent, reaching a total of 2,690 businesses. On average, though, businesses are still relatively small (NZ Government, 2020) and such employers can struggle to retain their key employees. With globally connected competitive labour markets, larger organizations abroad attract many highly skilled workers from New Zealand. Smaller organizations have fewer resources to offer competitive reward packages and career development programmes. This makes it difficult for New Zealand employers to retain staff, but also to recruit new employees, as the local labour market loses many young workers to offshore opportunities (Newshub, 2022).

Australia has a larger economy and a population approximately five times bigger than New Zealand. In 2020 in Australia there were over 4,300 companies with more than 200 staff (OECD, 2022c). Boxall et al (2018) pointed out that small businesses in Australia have similar HRM practices to those of their counterparts in New Zealand. However, larger companies in Australia have more developed *internal labour markets* – in other words systems where people are hired and promoted within the organization. This opens opportunities for more comprehensive succession planning and being able to offer a wider range of options for career development. Big companies may also be able to offer more attractive policies related to leave from work, e.g. flexible unpaid leave (Boxall et al, 2018).

Podgorodnichenko et al (2022) interviewed HR managers from New Zealand and Australian organizations that have a public statement about a sustainability programme. The study found various levels of engagement with sustainable HRM. It ranged from neglect, where little attention is paid to sustainable HRM, through limited and ad hoc approaches, to full recognition and a strategic role for sustainability in shaping HRM practices. The researchers concluded that where the sustainability agenda is implemented it broadens the scope of the HR function and helps to bring a 'stakeholder perspective and pluralist frame' to the practice of HRM (Podgorodnichenko et al, 2022) (this study is also discussed in Chapter 7).

Looking at GHRM, Parida et al (2021) surveyed employees and managers working in green office buildings across Australia. They confirmed that 'Green HRM has a central role to play in eliciting green behaviours in green office buildings and consequently improving employee outcomes'.

Skill check

Identifying external forces, in different parts of the world, which shape sustainable HRM. This is a key skill, especially important for organizations that operate in more than one country or plan to expand their operations abroad.

Multinational corporations and sustainable HRM

Multinational corporations (MNCs) have a significant amount of resources at their disposal. This can be used to create value for employees, communities and the environment, or inflict substantial harm. For example, in 2010, 18 migrant workers committed suicide while working in extreme conditions at a factory in China. The plant was owned by Foxconn, a multinational electronics manufacturer (BBC, 2010). Unsustainable practices carried out by MNCs for decades have been the subject of heated debate in the field of business ethics (Crane et al, 2019). Nowadays, with the proliferation of media platforms and different forms through which people consume news, there is increased pressure on global businesses to cease any forms of unethical practices. What's more, operating according to minimal legal compliance is often seen as no longer sufficient. MNCs are expected to champion best practices in sustainable development. In HRM this means maintaining standards in quality of employment across subsidiaries. For instance, Diageo, a multinational alcohol beverage company that owns brands such as Johnnie Walker, Guinness, Smirnoff and Baileys, introduced its own global standard of maternity and paternity leave. The company offers a minimum of 26 weeks of fully paid maternity leave and a minimum of four weeks of fully paid paternity leave in all markets where it operates. Moreover, in 14 selected countries the company offers 26 weeks of fully paid paternity leave (Diageo, 2020).

Academic research shows mixed findings on sustainable HRM performance in MNCs. For example, Bar-Haim and Karassin (2022) examined 11 Israeli industrial firms, a third of which were MNCs and the rest SMEs. The researchers found that socially responsible employment relations and HRM did not differ between the two types of organization. Both types of businesses failed to operate beyond the regulatory standards. The key challenge in the examined businesses was managers' negative and ambivalent orientation towards CSR and sustainable HRM. On the other hand, Haddock-Millar et al (2016) analysed GHRM introduced in British, German and Swedish subsidiaries of a US restaurant chain. The researchers found that across the subsidiaries there was 'evidence of proactive environmental management' with a range of 'people-centred initiatives'. Ehnert and colleagues (2016) wanted to check if the world's largest MNCs are more likely to disclose their CSR performance related to environmental protection rather than labour and decent work sustainability. The researchers were surprised to find that the biggest companies do not neglect 'people matters' in their social responsibility reporting. In fact, 'labour and decent work' was discussed by 73.7 per cent of the analysed reports, and it was the second most commonly discussed topic after economic sustainability (74.2 per cent of reports). The other CSR matters that Ehnert et al (2016) included in their study were:

- society (71.9 per cent)
- environment (68.6 per cent)
- human rights (65.9 per cent)
- product responsibility (64.5 per cent)

When MNCs engage in a transfer of sustainability practices this is often launched with the idea of headquarters sending information and management instructions to subsidiaries, but the exchange can be bilateral. Wehling et al (2009) studied the transfer of sustainable values from German multinationals to their Brazilian subsidiaries. They found that in some companies, sustainability ideas were also passed from Brazilian subsidiaries to the German headquarters.

HRM can be the subject of sustainable practices that are shared between the host and local country, for example encouraging subsidiaries to also introduce flexible work hours. However, we should remember that HRM is also the channel needed to share sustainability vision, practices and knowledge across MNCs' branches, for example through training and performance management.

Summary

External factors, such as government policies, demographic trends or economic development, have a significant impact on sustainable HRM practice. This chapter highlighted key similarities and differences between regions and identified challenges that the field is facing in various parts of the world.

In developing countries one of the concerns is breaking away from paternalistic management and shifting towards more democratic and participatory management. Rising economies are also facing the issue of building employee competences. For example, in sub-Saharan Africa there is a substantial gap between the large working population and the skills needed for decent jobs. HR professionals and managers in this region need to consider how to strategically and sustainably grow the capabilities of the local talent pool. Equality, diversity and inclusion continues to be a global effort and a pivotal element of sustainable HRM. However, in regions where the economy is still developing there is a particularly large scope for improving organizational EDI.

In many developed countries an ageing population forces HR professionals and managers to think more creatively about retaining and motivating staff. Moreover, in territories with more neoliberal governmental policies and weak union membership, there is pressure on employers to show initiative and provide good standards of job quality.

Sustainable HRM is an evolving area of management. Organizations' international connections add a dimension of difficulty to the study and practice of this field. However, the global markets also open opportunities to share knowledge and meaningful solutions in people management that balances social, environmental and business objectives.

Study questions

1 Do government policies in the US and Canada create different environments for sustainable HRM in these two countries? Support your answer with examples.

2 Discuss whether managerial paternalism correlates with sustainable HRM.

3 Is there a European model of sustainable HRM? Justify your answer by referencing key authors.

4 Discuss different ways in which CSR is perceived by Moroccan and French SMEs.

5 What are some of the contextual challenges that can affect sustainable HRM practice in Africa?

6 What is 'demographic window of opportunity' and how can it influence sustainable HRM practices?

7 What are some of the contextual challenges that can affect sustainable HRM practice in Australia and New Zealand?

Key reading

Brewster, C, Mayrhofer, W and Farndale, E (eds.) (2018) *Handbook of Research on Comparative Human Resource Management*, 2nd edn, Edward Elgar Publishing, Cheltenham

Diaz-Carrion, R, López-Fernández, M and Romero-Fernandez, P M (2019) Evidence of different models of socially responsible HRM in Europe, *Business Ethics: A European Review*, **28** (1), pp 1–18

Lewis, L (2016) The curse of the salaryman, as Shinzo Abe seeks reform, Japan's once-heroic symbol of dynamism is proving to be a roadblock, *Financial Times*, www.ft.com/content/d1a6aa18-1045-11e6-91da-096d89bd2173

References

Ababneh, O M A (2021) How do green HRM practices affect employees' green behaviors? The role of employee engagement and personality attributes, *Journal of Environmental Planning and Management*, **64** (7), pp 1204–226

Akpa, V O, Mowaiye, B, Akinlabi, B H and Magaji, N (2022) Effect of green human resource management practices and green work life balance on employee retention in selected hospitality firms in Lagos and Ogun states, Nigeria, *European Journal of Human Resource Management Studies*, **5** (4), pp 129–43

Al-Abdin, A, Roy, T and Nicholson, J D (2018) Researching corporate social responsibility in the Middle East: the current state and future directions, *Corporate Social Responsibility and Environmental Management*, **25** (1), pp 47–65

Alberton, A, Kieling, A P, Lyra, F R, Hoffmann, E M, Lopez, M P V and Stefano, S R (2022) Competencies for sustainability in hotels: insights from Brazil, *Employee Relations*, **44** (3), pp 555–75

Ali, A and Al-Kazemi, A (2006) Human resource management in Kuwait. In P Budhwar and K Mellahi (eds.) *Managing Human Resources in the Middle East* (pp 79–96), Routledge, London

Ali, F (2013) A multi-level perspective on equal employment opportunity for women in Pakistan, *Equality, Diversity and Inclusion: An International Journal*, **32** (3), pp 289–309

Ali, M and Guha, S (2018) Talent management in South Asia: prospects and challenges, *Bangladesh Journal of Public Administration (BJPA)*, **26** (2), pp 1–16

Allen, R S, Takeda, M B, White, C S and Helms, M M (2004) Rewards and organizational performance in Japan and the United States: a comparison, *Compensation & Benefits Review*, **36** (1), pp 7–14

Andonova, V, Gutierrez, R and Avella, L F (2009) The strategic importance of close employment relations in conflict-ridden environments: three cases from Colombia. In A Davila and M M Elvira (eds.) *Best Human Resource Management Practices in Latin America* (pp 39–50), Routledge, London and New York

Asrar-ul-Haq, M (2015) Human resource development in Pakistan: evolution, trends and challenges, *Human Resource Development International*, **18** (1), pp 97–104

Aust, I, Muller-Camen, M and Poutsma, E (2018) Sustainable HRM: a comparative and international perspective. In C Brewster, W Mayrhofer and E Farndale (eds.) *Handbook of Research on Comparative Human Resource Management* (pp 358–69), Edward Elgar Publishing, Cheltenham

Australian Bureau of Statistics (2020) Trade union membership, www.abs.gov.au/statistics/labour/earnings-and-working-conditions/trade-union-membership/latest-release (archived at https://perma.cc/E7KF-D5PB)

Axelsson, L and Hedberg, C (2018) Emerging topologies of transnational employment: 'posting' Thai workers in Sweden's wild berry industry beyond regulatory reach, *Geoforum*, 89, pp 1–10

Bachkirov, A A and Shamsudin, F M (2017) Reward allocation decision making in Arab-Islamic business organizations: an empirical examination through an emic lens, *International Journal of Islamic and Middle Eastern Finance and Management*, 10 (4), pp 536–53

Ball, D and Hagerty, J (2013) How to cut a job in Italy? Wait and wait some more, *Wall Street Journal*, www.wsj.com/articles/SB10001424127887324767004578488861272475972 (archived at https://perma.cc/P8Y8-L4SR)

Bar-Haim, A and Karassin, O (2022) CSR-related employment relations and HRM practices at small and medium-sized enterprises vs. multinational corporations, *Journal of Human Resource and Sustainability Studies*, 10 (1), pp 44–66

BBC (2010) Foxconn suicides: 'workers feel quite lonely', www.bbc.com/news/10182824 (archived at https://perma.cc/FGJ8-DA8P)

Bercusson, B (2002) *European Labour Law and the EU Charter of Fundamental Rights: Summary version*, European Trade Union Institute (ETUI)

Block, R N (2006) Industrial relations in the United States and Canada. In M J Morley, P Gunnigle and D Collings (eds.) *Global Industrial Relations* (pp 43–70), Routledge, London and New York

Boxall, P, Bainbridge, H and Frenkel, S (2018) Styles of HRM in Australia and New Zealand. In C Brewster, W Mayrhofer and E Farndale (eds.) *Handbook of research on comparative human resource management* (pp 614–30), Edward Elgar Publishing, Cheltenham

Brewster, C (2007) A European perspective on HRM, *European Journal of International Management*, 1 (3), pp 239–59

Budhwar, P and Mellahi, K (2007) Introduction: human resource management in the Middle East, *The International Journal of Human Resource Management*, 18 (1), pp 2–10

Budhwar, P, Pereira, V, Mellahi, K and Singh, S K (2019) The state of HRM in the Middle East: challenges and future research agenda, *Asia Pacific Journal of Management*, 36 (4), pp 905–33

Bureau of Emigration & Overseas Employment (2020) Labour Migration Report 2020, Government of Pakistan, https://beoe.gov.pk/files/statistics/yearly-reports/2020/2020-full.pdf (archived at https://perma.cc/57LV-JBNH)

Centre for Labour, Employment and Work (2020) Union membership in New Zealand shows further growth, www.wgtn.ac.nz/clew/news/union-membership-in-new-zealand-shows-further-growth (archived at https://perma.cc/9K4S-9WFY)

Chillakuri, B and Vanka, S (2022) Understanding the effects of perceived organizational support and high-performance work systems on health harm through sustainable HRM lens: a moderated mediated examination, *Employee Relations*, **44** (3), pp 629–49

Choi, J, Dutz, M A and Usman, Z (eds.) (2020) *The Future of Work in Africa: Harnessing the potential of digital technologies for all,* World Bank Publications, Washington, DC

Clark, J A (2006) Field research methods in the Middle East, *PS: Political Science & Politics*, **39** (3), pp 417–24

Claus, L (2003) Similarities and differences in human resource management in the European Union, *Thunderbird International Business Review*, **45** (6), pp 729–55

Colvin, A J and Darbishire, O (2013) Convergence in industrial relations institutions: the emerging Anglo-American model?, *ILR Review*, **66** (5), pp 1047–77

Crane, A, Matten, D, Glozer, S and Spence, L (2019) *Business Ethics: Managing corporate citizenship and sustainability in the age of globalization*, Oxford University Press, New York

Crombach, L and Smits, J (2022) The demographic window of opportunity and economic growth at sub-national level in 91 developing countries, *Social Indicators Research*, **161** (1), pp 171–89

Davila, A and Elvira, M M (2018) Revisiting the Latin American HRM model. In C Brewster, W Mayrhofer and E Farndale (eds.) *Handbook of Research on Comparative Human Resource Management* (pp 393–407), Edward Elgar Publishing, Cheltenham

Debroux, P (2010) The evolution of human resource management in East and South-East Asia, *Soka Gakkai Management Theory* [創価経営論集], **34** (2–3), pp 1–21

Diageo (2020) Leading the way on inclusion through equal parental leave, www.diageo.com/en/news-and-media/stories/2020/leading-the-way-on-inclusion-through-equal-parental-leave (archived at https://perma.cc/4K2E-9L9A)

Diaz-Carrion, R, López-Fernández, M and Romero-Fernandez, P M (2019) Evidence of different models of socially responsible HRM in Europe, *Business Ethics: A European Review*, **28** (1), pp 1–18

Dieke, P U (2020) Tourism in Africa: issues and prospects. In T Baum and A Ndiuini (eds.) *Sustainable human resource management in tourism* (pp 9–27), Springer, Cham

Edeh, F O and Okwurume, C N (2019) Green human resource management and organizational sustainability of deposit money banks in Nigeria, *Journal of Management Sciences*, **3** (1), pp 224–35

Ehnert, I, Harry, W and Zink, K J (2014) Sustainable HRM in Europe: diverse contexts and multiple bottom lines. In I Ehnert, W Harry and K J Zink (eds.)

Sustainability and Human Resource Management: Developing sustainable business organizations (pp 339–58), Springer, Berlin/Heidelberg, Germany

Ehnert, I, Parsa, S, Roper, I, Wagner, M, and Muller-Camen, M (2016) Reporting on sustainability and HRM: A comparative study of sustainability reporting practices by the world's largest companies, *The International Journal of Human Resource Management*, **27** (1), pp 88–108

El Baz, J, Laguir, I, Marais, M and Staglianò, R (2016) Influence of national institutions on the corporate social responsibility practices of small-and medium-sized enterprises in the food-processing industry: differences between France and Morocco, *Journal of Business Ethics*, **134** (1), pp 117–33

Ellem, B and Franks, P (2008) Trade union structure and politics in Australia and New Zealand, *Labour History*, **95**, pp 43–67

Eurostat (2022) Minimum wage statistics, https://ec.europa.eu/eurostat/statistics-explained/index.php?title=Minimum_wage_statistics (archived at https://perma.cc/JQ6E-B6MY)

Farndale, E, Raghuram, S, Gully, S, Liu, X, Phillips, J M and Vidović, M (2017) A vision of international HRM research, *The International Journal of Human Resource Management*, **28** (12), pp 1625–39

Fayyazi, M, Shahbazmoradi, S, Afshar, Z and Shahbazmoradi, M (2015) Investigating the barriers of the green human resource management implementation in oil industry, *Management Science Letters*, **5** (1), pp 101–08

Ferreira, P (2016) Is there a European convergence in HRM practices? A cluster analysis of the high-performance paradigm across 31 countries, *International Journal of Engineering and Industrial Management*, **6**, pp 139–64

Government of Canada (2022a) Rights on termination of employment, www.canada.ca/en/employment-social-development/services/labour-standards/reports/termination.html (archived at https://perma.cc/Y6HZ-UAEK)

Government of Canada (2022b) Types of leaves you can receive as an employee working in federally regulated industries and workplaces, www.canada.ca/en/services/jobs/workplace/federal-labour-standards (archived at https://perma.cc/X379-HES8)

Government of Canada (2022c) EI maternity and parental benefits, www.canada.ca/en/services/benefits/ei/ei-maternity-parental.html (archived at https://perma.cc/HRR9-4V35)

Gutiérrez Crocco, F and Martin, A (2022) Towards a sustainable HRM in Latin America? Union-management relationship in Chile, *Employee Relations*, **44** (3), pp 650–62

Haddock-Millar, J, Sanyal, C and Müller-Camen, M (2016) Green human resource management: a comparative qualitative case study of a United States multinational corporation, *The International Journal of Human Resource Management*, **27** (2), pp 192–211

Hernandez-Pozas, O, Murcia, M J, Ogliastri, E and Olivas-Lujan, M R (2021) Management and sustainability dilemmas in Latin America: introduction, *Academia Revista Latinoamericana de Administración*, **34** (1), pp 1–7

Huang, Z (2021) China spells out how excessive '996' work culture is illegal, *Bloomberg*, www.bloomberg.com/news/articles/2021-08-27/china-s-top-court-says-excessive-996-work-culture-is-illegal (archived at https://perma.cc/6ZET-A6WN)

Ikhide, J E, Timur, A T and Ogunmokun, O A (2021) The strategic intersection of HR and CSR: CSR motive and millennial joining intention, *Journal of Management & Organization*, 1–19

ILO (2016) Wages, productivity and labour share in China, www.ilo.org/wcmsp5/groups/public/---asia/---ro-bangkok/documents/publication/wcms_475254.pdf (archived at https://perma.cc/E9C8-EUVG)

ILO (2020) Report on employment in Africa (Re-Africa), tackling the youth employment challenge, www.ilo.org/wcmsp5/groups/public/---africa/---ro-abidjan/documents/publication/wcms_753300.pdf (archived at https://perma.cc/636K-5ML6)

ILO (2022) The ILO in China, about the ILO in China, www.ilo.org/beijing/WCMS_427363/lang--en/index.htm (archived at https://perma.cc/T7T3-HQDK)

ILOSTAT (2019) Statistics on union membership, https://ilostat.ilo.org/topics/union-membership/ (archived at https://perma.cc/JDU2-L7DZ)

Kajimoto, T (2021) Japan Inc to fall far short of goal for more female managers: Reuters poll, *Reuters*, www.reuters.com/world/asia-pacific/japan-inc-lag-far-behind-women-empowerment-management-roles-2021-06-17/ (archived at https://perma.cc/R8QT-TSVE)

Kawate, I (2019) Japan's lifetime employment and low pay risk brain drain: lobby, Keidanren chief Nakanishi leads charge against antiquated hiring practices, *Nikkei Asia*, https://asia.nikkei.com/Business/Technology/Japan-s-lifetime-employment-and-low-pay-risk-brain-drain-lobby (archived at https://perma.cc/6BNN-45YU)

Koleva, P (2021) Towards the development of an empirical model for Islamic corporate social responsibility: evidence from the Middle East, *Journal of Business Ethics*, **171** (4), pp 789–813

Kramar, R and Mariappanadar, S (2019) Global sustainable HRM practices. In S Mariappanadar (ed.) *Sustainable Human Resource Management: Strategies, practices and challenges* (pp 307–25), Red Globe Press, London

Legislative Assembly of Ontario (2021) Bill 27, Working for Workers Act, 2021, www.ola.org/en/legislative-business/bills/parliament-42/session-2/bill-27#BK4 (archived at https://perma.cc/99F3-NSLB)

Lewis, L (2016) The curse of the salaryman, as Shinzo Abe seeks reform, Japan's once-heroic symbol of dynamism is proving to be a roadblock, *Financial Times*, www.ft.com/content/d1a6aa18-1045-11e6-91da-096d89bd2173 (archived at https://perma.cc/KBK7-5K6C)

Lin-Hi, N, Rothenhöfer, L and Blumberg, I (2019) The relevance of socially responsible blue-collar human resource management: an experimental investigation in a Chinese factory, *Employee Relations,* **41** (6), pp 1256–72

Macini, N, Alves, M F R, Cezarino, L O, Liboni, L B and Caldana, A C F (2022) Beyond money and reputation: sustainable HRM in Brazilian banks, *Employee Relations,* **44** (3), pp 702–28

Mamman, A, Kamoche, K, Zakaria, H B and Agbebi, M (2018) Developing human capital in Africa: carving a role for human resource professionals and practitioners, *Human Resource Development International,* **21** (5), pp 444–62

Mariappanadar, S (2020) Do HRM systems impose restrictions on employee quality of life? Evidence from a sustainable HRM perspective, *Journal of Business Research,* **118**, pp 38–48

Metcalfe, B D (2007) Gender and human resource management in the Middle East, *The International Journal of Human Resource Management,* **18** (1), pp 54–74

Mishra, P (2017) Green human resource management: a framework for sustainable organizational development in an emerging economy, *International Journal of Organizational Analysis,* **25** (5), pp 762–88

Mohiuddin, M, Hosseini, E, Faradonbeh, S B and Sabokro, M (2022) Achieving human resource management sustainability in universities, *International Journal of Environmental Research and Public Health,* **19** (2), p 928

Muhl, C J (2001) The employment-at-will doctrine: three major exceptions, *Monthly Labor Review,* **124**, pp 3–11

Murcia, M and Tomaselli, M F (2020) Ready to 'escape the economy'? Latin American MBAs' cognitive disconnects concerning degrowth, societal well-being and environmental sustainability, https://papers.ssrn.com/sol3/papers.cfm?abstract_id=3576551 (archived at https://perma.cc/W623-JYTJ)

Newshub (2022) The Detail: Kiwi employers at risk of losing talent to offshore employers once borders reopen, www.newshub.co.nz/home/money/2022/02/the-detail-kiwi-employers-at-risk-of-losing-talent-to-offshore-employers-once-borders-reopen.html (archived at https://perma.cc/AMC6-6YZD)

Novianti, K R (2018) Cultural dimension issues in Indonesia human resource management practices: a structured literature review, *MEC-J (Management and Economics Journal),* **2** (3), pp 245–56

Nwosu, B and Ogunyemi, K (2020) A view from the top: hotel HR directors' perspectives of Sustainable HRM in Nigeria. In T Baum and A Ndiuini (eds.) *Sustainable Human Resource Management in Tourism* (pp 61–76), Springer, Cham

NZ Government (2020) Nearly 1,000 more big businesses now than two decades ago, www.stats.govt.nz/news/nearly-1000-more-big-businesses-now-than-two-decades-ago/ (archived at https://perma.cc/EFR6-G3L8)

OECD (2021) Creating responsive adult learning opportunities in Japan, implications for the Japanese employment system, www.oecd-ilibrary.org/employment/creating-responsive-adult-learning-opportunities-in-japan_cfe1ccd2-en (archived at https://perma.cc/XVC9-M3CV)

OECD (2022a) Work–life balance, www.oecdbetterlifeindex.org/topics/work-life-balance/ (archived at https://perma.cc/QK3M-86P2)

OECD (2022b) Financing SMEs and entrepreneurs 2022: an OECD scoreboard, 32. New Zealand, www.oecd-ilibrary.org/sites/5e4c6af5-en/index.html?itemId=/content/component/5e4c6af5-en (archived at https://perma.cc/L6L8-3PV7)

OECD (2022c) Financing SMEs and entrepreneurs 2022: an OECD scoreboard, 3. Australia, www.oecd-ilibrary.org/sites/4990a332-en/index.html?itemId=/content/component/4990a332-en (archived at https://perma.cc/D5VE-8BQS)

Okupe, A (2020) Plugging the gaps in Africa's tourism system: the need for tourism leadership. In T Baum and A Ndiuini (eds.) *Sustainable Human Resource Management in Tourism* (pp 29–44), Springer, Cham

Ollus, N (2016) Forced flexibility and exploitation: experiences of migrant workers in the cleaning industry, *Nordic Journal of Working Life Studies*, **6** (1), pp 25–45

Osland, A, Osland, J S and Tanure, B (2009) Stakeholder management: the case of Aracruz Celulose in Brazil. In A Davila and M M Elvira (eds.) *Best Human Resource Management Practices in Latin America* (pp 24–38), Routledge, London and New York

Parboteeah, K P, Seriki, H T and Hoegl, M (2014) Ethnic diversity, corruption and ethical climates in sub-Saharan Africa: recognizing the significance of human resource management, *The International Journal of Human Resource Management*, **25** (7), pp 979–1001

Parida, S, Ananthram, S, Chan, C and Brown, K (2021) Green office buildings and sustainability: does green human resource management elicit green behaviors? *Journal of Cleaner Production*, **329**, p 129764

Patterson, L, Varadarajan, D S and Salim, B S (2020) Women in STEM/SET: gender gap research review of the United Arab Emirates (UAE)–a meta-analysis, *Gender in Management: An International Journal*, **36** (8), pp 881–911

Pinto, A M G L R S, da Silva Ramos, S C M and Nunes, S M M D (2014) Managing an aging workforce: what is the value of human resource management practices for different age groups of workers?, *Tékhne*, **12** (1), pp 58–68

Pipoli, G, Fuchs, R M and Prialé, M A (2014) Sustainable HRM in Peruvian companies. In I Ehnert, W Harry and K J Zink (eds.) *Sustainability and Human Resource Management: Developing sustainable business organizations* (pp 359–77), Springer, Berlin/Heidelberg, Germany

Pison, G (2019) The number and proportion of immigrants in the population: international comparisons, *Population Societies*, **563** (2), pp 1–4

Podgorodnichenko, N, Akmal, A, Edgar, F and Everett, A M (2022) Sustainable HRM: toward addressing diverse employee roles, *Employee Relations*, **44** (3), pp 576–608.

Ridho, T (2017) CSR in Indonesia: company's perception and implementation, *The EUrASEANs: Journal on Global Socio-Economic Dynamics*, **3** (4), pp 68–74

Shimoda, S A (2015) Time to retire: is lifetime employment in Japan still viable? *Fordham International Law Journal*, **39** (3), pp 753–90

Sitorus, J H E (2016) Pancasila-based social responsibility accounting, *Procedia-Social and Behavioral Sciences*, **219**, pp 700–09

Soehardjojo, J, Delbridge, R and Meardi, G (2022) The hidden layers of resistance to dominant HRM transfer: evidence from Japanese management practice adoption in Indonesia, *Economic and Industrial Democracy*, pp 1–24

Sohail, I and Habib, M (2016) Brain drain: doctors' career intentions and associated factors, a questionnaire survey in Pakistan, *Journal of Postgraduate Medical Institute*, **30** (2), pp 189–93

Strachan, G, Adikaram, A and Kailasapathy, P (2015) Gender (in)equality in South Asia: problems, prospects and pathways, *South Asian Journal of Human Resources Management*, **2** (1), pp 1–11

Supangco, V T and Los Baños, J A (2018) Comparative HRM research in Indonesia, Malaysia and the Philippines. In C Brewster, W Mayrhofer and E Farndale (eds.) *Handbook of Research on Comparative Human Resource Management* (pp 597–613), Edward Elgar Publishing, Cheltenham

Suram, R (2015) Role of human resource management in sexual harassment at workplace, *International Conference on Trends in Economics, Humanities and Management* (ICTEHM'15) 27–28 March, 2015, Singapore

Tahir, M W, Kauser, R and Tahir, M A (2011) Brain drain of doctors; causes and consequences in Pakistan, *The International Journal of Humanities and Social Sciences*, **5** (3), pp 302–08

Tayeb, M (2005) *International Human Resource Management: A multinational company perspective*, Oxford University Press, Oxford

Taylor, S and Lewis, C (2014) Sustainable HRM in the US. In I Ehnert, W Harry and K J Zink (eds.) *Sustainability and Human Resource Management: Developing sustainable business organizations* (pp 297–314), Springer, Berlin/Heidelberg, Germany

Thorne, L, Mahoney, L S and Bobek, D (2010) A comparison of the association between corporate social responsibility and executive compensation: United States versus Canada. In C Jeffrey (ed.) *Research on Professional Responsibility and Ethics in Accounting Vol. 14* (pp 37–56), Emerald Group Publishing Limited, Bingley

Thorne, L, Mahoney, L S, Gregory, K and Convery, S (2017) A comparison of Canadian and US CSR strategic alliances, CSR reporting and CSR performance: insights into implicit–explicit CSR, *Journal of Business Ethics*, **143** (1), pp 85–98

UN (2021) World economic situation and prospects 2021: South Asia, www.un. org/development/desa/dpad/wp-content/uploads/sites/45/WESP2021_CH3_SA. pdf (archived at https://perma.cc/4QT9-AEAJ)

UN (n.d.) Young people's potential, the key to Africa's sustainable development, www.un.org/ohrlls/news/young-people%E2%80%99s-potential-key-africa%E2%80%99s-sustainable-development (archived at https://perma.cc/FNM9-MAQ6)

UNCTAD (2000) World investment report 2000 cross-border mergers and acquisitions and development, https://unctad.org/system/files/official-document/wir2000_en.pdf (archived at https://perma.cc/B4YG-CH27)

UNCTAD (2022) World investment report 2022: international tax reforms and sustainable investment, https://unctad.org/system/files/official-document/wir2022_en.pdf (archived at https://perma.cc/W873-KU4N)

UNICEF (2019) More than half of South Asian youth are not on track to have the education and skills necessary for employment in 2030, www.unicef.org/press-releases/more-half-south-asian-youth-are-not-track-have-education-and-skills-necessary (archived at https://perma.cc/X2NT-85MR)

US Department of Labor (2022) Family and medical leave act, www.dol.gov/general/topic/benefits-leave/fmla (archived at https://perma.cc/8969-QLU8)

US News (2021) Best countries to invest in, www.usnews.com/news/best-countries/best-countries-to-invest-in (archived at https://perma.cc/TH7V-DCP5)

Uzama, A (2008) A critique of lifetime employment in Japan (Shushinkoyou), *Ritsumeikan Journal of Asia Pacific Studies*, **24**, pp 71–83

Vaughan-Whitehead, D (ed.) (2015) *The European Social Model in Crisis: Is Europe losing its soul?* Edward Elgar Publishing, Cheltenham

Vives, A (2006) Social and environmental responsibility in small and medium enterprises in Latin America, *Journal of Corporate Citizenship*, **21**, pp 39–50

Vollers, A C (2019) These Alabama companies get generous with paid maternity leave, *Advance Local Media*, www.al.com/news/2019/10/these-alabama-companies-get-generous-with-paid-maternity-leave.html (archived at https://perma.cc/33D9-GSV8)

Vraňaková, N, Gyurák Babel'ová, Z and Chlpeková, A (2021) Sustainable human resource management and generational diversity: the importance of the age management pillars, *Sustainability*, **13** (15), p 8496

WEF (2021) Global Gender Gap Report 2021, www.weforum.org/reports/global-gender-gap-report-2021 (archived at https://perma.cc/8L3B-GSLW)

Wehling, C, Guanipa Hernandez, A, Osland, J, Osland, A, Deller, J, Tanure, B et al (2009) An exploratory study of the role of HRM and the transfer of German MNC sustainability values to Brazil, *European Journal of International Management*, **3** (2), pp 176–98.

World Bank (2018) Legal barriers to women's employment are widespread in South Asia, says WBG Report, www.worldbank.org/en/news/press-release/2018/03/29/legal-barriers-to-womens-employment-are-widespread-in-south-asia-says-wbg-report (archived at https://perma.cc/ZT86-UNS7)

World Bank (2020) *Women, business and the law 2020,* World Bank Publications, Washington, DC

World Bank (2022a) Reshaping norms: a new way forward, South Asia Economic Focus, https://openknowledge.worldbank.org/bitstream/handle/10986/37121/9781464818578.pdf (archived at https://perma.cc/X3WM-FDXV)

World Bank (2022b) World Bank Open Data, https://data.worldbank.org/ (archived at https://perma.cc/6G42-HVGP)

World Bank (2022c) GDP, https://data.worldbank.org/indicator/Ny.Gdp.Mktp.Cd?most_recent_value_desc=true (archived at https://perma.cc/5B5L-NMEJ)

Wu, X and Hąbek, P (2021) Trends in corporate social responsibility reporting. The case of Chinese listed companies, *Sustainability,* **13** (15), p 8640

Zoogah, D B (2016) Tribal diversity, human resources management practices and firm performance, *Canadian Journal of Administrative Sciences/Revue Canadienne des Sciences de l'Administration,* **33** (3), pp 182–96

GLOSSARY

996 work culture: A long-hours work culture with companies demanding their employees to work from 9 am to 9 pm six days a week.

Aesthetic capital: Employee assets and attributes related to physical attractiveness and presentation.

At-will employment: A term describing a US law that allows employers to fire an employee for any reason and without warning, providing that it is not an illegal dismissal.

Atypical contract: Employment contracts that do not conform to standard, open-ended and full-time employment arrangements.

Brain drain: A substantial departure of highly educated or skilled people from one country, area or economic sector to another.

Corporate social responsibility: An umbrella term describing theories and practices which emphasize that corporations have not only financial but also social, environmental and ethical responsibilities.

Counterproductive work behaviour: Employee intentional behaviour contrary to its employer's legitimate interests.

Cross-training: A development initiative where employees train how to do work in different roles.

Disconnecting from work: Being able to stop receiving work-related communication and enjoy personal time without the guilt of not working.

Distributive justice: The perceived fairness of how outcomes, such as rewards, resources or opportunities, are shared in an organization.

Diversity and inclusion (D&I): An organizational strategy of recognizing, accepting and valuing differences among employees, as well as striving to integrate a range of perspectives of different groups of people into the work environment.

Diversity training: A training programme that raises awareness about diversity issues in the workplace and explains how to approach individual differences with understanding.

Downsizing: A management strategy that involves intended, permanent and significant reductions of personnel.

Employability: Attributes that would allow a person to gain and maintain employment.

Employee commitment: A degree to which an employee identifies with their organization and demonstrates involvement with it.

Employee green behaviour (EGB): Employee scalable actions linked with environmental sustainability.

Employee vitality: A state where an employee is in a good physical and mental condition, shows resilience against work difficulties and is willing and able to invest effort into their work.

Employee voice: Formal and informal mechanisms through which employees can have a say about aspects of their work.

Environmental management (EM): An umbrella term for processes, practices, policies and application of tools addressing various ecological issues and improving an organization's impact on the natural environment.

European social model: A vision of European society based on principles of social protection and dialogue, with emphasis on employee rights, workplace preventative measures and democracy, as well as promotion of equality, diversity and inclusion.

Exit interview: An interview with an employee who is about to leave the organization.

Externality: A result of one agent's actions affecting the welfare of an uninvolved third party.

Extrinsic rewards: Rewards that come from an external source, e.g. employer providing financial bonuses or vouchers.

Great Resignation: An economic trend in different parts of the world, which started in 2021, where employees in large numbers voluntarily resign from their jobs.

Green empowerment: Giving employees the autonomy, resources and support they need to act independently towards environmental goals, as well as providing a degree of freedom to tackle and solve green work-related problems.

Green HRM (GHRM): Parts of sustainable HRM focusing on environmental sustainability.

Green human capital: Employee knowledge, skills and abilities about environmental protection.

Green innovation: A form of innovation that helps to achieve environmental goals, such as minimizing environmental damage.

Green involvement: The practice of presenting employees with opportunities to participate in environmental management.

Green performance management (GPM): A process of establishing goals, measuring performance and providing feedback on how employees, departments and the organization as a whole achieve environmental results.

Green recruitment and selection: A process of recruiting and selecting candidates who have personal qualities and attributes considered useful for an organization's environmental goals.

Green reward system: A combination of policies, practices and standards used to allocate financial and non-financial benefits, which are meant to motivate and recognize employees' green performance.

Green rewards: Financial or non-financial benefits used to motivate and recognize employees' green performance and their contribution to the organizational green goals.

Green team creativity: A development of environmentally sustainable ideas among organizational teams.

Greenwashing: A practice where an organization releases false or misleading information to present itself as environmentally responsible.

Groupthink: A phenomenon that tends to occur in small groups, when individuals prioritize group solidarity over making best choices.

High-performance work systems (HPWS): Bundles of HRM practices that are strategically linked with one another, with the aim to advance employee abilities and motivation, and provide cost-efficient results that could increase organizational profitability.

Human capital (HC): Employee knowledge, skills and abilities.

Human resources (HR): All the assets and characteristics that people possess and contribute to an organization, for example knowledge, passion, motivation, technical abilities, soft skills, social networks and experience.

Individual environmental commitment: A degree to which an employee is dedicated to environmental sustainability.

Industrial betterment: An industrial and managerial movement to improve working conditions of the employed.

Internal labour market: A system where people are hired and promoted within the organization, as opposed to interviewing and appointing someone from outside the organization.

Intrapreneur: An employee who develops innovative ideas and solutions within an organization.

Intrinsic rewards: Psychological rewards that employees achieve from performing well or engaging in meaningful work.

Isomorphism: A phenomenon where organizations in a given environment resemble one another because they conform to similar pressures.

Job sculpting: A process of structuring jobs around people who you want to bring to and keep in an organization.

Labour force participation rate: An estimate of a region's active workforce, calculated by summing employed and unemployed people, then dividing it by the total number of working age population.

Laying off: An act of terminating a worker for reasons other than their work performance.

Living wage: The minimum income necessary for a worker to meet their basic needs and afford food, housing, clothing and other necessities.

Loose labour market: A labour market where the demand for employees is relatively low and the supply of labour is relatively high.

Lying flat: A Chinese social movement, which began in 2021, protesting the pressures of overworking.

Management support: Managers providing their employees with necessary resources, time and attention.

Occupational burnout: A state of emotional exhaustion resulting from work demands consistently exceeding an employee's capacity to manage them.

Organizational citizenship behaviours (OCB): Employee voluntary contributions that go beyond what is normally expected and bring benefits to the organization.

Organizational commitment to environmental sustainability: The degree to which an organization is dedicated to reducing its environmental impacts.

Organizational culture (OC): A set of creations, values and assumptions that are shared within an organization, and guide employees' interpretations of, and behaviour in, their professional environment.

Organizational identification: A degree to which an employee identifies with their organization and believes they belong to it.

Organizational justice: The extent to which an employee perceives that its organization treats them in a fair and just manner.

Organizational values: Shared convictions about what is or is not good for the organization, that guide employees' behaviour.

Paternalistic management: A system where employers offer a form of protection for employees in exchange for strict autonomy in the decision-making process, loyalty and obedience.

Performance management (PM): Identifying, measuring and developing the performance of individuals and teams in line with the needs of the organization.

Personnel management (PM): A term for people management which has been mostly replaced with human resource management. Its distinctive feature was specialization in administrative function.

Presenteeism: Instances when employees attend work while being ill.

Procedural justice: The perceived fairness of organizational procedures, policies and decision-making processes.

Psychological contract: Employee's and employer's perceptions of their employment agreement, including implied work-related promises and obligations.

Psychological safety: A belief that you can be yourself at work without fear of negative consequences, such as punishment or humiliation.

r/antiwork: An online community on Reddit.com dedicated to a critique of work, and the anti-work movement.

Recruitment: A process of attracting qualified applicants for employment in an organization.

Selection: A process of choosing from the pool of applicants the best candidates for the job.

Social cohesion: A shared sense of solidarity among group members, and the motivation to build and maintain social relationships within the group.

Stakeholder: A person or a group who can affect or is affected by the organization's actions.

Strategic HRM: The use of human resource policies and practices to enable the organization to achieve its goals.

Strategy: A composition of long-term goals and objectives of an organization, combined with acting towards the set targets.

Stress: An adverse response to external stimuli that puts an excessive amount of physical or psychological pressure on a person.

Stressor: An external factor that impinges on a person and results in stress, at work it can be challenging deadlines, for example.

Survivor syndrome: Feelings that employees experience after they remain in an organization that had involuntary staff reductions.

Sustainability: A long-term maintenance of social, environmental and economic resources.

Sustainability council: An internal body that guides the organization towards social and environmental sustainability.

Sustainable human resource management: The use of HRM to achieve long-term social, environmental and business goals.

Thriving at work: Experiencing vitality and learning, which allow sustained performance at work.

Tight labour market: A labour market where the demand for employees is relatively high and the supply of labour is relatively low.

Triple bottom line (TBL): A sustainability framework that measures a business's success in three key areas: profit, people and the planet.

Turnover contagion: En masse resignation of employees in a relatively short period of time.

Union density: The proportion of paid employees who are union members.

Unitarist managerial perspective: An assumption that managers and employees share the same interest.

Wasta: An Arabic word for favouritism and providing someone who we know with benefits such as getting hired or promoted.

Work ability: A combination of good health and occupational competencies which allow an individual to perform work tasks.

Work intensification: A substantial increase in work demands, and the amount of effort an employee needs to exercise.

Work–family conflict: A conflict that occurs when the energy, time or behavioural demands of the work role interfere with those of the family role.

Workforce planning: A process of analysing the current staff, determining future personnel needs and identifying gaps between the labour demand and supply.

Zero-hours contracts: Employment contracts whereby the employer is not obliged to provide any minimum working hours to the employee.

INDEX

The index is filed in alphabetical, word-by-word order. Acronyms are filed as presented. Numbers are filed as spelt out, excepting ISO Standards, which are filed chronologically.